Advance Praise for *Winning from Within*
and Erica Ariel Fox

"Erica Ariel Fox knows how to transform her audience and really make them think, question their beliefs, and change for the better. She is a cutting-edge thought leader and change agent."
> —Puja Sehgal Jaspal, principal, Google Compensation Team, Google

"As a colleague, I've watched Erica develop groundbreaking work over many years at Harvard Law School. She is the right person at the right time to offer a new, more integrated, model of negotiation for people practicing leadership in business, in government and in non-profit organizations."
> —Ronald Heifetz, founding director, Center for Public Leadership at the Harvard Kennedy School; author of *Leadership Without Easy Answers*

"*Winning from Within* offers a powerful and practical method for character development, a missing link in leadership development that is increasingly essential for new and seasoned executives alike. Fox's unerring, beautiful prose makes the journey toward a better self one that you won't want to miss."
> —Amy C. Edmondson, Novartis Professor of Leadership and Management, Harvard Business School, author of *Teaming: How Organizations Learn, Innovate, and Compete in the Knowledge Economy*

"Every so often a star is born, illuminating what we thought was commonplace or inevitable and fundamentally rearranging the way we think. Erica Ariel Fox is one such star. She offers dazzling, effective, deeply transformational insights, not merely into what we *do*, but into who we *are* and can become. Read her. Your life could change as a result."
> —Kenneth Cloke, author of *Mediating Dangerously*, founder of Mediators Beyond Borders

"After twenty-five years in the business, I found *Winning from Within* to be simply the most impactful training I have ever experienced."
> —Brian Ratte, North America sales leader, Industry Solutions, IBM

"Erica Ariel Fox and *Winning from Within* provide critical insights and skills for attaining the holy grail of any professional services firm: how to become a trusted business advisor!"
> —Edward Goodman, partner, Financial Services, Ernst & Young LLP

"To spend several days with Erica Ariel Fox exploring the inner dynamics of negotiation is to discover an entirely new way of seeing oneself as a leader, spouse, and human being. The deep conversations, experiential learning, and self-directed practices all help 'interesting ideas' drop from the head down into the heart, where they were transformed into personal commitments."
> —Larry Dressler, author of *Standing in the Fire*

WINNING FROM WITHIN

A Breakthrough Method for Leading, Living, and Lasting Change

ERICA ARIEL FOX

HARPER
BUSINESS

An Imprint of HarperCollins*Publishers*
www.harpercollins.com

WINNING FROM WITHIN. Copyright © 2013 by Erica Ariel Fox. All rights reserved. Printed in the United States of America. No part of this book may be used or reproduced in any manner whatsoever without written permission except in the case of brief quotations embodied in critical articles and reviews. For information, address HarperCollins Publishers, 10 East 53rd Street, New York, NY 10022.

HarperCollins books may be purchased for educational, business, or sales promotional use. For information, please e-mail the Special Markets Department at SPsales@harpercollins.com.

first edition

Designed by William Ruoto

Library of Congress Cataloging-in-Publication Data has been applied for.

ISBN: 978-0-06-221302-0 (Hardcover)
ISBN: 978-0-06-229530-9 (International Edition)

13 14 15 16 17   OV/RRD   10 9 8 7 6 5 4 3 2

This book is dedicated in loving memory of my parents,

David Joseph Fox

and

Louise Weiss Fox

May your memory be for blessing

And in loving honor of

Hillie,

who expresses kindness in every breath, and who allowed me

to become a daughter again

In pursuit of "the centuries-old tradition of self-mastery—
the rigorous struggle to transform our limitations into
strengths and to invigorate our virtues into skillful action."
—Richard Strozzi-Heckler, *The Leadership Dojo*

CONTENTS

It is a true privilege to write a foreword for such an inspiring and pioneering book as Erica Ariel Fox's *Winning from Within*. The pleasure is particularly great since I have known Erica for many years and watched her as she developed and honed the ideas that are now crystallized in this lively and lucid introduction to the inner realms of negotiation.

More than thirty years ago, Roger Fisher, Bruce Patton, and I had the pleasure and privilege of collaborating on codifying a cooperative approach to negotiation in a slim volume called *Getting to Yes*. We sought to inspire readers to change the game of negotiation from its customary form of winning and losing to a game in which both sides could benefit. This approach, commonly known as "win-win," helped change the way people understand and practice negotiation from business to diplomacy to debates around the kitchen table.

In the three decades since, perhaps the most important lesson I have learned in my work as a mediator and negotiation advisor is that the biggest obstacle to success in negotiation is not the other, however difficult they might be. It is ourselves. The true difficulty lies within in our all-too-human tendency to react—to react impulsively out of fear or anger. The foundation of successful negotiation, I have found, is learning how to "go to the balcony"—to a mental and emotional place of perspective, calm, and self-control. I made the importance of going to the balcony a principal theme of *Getting Past No*, a book that I wrote twenty years ago.

Over the years, however, I have come to realize just how difficult it is for people to go to the balcony, and even more difficult, to stay on the balcony during their conflictual interactions with others. Each of us has a strong tendency to be controlled by our destructive emotions and thoughts and then to react impulsively in ways that do not serve our long-term interests. In other words, we tend to "fall off the balcony." My clients and readers often report this and ask me repeatedly for help on how to stay on the balcony. While the basic techniques—of stopping, naming what's going on, and keeping one's eyes on the prize—can be very valuable, they need elaboration and reinforcement, particularly in the problematic relationships that many of us encounter every day.

What I have increasingly come to appreciate is that success in getting to yes with others can go only so far unless we also engage in a parallel work, an internal work on ourselves that accompanies the external work we do in the world. To be successful in traveling the external behavioral path to agreement, we need to travel an internal psychological path as well. We need to get to yes not only with others, but first and perhaps foremost with ourselves, strange as this may sound. In order to go outside into the world to relate successfully with others in challenging situations, we need to go inside first to relate successfully with ourselves. For how can we expect to influence others effectively if we cannot *first* influence ourselves?

This is where this seminal book by Erica Ariel Fox makes its contribution. *Winning from Within* invites us to think about negotiation in a new way, before we get to the table or ever talk to the other side. It opens the door for us to look inside at how we negotiate with ourselves. Erica offers us an anatomy of the negotiation within, giving us a working vocabulary of the Dreamer (in business language, the CEO), the Thinker (the CFO), the Lover (the VP of HR), and the Warrior (the COO). These are our inner negotiators, what Erica calls the Big Four, all led by the Captain with the invaluable help of the Lookout and the Voyager. And there is much more, presented in lively and stimulating language, and accompanied by vivid and inspiring examples that bring the inner characters and practical methods to life.

In the 1980s, when *Getting to Yes* came out, the world we lived in was in real need of a new way for people to solve problems together. Principled negotiation provided one such alternative. Today, our world is in need of road maps for people to understand themselves so they can make wise and conscious choices about their lives and their leadership. We need a practical and accessible set of tools that explains how we operate to enable us not only to broker deals with others, but to make peace with ourselves. Until we can understand and engage with ourselves, our deepest aspirations will elude us—from meeting our potential for professional performance to creating a secure and sustainable peace in the world.

Winning from Within offers us such a road map. I truly hope that it will help readers understand and practice both leadership and negotiation in a more effective, more centered, and more satisfying fashion, whether in the corporate offices or in public policy debates, or simply in talks among family and friends. I am convinced that, in order to change the outer game of negotiation, we need to learn to change the inner game of negotiation. This pathbreaking book by Erica Ariel Fox offers us a great place to begin. I hope that you enjoy and benefit from it as I have!

WILLIAM URY
COFOUNDER, HARVARD NEGOTIATION PROJECT

Once upon a time, before I went to college, my mother worried. I didn't know how to prepare what she called "any decent meals." So she bought me a copy of *The Joy of Cooking*, and sat me down to watch and learn. She opened the cookbook to a favorite recipe and began to show me how to make it.

"Here it says use vegetable oil, but I always use olive oil."

And then "here it says use chili peppers, but I always leave those out, because the dish gets too spicy."

And on it went. Just like that.

"It says here to add salt, but *never* do that—salt is bad for your heart."

After some time, I interrupted the process.

"What is the point of the recipe if you do whatever you want anyway?" I asked.

And then, as sometimes happened in my mother's bright red kitchen, a pearl of wisdom was passed down to me in the uniquely memorable Louise Fox way.

"Listen to your mother. A meal becomes good by starting with quality instructions. It becomes great when you add a quality chef."

Since that day more than twenty years ago, I've come to understand my mother's teaching as a proverb that applies far beyond cooking. Actually, it applies to every important activity in our lives. In negotiating the highways and byways of life, recipes can take us only so far. Beyond getting the right ingredients or dutifully following instructions, to become a "quality chef"—in cooking and in life—we need to reach beyond the fundamentals and learn to adapt, improvise, and innovate as life demands. We need to use not only our utensils—our "best practices" and techniques—but also our inner strengths and deeper wisdom.

The key to mastery, to achieving greatness, in the kitchen or in the boardroom, is not your toolbox. *It's you.*

Getting Out of Our Own Way

Life is a series of attempts to get things right. You work to achieve your goals. You hope to fulfill your potential. And you want to be a good person. You aim to live well, love and be loved, and if all goes well, make a contribution. Some of these come easily; others don't. You do the best you can.

Still, despite your best efforts, things don't always go according to plan.

Who hasn't said or done the wrong thing, making a bad situation worse? Or said nothing, when we might have made a difference if we had? Who hasn't lain in bed at night thinking, "I can't believe I said that!" or "Why didn't I speak up when I had the chance?" We may especially beat ourselves up when we fall into the same old traps. "*I did it again* . . . even though I knew better."

Everyone has some version of this experience. You prepare for an important meeting, or a weighty conversation. You think in advance about what you want to say. And then, in the moment of truth, it doesn't go the way you pictured it the night before.

The interesting thing is how often the difference doesn't come from what other people said or did. We like to point fingers, yes. But in truth, the reversal of fortune from the night before quite often *comes from us.* We go in with one plan. Yet we end up doing something else entirely.

Why?

Consider the following scenarios:

> In a conversation for a promising contract, Tonia, who owns her own business, is surprised when a potential client pushes back on her fees. She'd gone into the meeting intending to be flexible—new opportunities had all but disappeared since the economy tanked. But in the moment, Tonia feels insulted and undervalued. She walks away from the engagement, despite needing the work and having a decent offer on the table.
>
> While meeting with a valued client of his firm, Pierre learns that the client rejected his recommendations for upgrading their IT system. The client tells Pierre why he doesn't think the strategy will work for them. Pierre knows he should use the "active listening" he learned in a seminar. But he's proud of the strategy, and believes it's right for the client. Pierre explains why the reservations are unfounded, laying out again the merits of the proposal. The client doesn't want to argue. Instead, he asks Pierre's boss for a different consultant.
>
> Susan comes home from a long day at work and wants to connect with her family. At the dinner table, she describes her taxing day at the office. Her husband, Mike, complains that Susan isn't paying enough attention to their daughter Jennifer, who's struggling at school. Susan bristles. "My job isn't the cause of Jenny's problems," she says. Mike disagrees. "You seem more concerned with your

customers than with our daughter!" Susan snaps back. "*You* have no idea what it's like to be a working mother!" Jennifer shrinks into her chair as Susan and Mike finish dinner in a tense, uncomfortable silence.

Despite our best intentions, we often miss opportunities and generate breakdowns. We walk away from good deals, harm relationships, and generally act against our own interests. Plenty of books tell us what to do about "difficult people." The truth is we need advice for succeeding when the difficult person *is us*.

Until now, experts have paid little attention to mapping the myriad ways we get in our own way. Yet when push comes to shove, we are often our own worst enemy.

The advice we do get about improving ourselves emphasizes changing our behavior to get better results: we should assert less, or assert more; listen, and ask more questions. The problem is that focusing on tactics and techniques misses the mark in many cases, because you're throwing darts at the wrong board.

Remember my mother's advice on cooking. Trying to fix behavior is like focusing on a recipe. It's necessary, but insufficient to achieve high performance. You'll start seeing big impact when you pay attention to what you, the "chef," are bringing to the meal. Lasting change starts with you.

Despite what you might think, what happens inside you is something **you can change**. If you know how. When you do that, you start making new choices, and getting better outcomes. You feel good about how you get things done. And you're much more likely to make a meaningful difference.

This book takes that challenge head-on.

Winning from Within provides insight into how you get in your own way and what to do about it. It gives you a map for understanding your inner world, and a method for sorting yourself out. By understanding yourself and the common traps you fall into, you'll learn to turn breakdowns into breakthroughs, whether you're struggling with a difficult colleague or arguing with your teenage son. If you practice the steps in this book, over time you'll stop planting your own minefields. And better yet, you'll finally be able to capture life's wonderful opportunities when they come your way.

My Journey

I came to write this book by standing on the shoulders of giants. In 1981, my mentors in the Harvard Program on Negotiation (PON), William Ury and the late Roger Fisher, wrote the landmark *Getting to Yes: Negotiating Agreement Without Giving In*, a book that has since sold more than 3 million copies. Their work changed the negotiation game by introducing the famed "Harvard Concept"— how to "separate the people from the problem"—and calling for "win-win" collaboration over blind competition for the mutual benefit of all concerned.

In 1999, my friends Douglas Stone, Bruce Patton, and Sheila Heen built on those ideas in their best-selling book, *Difficult Conversations: How to Discuss What Matters Most*. They shared the new best practices from PON, addressing what had become a recurring question about the first theory: what happens when you *can't* separate the people from the problem, because, in fact, the other people *are* the problem? They introduced the notion of the "three conversations" to help resolve that quandary.

I'd graduated from Harvard Law School (HLS) in 1995 and

started teaching there in 1996. HLS is the home of PON, the leading think tank in the world on making deals and resolving disputes. PON has been my professional home for nearly two decades, for which I am profoundly grateful. I was blessed with the mentorship of luminaries in the field, from thought leaders to pioneers in practice. I also built friendships in my early years at PON, with people who remain my inner circle to this day.

As a protégé of Roger and William, and as a colleague of Doug, Bruce, and Sheila, I taught the material contained in these books to Fortune 500 corporations, government agencies, not-for-profits, and every kind of organization in between. I had the privilege to share these ideas on nearly every continent. I also learned the art of developing new frameworks and methodology.

In addition to taking negotiation workshops like ours, our clients had often studied the bestselling books on effective habits and how to influence people. They certainly knew what they "should" do to succeed. Yet all too often, in the heat of the moment, they'd lose sight of their goals. They'd find themselves failing to speak up at a meeting; lambasting a co-worker before hearing her out; leaving money on the table when they might have gotten more; or vowing to communicate gently with a spouse but snapping sarcastically instead.

I had to wonder. Why weren't the best practices we'd taught these professionals—such as focusing on interests rather than positions, or listening carefully to people with strong emotions—enough? When push came to shove, why did people shut down, lash out, or avoid the conflict altogether?

I saw a clear need for a new and deeper approach to leading and living. I was inspired to resolve this disconnect between what people know they *should say* and what they *actually do* every day. I was determined to work toward a practical solution, following in the PON tradition of linking theory and real-world usefulness.

The ideas in this book sprang from these realizations, but also from two other experiences: the death of both of my parents within one year and, during that same twelve-month period, the events of September 11, 2001.

The Personal Side of the Story

On Friday afternoon, November 10, 2000, I called my mother to wish her a peaceful Sabbath, as I always did before lighting my candles. That Saturday night, my sister called to tell me that Mom was in the hospital. She had collapsed from a stroke. By Sunday, November 12, she was gone.

For the next year I said memorial prayers for my mother every day. My main focus was to support my dad. He'd lost his companion of forty years.

As I weathered this year of personal challenge, a national tragedy took place: the events of September 11, 2001.

The sense of shock, grief, loss, and disarray was overwhelming for everyone. Stories poured forth about the workers in the towers, the passengers on the planes, the fire and police crews who had rushed to the rescue.

As a conflict resolution professional, I found myself profoundly disturbed. *Getting to Yes* and the worldview behind it helped to usher in a new era of negotiation strategies, ones built on fairness and mutual understanding. The notion of a "win-win" outcome had become conventional wisdom in many parts of the world. With my colleagues and friends, I'd fanned across the globe teaching these methods and tools to help people work out their differences without violence. Yet here in my own backyard, people were flying planes into buildings. Thousands of innocents went to work in the morning and never came back.

The ashen faces of New Yorkers streaming away from the flames haunted me. What were we negotiators doing wrong? What were we missing?

As the public grappled to make sense of this horrific bloodshed, I approached the milestone that would end my private mourning period. By marking the first-year anniversary of my mother's death, I wanted to turn the page and move forward with my life. But that didn't happen. Not two months after September 11, and the week before commemorating that first anniversary, my father very suddenly passed away.

When my father died, I felt profound grief. I also inherited a large responsibility. As the only lawyer in my family, I took over all legal matters. I dealt with a mountain of paperwork while continuing every day for another year to say the Jewish memorial prayers for a deceased parent.

The Negotiation Cyclone

Ironically, when I took a break from my professional world of engaging conflict to focus on my family, I was thrust into a negotiation cyclone of my own. In the days before my father passed away, it was with doctors, ICU nurses, my rabbi, my siblings. Then came the lawyers, insurance agents, tax accountants, art appraisers, and myriad other estate professionals.

One of the more memorable negotiations was with "Al the Garbage Guy," who wanted thousands of dollars to take away our trash. And then we faced the sea of Donation Ladies—some wanted clothes sorted by color, some by size, others by season. Some wouldn't take summer clothes at all. If there was a method to their madness, I never figured out what it was.

Friends watched me navigate this tender, endless process and would invariably ask me the same thing: "You know, Erica, you're an international leader in negotiation. You've taught this stuff all over the world. After all of your training and the hundreds of workshops you've led . . . *does any of this stuff really help?*"

I had to pause and think about this. I'd spent countless hours negotiating with doctors, lawyers, insurance agents, and hospital bureaucracies. I'd dealt with high-stakes, high-pressure situations, literally the stuff of life and death. I'd had incredibly raw conversations with my sisters. I'd negotiated from morning until night. Had my immersion in negotiation skills prepared me to engage all of this successfully?

Yes and no.

On the one hand, of course, years of teaching best practices for managing conflict had helped me. I had tools for breaking down complex situations and problem solving. I knew how to consider different points of view. I could mediate among people holding strong emotions and the conviction that their perspective was the only correct one. I could generate a range of potential solutions to disputes that seemed to have no answer. And I had the communication skills to keep very challenging conversations moving forward when impasse loomed.

At the same time, as I reflected over the course of a year on this question, I saw that the skills and capabilities we had taught for all these years were insufficient to the task. People had come from around the world to Harvard to learn the fundamentals of negotiation, and we had delivered that. We offered a sound conceptual foundation and core behaviors that foster competence. But when push came to shove, this foundation by itself hadn't been enough to produce results when it mattered most. When the going got rough, real-time effectiveness required something more. I wondered: *What else is there?*

The nexus of my personal odyssey and the public catastrophe of September 11 made this question unavoidable and urgent. I took a yearlong sabbatical to explore and learn. I contemplated why, in the heat of the moment, I wasn't always able to use commonsense negotiation tips or prevent discussions from escalating into hostile debates. What made the stuff work, or not?

I noticed that during the more "successful" interactions, I'd relied on techniques I'd learned beyond the Harvard classrooms, some based in wisdom traditions thousands of years old. These same tools were gaining recognition at the time through discoveries in neuroscience. Brain science and philosophy were converging on the power of looking within to generate powerful and lasting change.

The Next Step in Best Practice

What I came to realize during that complex time is a simple truth: that what makes the difference in successful negotiation and leadership lives *inside* of us. The key to a good outcome, whether around a conference room table or the dining room table, is to undertake a negotiation within ourselves. Yes, we can learn to say and do helpful things. But ultimately the ability to achieve mastery over how we lead and live with each other comes from a place within, what I call "center of well-being," or our "center."

When we anchor ourselves in our center, we are mindfully aware of our reactions and choices. The actions we then take produce better results, stronger relationships, and more of life's deeper rewards.

I realized I needed to bring this insight into my teaching. So I founded the Harvard Negotiation Insight Initiative (HNII) in 2002 at PON. The mission of HNII was to explore the integration of the world of action and the world of reflection. HNII served as a living laboratory, bringing professionals together for executive education from around the world.

One summer, people came from more than forty-five countries to experience the innovation that was stretching the Harvard Concept to a new level. Our programs gave equal weight to neuroscience and to the creative arts; we taught PON's best practices combined with the insights of psychologists, poets, and theologians. Across these diverse disciplines, the consistent wisdom pointed people back to themselves. Out of this eclectic melting pot, the ideas and methods in this book were born.

In the years since this research started, my personal life has changed course dramatically. My parents' memory now brings me warmth instead of sadness. The estate is long behind me. My focus is now on my new family—my wonderful husband, Bernardus, and his beautiful son, whom we affectionately call the Little Dude. I'll share more of *that* part of the story in the pages to come.

An Idea Whose Time Has Come

At the beginning of this journey I wondered if the idea of self-exploration would fly in corporate environments. It turned out the answer is yes. More than a decade after its inception, Winning from Within isn't an experiment anymore. Thousands of people have used the map and the method to get out of their own way and get the results they really want.

At Mobius Executive Leadership, a company I cofounded with my sister Amy Elizabeth Fox, my partners and I now have substantial experience teaching this material to senior teams, managers, and emerging leaders. In turbulent times, when the pace of change makes your head spin, business leaders and public servants alike want a system that helps them stay balanced as they face unprecedented complexity and uncertainty.

Consensus is growing in the business community that "the next big thing" in leadership relates to transforming the capabilities of leaders themselves. Reality has leapt ahead of people's capacity to cope, no less thrive. Leaders need tools for examining how they operate, and methodologies for evolving to new mindsets and behaviors. The ability to "lead yourself" is emerging as today's new leadership requirement. Winning from Within provides a necessary road map for that leadership development.

Your Journey, Our Journey

I've now shared part of my journey. I'll tell you more of my story to illustrate ideas. But the rest of this book is fundamentally about *your* journey.

Winning from Within is about reconnecting all the parts of yourself and engaging them skillfully as you navigate your interactions with the world around you. It explains the links between personal mastery and high performance. It provides you with a way to fulfill the broadly felt wish to experience a world in which daily life at work and at home reflects the best of who you are.

As you will soon see, the method is not a quick fix. It doesn't offer shortcuts or tricks to get your way. Instead, it provides a map for lifelong learning. While the path is challenging, and the results at times hard won, the process fosters genuine and lasting transformation.

PART ONE

Create Lasting Change

CHAPTER 1

Uncover Your Performance Gap

You are unique, and if that is not fulfilled,
then something has been lost.
—MARTHA GRAHAM

Mark is an engineer working with a team in the high-tech industry. Like many managers, he finds himself torn between the people who report to him, and his boss Stefan, the head of his business unit. Mark and Stefan are in a heated exchange:

STEFAN: You should never have told the staff about this decision!

MARK: I should have talked to you first, yes. But I needed to tell the team before they took irreversible action.

STEFAN: That's absurd! You've completely tied our hands and damaged management's credibility.

MARK: Everyone knew something was up, and they won't trust me if I don't tell them what's going on.

STEFAN: Well, be glad you have their trust, because I don't trust you at all! Don't expect me to come to you for advice again anytime soon.

As the shouting match erupted in the hallway, Mark's stomach was in knots. He tried to stay calm. But he was losing his cool.

Part of him knew he should play nice. Stefan was his boss, after all. Another part of him wanted to strike.

Mark could picture a tennis match in his own mind, with balls lobbing back and forth across the mental net:

Take a stand against this jerk.

No, be a team player.

No one should treat you like this and
  get away with it.

Let it go—he isn't worth making a scene.

Then the conversation in his head grew heated:

Is he kidding?
He thinks I broke the bad news?
He doesn't get it.
People have been talking about
  this for weeks!

Stay calm, or this won't end well.

This is why no one likes you,
  Stefan—because you're a bully!

Shut up! He's still your manager!

Mark finally gave in to his anger. He couldn't hold his tongue for one more minute.

"If I'm so untrustworthy, why do I have the highest employee loyalty in the company?" Mark asked Stefan flatly. "Frankly, I'd be glad for you to not come to me for advice. With any luck, I won't need to talk to you at all. You text me, and I'll reply. Consider my door closed."

When he got back to his office, Mark felt relieved. It was good to tell Stefan how he really felt.

But within minutes, a familiar sense of regret washed over him. He *knew* he should have kept his mouth shut, at least until he calmed down. Telling his boss he'd prefer never to talk to him again wasn't the greatest idea. Yet time and again, in those hot moments of confrontation, he just couldn't keep his cool.

If We Don't Explode, We Withdraw

At the other end of the spectrum, there's my former student Rafiq. Unlike Mark, Rafiq didn't explode. In fact, he could hardly speak at all.

For three years, Rafiq had studied at Harvard Law School. After graduation, he'd planned to return to Pakistan and his family. Much to his surprise, while at Harvard, Rafiq fell in love with an American woman from the Midwest. Their relationship was a source of joy, but also dread. Rafiq knew that one day he'd have to tell his mother that he wouldn't be returning to Pakistan as she assumed. He planned to marry Stacy and live in the United States.

On several occasions, the conversation almost happened. He'd phone home to discuss graduation plans since his mother, father, and extended family were all coming to America for the ceremony. He'd gone over and over it in his head—what he would say, the firm but gentle tone he would take. He visualized the conversation ending well.

But then the real moment would arrive, and he would freeze.

"When are you coming home?" his mother would ask. Rafiq would say nothing. "You'd better buy a plane ticket soon before the fares go up," his mother continued. More silence.

During these actual conversations with his mother, part of Rafiq urged, "Go on, tell Mom the truth." But before he could open his mouth, the counter-point emerged: "No! It will kill her." With each of his mother's questions, he felt the weight of her expectations. Waves of anguish accompanied opposing thoughts: "You have to tell her sometime," followed by, "Keep quiet. You'll break her heart."

Rafiq wanted to be honest with his mother about his plans to stay in America—he knew he would have to, eventually. But he continued to teeter on the precipice of telling the truth. He deferred questions about plane tickets for later, not even fully aware of all the reasons why, but knowing that he couldn't bring himself to tell her. Not today.

Succeed from the Inside Out

For many years at the Harvard Negotiation Project, my peers and I taught an Executive Education program in the summer. At the highpoint of the seminar, we ran an exercise to help people develop interpersonal skills. For this special session, we assigned one instructor to every three delegates, in order to provide a high level of individual coaching.

Workshop participants brought a real negotiation challenge from their lives, and we worked with them in trios to help each person improve in their chosen scenario. This all worked just fine, until one day, when a member of my trio was a Supreme Court justice.

Nothing had prepared me to run this high-stakes exercise with such a prominent person. This intimidating seventy-five-year-old gentleman had served on the High Court of his country for the previous thirty-five years.

Before his turn, I strained to imagine the kind of negotiation he would pick to get my advice. Would it involve confrontations with his fellow justices over the rule of law? Do people like him negotiate with the prime minister, I wondered, or members of Parliament? When the time came for his exercise, the judge described a difficult situation that had haunted him for decades.

"Every day for fifty years my wife has picked out my tie," he told me. "I *hate* that. I can dress myself. Why does she do that?"

I was stunned. *This* was the big issue that kept him up at night? I asked the obvious question.

"Have you ever told your wife that you prefer to choose your own tie?"

"That's *exactly* my problem," he said. "No matter how many times I rehearse it in my head, *I just can't bring myself to tell her.*"

After years of pondering the same question, something clicked. I got it.

Mark, Rafiq, and the High Court judge are smart people. They're honest people. They know what makes communication work. Yet they betray themselves: by not holding their ground gracefully, by not telling the truth, and by not standing their ground while also protecting their important relationships.

Usually in the communication skills exercise I did with the Supreme Court judge, we practiced lines people could say when they returned to "real life." But this time, suggesting to this towering figure that he rehearse the phrase "could you please not pick out my tie" seemed ridiculous. He was an exceedingly powerful person, a man who'd given orders for decades from the bench, issuing opinions that impacted a nation. He didn't need help with assertiveness skills.

So, practicing behavior was not going to help. He **knew** the words he could say. The nut to crack was whatever stood in his way from **actually saying them**.

Working with the justice that day opened my eyes to the problem in a whole new way. Like others before him, when it came to the conversation that truly challenged him, he couldn't say what he meant, or get what he wanted. But for the first time I saw clearly why focusing on behavior wasn't the answer.

Beyond the shadow of a doubt, this person *possessed the skills* that he needed to meet his challenge. The way to help him succeed was to shift something inside him, *to work with the voice that told him not to say anything*. If he got the green light from that voice inside, he'd have no problem finding the words to talk with his wife. And that is indeed what happened.

Your Current Reaction vs. Your Optimal Reaction

Once I had this insight, I saw the phenomenon everywhere. It turns out that most people find a disparity between what they know they *should* say and do to behave successfully—their *optimal reaction*— and what they *actually* do in daily life—*their current reaction*. I call this phenomenon *The Performance Gap* (see Figure 1.1).

It doesn't matter how accomplished you are. Anyone can fall into the Performance Gap. The fact that you're respected in your career, have a high IQ, or are an eloquent communicator doesn't necessarily matter. You aren't mostly falling into the Performance Gap because your problem is beyond your skill set. You're likely stumbling because of what's going on inside of you. *You're getting in your own way without even realizing it.*

Going Left When We Meant to Go Right

How often do you plan to do one thing, but then in the moment, *you do something else?*

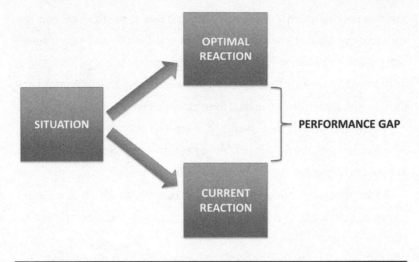

FIGURE 1.1

- Do you ever plan to listen to your partner, but find yourself yelling—or shutting down—instead?
- Do you ever intend to collaborate with other people, but then get rigid and stuck in your opinions?
- Do you ever become defensive or reactive, when you want to keep your cool?
- Do you say yes when you want to say no?
- Do you say things and later wish you hadn't?
- Do you ever sit quietly, wishing you would speak up or take a stand?
- Are you tempted to break away from everyone's expectations, but feel too scared or "too responsible" to rock the boat?
- Do you ever feel at odds with your passion and life purpose?

You may practice a dialogue on the drive to work. You can see yourself saying just the right thing. But it's often not enough, no matter how senior or how experienced you are. Steps like these didn't work for the High Court justice. And it hasn't worked for thousands of people I've advised around the world.

Why, like Mark and Rafiq, do we fall victim to the Performance Gap again and again? Where do we go wrong? And most important, what *can* we do to *change these outcomes*?

One obvious answer is to learn better skills. With a stronger toolbox, you'd get the results, the process, and the relationships that you want. Right?

Actually, no. If you want lasting change, it doesn't work this way much of the time. Most people think that learning new skills is the answer. It isn't—at least not by itself. As my mother knew, you need more than a better toolbox.

New Skills Don't Come from Just Learning Behaviors

As I consult to companies across multiple industries, I'm struck by how many of them apply "competency grids" to their leaders and general workforce. It seems virtually everyone needs a way to measure the potential and performance of their people. Here's an example of the kind of grid I'm talking about, listing the "competencies" that people will get measured by (see Table 1.2).

Since they hold people accountable to perform these competencies, companies need to build capability in their leaders and workforce to do them. So they routinely send their people through training to teach them the skills required to perform these competencies.

Vision	People
Aspiration Setting	Communication and Influence
Inspire Others	Teamwork
Innovation and Creativity	Emotional Intelligence
Passion and Purpose	Coaching Others

Analysis	Execution
Risk Management	Accountability
Smart Decision-Making	Results-Focus
Measuring Success: KPIs and ROI	Project Management
Compliance	Operational Efficiency

TABLE 1.2

But remember Mark, Rafiq, and the judge? *Learning the behaviors of leaders doesn't translate into performing the practices of leadership.* To generate real change—to see new behavior and get new results that last over time—*you need to activate something inside you that enables you to perform the skill.*

If you do that, new behavior will come naturally. If you don't, when the pressure's on and the stakes are high, you're unlikely to see new behavior outside of the seminar room.

Taking My Own Medicine

While I researched this book on creating lasting change, I went through a personal transition that gave me a look at "change" from up close.

My life was stable if predictable: I'd lived outside of Cambridge, Massachusetts, for nearly twenty years. I'd remained in the same career throughout those years. I ate in the same Chinese restaurant, went to the same movie theater, and belonged to the same synagogue. I lived fifteen minutes from my sister.

Then, in what felt like the blink of an eye, I fell in love, got married, wed a divorced man from The Netherlands, moved to Amsterdam to live with my new husband, Bernardus, and to live near his son, became a stepmother to a little boy who speaks no English, and landed in a foreign country with no family or friends.

If I wasn't an expert on change before, I am now.

Before coming to live in The Netherlands, I saw myself as a strong, confident, resourceful person. In fact, if you'd asked me to choose one word to describe myself, I might've chosen *self-reliant*.

A downside of my personal profile is that I couldn't easily ask for help. But that wasn't too bad. I didn't like "needy" people much anyway, and didn't want to be one of them. Indeed, as the youngest of four, I'd learned early about the folly of weakness. I'm told that as of three years old, I described myself as "a tough cookie."

Relocating from the United States to Western Europe involves a punishing illusion: everything *appears* to be basically the same, when it is, in fact, *just different enough* that a formerly competent person can do nothing. And I mean nothing.

When I first arrived last year, I felt overwhelmed by my new situation. I figured that doing some "normal" things around the house would make me feel—well, normal. So I headed upstairs with a basket of laundry.

Kreukherstellend *and* Overhemden

To start with, I couldn't figure out how to turn the machine on. And try as I might, I couldn't get the door to open to put in any clothes. When I did triumph over the washing machine door, I faced the following panel of choices:

- *Witte was/Bonte was*
- *Voorwas*
- *Kreukherstellend*
- *Overhemden*

Are you kidding me?

Laundry was not going to work as my "comfort" activity.

So I turned to other presumably familiar activities to find solid ground: things like making coffee, or roasting a chicken.

No dice.

I couldn't figure out the coffeemaker if my life depended on it. All I wanted was a plain old Mr. Coffee machine. But here they take coffee *so seriously*. Everyone has a cappuccino machine, or—as in the house I moved into—one that makes espresso. I'm not sure at that time I even knew the difference between cappuccino and espresso, but I'll tell you one thing they have in common. I cannot make either one of them in a European, fancy coffee-making device.

Roasting the chicken was out of the question. In our house in The Netherlands, we don't have an oven. Seriously. We have a microwave, but not something you'd use to roast a chicken.

Apparently, "everyone" here cooks on the stovetop. Of course, I *could* warm up my coffee in the microwave. But that would have required success where I was already an abject failure, as you know.

I was starting to break down. And I was out of ideas.

I finally called a friend in the States, and she had the *most* annoying thing to say.

"Maybe life has brought you to The Netherlands to learn about your vulnerability."

"My what?" I asked in disbelief.

"You're always the strong one, cooking up visions and making things happen. Now you can't make a cup of coffee. Maybe you're on a journey to discover a new side of yourself, one you don't see very often. The part of you that feels vulnerable."

I thought, "*This* is what I get when I call my friend? Some friend!"

And she really was.

Integrating Our Hidden Sides Closes the Performance Gap

The past year of struggle, minor successes, and seemingly infinite confusion has forced me to deal with the Vulnerable Erica. Not something I admit lightly. But I had nowhere to hide.

The irony is that I teach my clients to look for new sides of themselves, to tap inner resources they haven't discovered. I assure them this is productive and meaningful, that it will improve their lives at work and at home. I also say that such exploration and discovery will build power in their center, the inner core that gives them strength and capacity for skillful action.

Now I was taking a dose of my own medicine.

My Year of Living Vulnerably reinforced several points that we'll explore throughout this book:

1. We are more multi-faceted than we realize.
   I'd defined myself narrowly, both to the world, and to myself.

2. We pick parts of ourselves to define who we are.
   Based on what I saw as my strengths, I'd defined myself as a highly competent woman who could do it all on her own.

3. The identities we form have some truth to them.
   I am generally a capable and resourceful person. In most situations I feel confident. I like to initiate things and make them happen.

4. Yet, they don't tell the full truth. We create profiles of ourselves by elevating certain elements of who we are and leaving others behind. That distorts the full truth.
   I am vulnerable as well as powerful.

5. The identity we show the world, and ourselves, isn't necessarily false. But it isn't fully true. What we amplify and diminish in our profile leads to our Performance Gap. That keeps us from fulfilling our potential in all areas of our lives.
   If people, starting with me, see only my powerful side, they don't see all of me. Trouble is, the parts that I've

deleted from my profile have a lot to offer. Like my vul-
nerable side, who knows how to ask for help. I can only
exercise that skill when I integrate that missing piece into
my profile.

6. We gain something when we recognize a part of ourselves that's missing from our profile—the way we
define who we are—and expand it to include what we
left out. We also gain by right-sizing parts of our profile that we express now in excess. Doing *both* gives
us a sense of centeredness. And that leads straight to
high performance.
I can make coffee in The Netherlands now. Believe it or
not, I can choose on my own between Bonte Was *and*
Overhemden. *Bernardus' family is part of my family.*
And Bernardus' son, whom we call the Little Dude, is
teaching me to speak Dutch. That's all because I learned to
ask for help. To let people see that I'm struggling. And to
accept that while I'm powerful to my core, I am vulnerable
to my core, too.

7. Lasting change doesn't happen overnight.
Yes, I can do the laundry. Yes, I love Bernardus' family. But
I have all of one friend in The Netherlands. We haven't
found a synagogue yet. I have no familiar restaurants.
No idea where to find a movie theater. Stepparenting is
a world unto itself. I miss my sisters terribly. I long for
my house, my friends, and people speaking English. I'd be
stretching it to say that Amsterdam feels like "home." It's
not easy, but it's the voyage I'm on.

The Bottom Line

Ideally, we'd like to deliver our optimal reactions. Most of the time, we don't. Instead, we fall into the Performance Gap.

This happens in part because of who we tell ourselves we are—the profile we hold that defines us. It also comes from disconnecting from the strengths and centeredness at our core. To close your Performance Gap, you need to look closely at your current profile, and learn to develop it. Your profile can adjust—a little here, a little there—so it can serve you and the world in whatever circumstances you're living in now. Leading and living in a centered way will enable that adaptation.

The Winning from Within method of balancing your profile and connecting to your core isn't about my adventure to a new land. *It's about the voyage we're all on*: to stretch and grow, to live fully, to figure out who on earth we really are. It's a method for waking up to the wide range of our experiences, both out there in the world as well as in our inner lives. This voyage is both joyful and painful. But ultimately, we want to water the seeds of possibility that are dormant within us. That's how we live and lead from our full power, our full potential, our full beauty and grace. It's how we find our way home.

Appreciating the interplay of our internal experience and the world we see around us is also central to leading wisely and fostering lasting change. Madeleine Albright expressed this well when she said, "Opportunities for leadership are all around us. The capacity for leadership is deep within us." From centuries-old philosophy to contemporary physics, we find this nexus: of inner and outer; microcosm and macrocosm; heaven and earth; immanence and transcendence. In the language of my lineage, Kabbalah: as above, so below. From different directions we come back to the mirror between the grandeur of the universe and the wonder of being human.

This wisdom is driving a new conversation about developing leaders because our times demand it. It's hard to miss that we're living through massive change on a global level that impacts each of us on a direct level. Whether you're coaching a local team, working at a medical clinic, running a law firm or a nonprofit. If you're trading stocks, working in government, serving meals, attending to passengers, or flying the plane. If you go to school, write blogs, make movies, do research, give lessons. If you counsel or nurse or teach. The deal is the same. *You'll find success and satisfaction from contributing to the world around you with the full breadth of your inner resources.* **No matter what you do.**

You'll discover that navigating the bumpy road outside gets easier when you can tap the innate wisdom at your core. Indeed, as you get to know yourself from the inside out, you learn to your surprise that some of the bumps out there actually reflect the ones in here. Paradoxically, you can ease your way through the world outside by engaging, embracing, and integrating more of yourself on the inside.

Workshop participants ask me what I mean when I talk about integrating more of you "on the inside." I say, "Think about everything that happens in you from the neck down. How much attention do you pay to all of that?" I don't mean you should forget about your head. But the question helps draw attention to embracing more of what's going on inside of you.

All of that starts with seeing and expanding your profile, the story you tell yourself about who you are. Broadening your profile is what we'll look at next, in chapter 2.

Discover Your Inner Negotiators

Every game is composed of two parts, an outer game and an
inner game. The outer game is played against an external
opponent to overcome external obstacles, and to reach an
external goal. . . . The inner game . . . is the game that takes
place in the mind of the player . . . and it is played to overcome
all habits of mind which inhibit excellence in performance.

—W. TIMOTHY GALLWEY

Giovanna was a sales manager at a national insurance carrier. She was in charge of driving new business and increasing premium income in her territory. She also oversaw several teams of sales representatives.

Giovanna was frustrated at getting passed over for promotion twice in a row. She couldn't understand the problem, since her performance was stellar. Her sales reps met their premium targets; her agents offered competitive prices to consumers; she paid out losses when it was fair, and she refused to pay when her investigators found fraud. Her territory improved its profitability every year she was in charge. She'd even extended the company's service lines—it now offered life insurance in packages that covered only auto and home in the past.

The first time she came up for promotion and didn't get it, Giovanna didn't say anything. The second time, she confronted her director of sales and demanded an explanation.

"To be perfectly blunt," he told her, "your sales teams don't want to work for you."

He continued.

"Several team members have complained about your forceful-ness when negotiating over sales targets, or commented on your hostility when you're under stress." He claimed that someone had mentioned her "aggressive" behavior as their reason for leaving the firm. "Frankly, until you get your management style under control, you're not going to see any promotions."

Giovanna was shocked.

I met with her a few weeks after that conversation, because she'd asked for a coach. When I asked her about how she worked with teams, she described herself as friendly, motivated, and apply-ing high standards of excellence. I asked if she worked people very hard, and she said no, not really. "I don't ask them to do anything I don't do myself."

We agreed that I'd speak with a range of her co-workers, and bring back my observations for further discussion.

To Close Your Performance Gap, You Need to *See* It

After talking with a bunch of people, I learned that the feedback Giovanna's boss had shared wasn't far off base. Her teams were alarmed by her temper and felt too intimidated to state their opin-ions. One person acknowledged her ability to get results. He quickly added that she was "a bully," so he didn't want to work with her.

I collected more information to test what I was hearing. A former team member who'd switched territories commented on Giovanna's intelligence and integrity. She'd made the change be-cause she wanted a better quality of life. "Giovanna is one of the best in the business. I know I could learn a lot from her. She's just so driven—I could never keep up. She only saw how I could do better—she never noticed what I did well. And sometimes I just needed a break. But I was afraid to ask."

When I brought these impressions back to her, Giovanna was taken aback. She said she had "no idea" why anyone would say those harsh things. In fact, she came up with several theories to explain it, none of them relating to her management style. Maybe people were jealous of her all-star results? Or maybe they didn't want another woman rising into the ranks of leadership? I had my work cut out for me to help her connect *herself* in any way to the delay in her career progress.

Seeing Your Gap Means Expanding Your Profile

The first step in closing your Performance Gap is seeing your own role in the results you're getting. Giovanna can muse about jealous colleagues all she likes. It isn't going to get her promoted any faster.

Here's the tricky part. In order for her to see how she's getting in her own way, Giovanna needs to admit and accept something about herself that she doesn't recognize yet. It's not that she hasn't heard the feedback. *It's that she can't believe it without changing something about her profile, the way she defines herself **to herself**.*

In the story she tells about herself, Giovanna is a principled, hardworking, and very successful businesswoman. She sees herself as a mentor who's committed to developing her teams. In fact, she goes out of her way to show them opportunities for improvement. She connects people on LinkedIn. She gives that little extra push so they'll stretch and grow. Her teams do work hard. But she always gives time off when people ask for it, no questions asked. Nowhere in her current autobiography is there room for Giovanna the Bully.

Seeing Your Performance Gap Enables Accountability

Normally we'd think someone needs to be honest with her, to tell her the hard truth. But she has the facts. People say she's a bully. They feel intimidated by her. They change territories or leave the company to avoid working with her. Until she registers that she has an aggressive side, and *integrates the information* that she becomes hostile under stress, she has no way to take accountability for the reactions she's getting.

Here's the rub: *Giovanna will only close her Performance Gap for real when she meets those sides of herself, and lets them into her profile.* Until then, she'll keep doing what she's doing now: make things up about the motivations of other people to explain why they say these mean—and untrue—things about her. In other words, she'll point fingers rather than take accountability. What else can she do? No one wants to take responsibility for something they believe they didn't do.

Once she knows about Giovanna the Bully, she can make a deal, negotiate an arrangement where Bully Giovanna can use her strength for good, and temper her hostility by partnering with Giovanna the Mentor. She can't broker any internal agreements, though, until she knows which negotiators to bring to the table.

Now, you might ask, why should she "negotiate" with her inner bully? Shouldn't she just get rid of the bully?

Fair question. Certainly the world doesn't need more bullies. The short answer is no, she shouldn't. For one, because she can't eliminate the drive that comes out in the bully. And for two, that drive has constructive potential, if she *directs it differently*. She's pushing now in *unconstructive* ways, partially because *that drive isn't balanced* by something else. But that doesn't mean she can't change her ways.

When the forceful part of her works *in tandem* with the supportive mentor in her profile, she can combine her inner achiever's drive with care for her team. Giovanna can still crusade for great results while leaving the hammer at home.

Now, let's say Giovanna gets the right parties to the inner table. She wants an arrangement that works better. But she doesn't know how. She can't work this out *until she knows how to negotiate with herself.*

Close the Performance Gap by Negotiating with Yourself

The next step in closing your Performance Gap and developing lasting change is learning to negotiate with yourself.

Negotiate with yourself?

At first this idea sounds strange. Can you talk to yourself without being crazy? Can you disagree with yourself? If you have an argument with yourself, who wins?

As we just saw, our sales manager needs to negotiate a new deal with herself. Mentor Giovanna needs to bargain with Bully Giovanna, so she can get promoted. The two sides need to forge a new way to make friends and influence people. Mentor Giovanna can try to sidestep her inner bully. But she'll start to see lasting change only when she brokers a truce that *both sides* accept.

At the start of my workshops, I ask people for examples of "negotiating with yourself." It's actually not hard to brainstorm a list once you think about it.

People usually come up with personal examples first: Should I eat the ice cream or stick to my diet? Make a scene with the garage for charging more than the estimate, or just pay the bill and move on? Accept the "friend" request from my high school nemesis, or have twenty years not removed the sting?

Soon, the list of topics grows more serious, and often turns to work:

- Should I raise that difficult topic today?
- Say yes to please my boss, or admit my plate is full?
- I want to approach my colleague who's back from bereavement leave, but then I tell myself it's none of my business.
- My client is pushing me hard to do something questionable. Technically speaking, it's not against the written rules. On the other hand, it feels a bit unethical. Should I say no?
- We're nearing our fund-raising target, but we're not quite there. Our biggest donor said I could ask him for more money if we fell short, but I feel awkward going back to him *again*.

As we go about the ordinary business of every day, there are inner commentators competing for our attention. At times they speak nicely. But often their voices debate each other like hostile adversaries on talk radio.

As you know by now, I think of them as negotiating parties—

your inner negotiators. Like actual individuals, these internal negotiators have a range of styles, motivations, and rules of engagement. They have their own interests and preferred outcomes.

I suspect you're no stranger to this inner tug-of-war. A sarcastic part of you wants to make a cutting remark when a colleague "forgets" again to do his part. Your kinder side tells you to talk to him about what's distracting him. The fed-up parent in you wants to scream your head off at your teenager for leaving *another* mess. Your more grounded side knows you should set up a family meeting about chores and responsibilities. Your generous side leans toward loaning more money to your friend who can't seem to manage her debts. But a self-protective voice in you hesitates, whispering in your ear, "She's never paid you back before, and she won't pay you back this time. You need money, too, you know."

These voices can become like bullhorns on a football field, roaring for your attention, when you turn to the most important questions and choices in your life. The risk-taker in you demands that you walk out on a lousy job; the side that worries about the mortgage begs you to keep trying. The dream of your own baby pulls you to do one more round of IVF. Meanwhile the voice of reason looks at the statistics and counsels you, "Just face it. You're not going to conceive, and you should let this go."

Whether these debates continue all day—or for weeks or months—these conflicting voices and the inner turmoil they create leave you ill equipped to make good choices, take effective action, or sleep well at night. They make it difficult to lead your life, and sometimes nearly impossible to lead your organization. Unresolved inner conflicts also prevent you from jumping on opportunities that could take you to a whole new level.

Like Giovanna, your journey toward self-mastery involves:

1. Learning to recognize your inner negotiators
2. Learning to accept and appreciate them
3. Learning to negotiate with them to broker a new deal
4. Learning to anchor in your center of well-being
5. Learning to maintain centering practices over time.

Discover Your Team of Inner Negotiators

Since you first learned about Freud and what he called the ego, id, and superego, you've heard the idea that there's more to you than meets the eye. You might have come across newer ways to name different parts of you: the inner critic; the people-pleaser; the perfectionist; the inner child. Or this concept might seem completely new to you. You might be asking, how can you negotiate with yourself? You might wonder whether distinct "parts" of you even exist.

They really do.

Today, science can prove what theorists have long believed: you are a complex ecosystem, delicately balancing interdependent parts in the shared habitat called "you." Neuroscientists who've mapped the brain confirm that what appears to you and me like a singular mind is, in fact, a combination of many interconnecting parts.

Science writer Steven Johnson describes this in *Mind Wide Open*:

[T]he more you learn about the brain's architecture, the more you recognize that what happens in your head is more like an orchestra than a soloist, with dozens of players contributing to the overall mix. You can hear the symphony as a unified wash of sound, but you can also distinguish the trombones from the timpani, the violins from the cellos.

Sophisticated technology now shows what social science had already claimed: that we're multi-faceted, made of distinct parts with various functions.

Psychologist Jay Earley described this well when he wrote, "the human mind isn't a unitary thing that sometimes has irrational feelings. It is a complex system of interacting parts, each with a mind of its own." Daniel Goleman expressed a similar idea in *Emotional Intelligence*, writing that "in a very real sense we have two minds, one that thinks and one that feels."

Long before this era of modern psychology, this same idea was famously expressed by Walt Whitman in *Song of Myself*: "I am large. I contain multitudes."

Who Was *That Masked Man?*

If you're still not sure about these "inner negotiators," that's fine. See if this helps.

Have you ever found yourself thinking or saying anything like this?

I don't know why I said that—I didn't mean it.
That was strange—something just came over me.
Where did *that* come from? I didn't know I felt so strongly.
I just wasn't myself.
I'm sorry. I'm *really* not like that.

If you recognize any of these thoughts, then you might ask yourself, who or what "comes over you" in those moments? If you weren't yourself, then *who were you*? Is it *possible* that one of your internal negotiators took center stage, if only for a minute?

Maybe you went to shake hands with your son at his graduation, and felt tears welling up in your eyes. If you haven't cried for twenty years, you could ask yourself, "What *was* that?" Or maybe you approached the nurse's station *every ten minutes*, until someone *finally* came to your mother's hospital room with painkillers. If you see yourself as an easygoing, laid-back person, you might feel surprised by the insistent tone coming out of your mouth to command the nurse's attention.

The good news is that our variable nature is adaptive, necessary, and helpful, once understood. Dr. Daniel Siegel, a renowned brain researcher and professor at the University of California, Los Angeles, explains it this way in his book *Mindsight*: "We must accept our multiplicity, the fact that we can show up quite differently in our athletic, intellectual, sexual, spiritual—or many other—states. A heterogeneous collection of states is completely normal in us humans."

If you're worried about multiple personalities, fear not. The "multiple minds" phenomenon we're talking about is universal.

Think about it. Sometimes you go about your day, living like an ordinary Clark Kent. Other days you get the kids out the door, rescue three projects at work, advise your squash partner about his retirement accounts, and help your wife resolve a conflict with her sister. *That* day you're a living, breathing Superman. Women feel these swings inside, too. Some days we feel small. We want someone to step up and fight our battles for us like Prim, Katniss Everdeen's little sister in the *Hunger Games*. Other days we're the Bionic Woman, superpowers and all.

Recognizing how this works is not only a sign of positive mental health. It also opens the door to using the range of your potential in targeted ways. Mythologist Sam Keen wrote: "Few of us know the fantastic characters, emotions, perceptions, and demons that inhabit the theaters that are our minds. We are encouraged to tell a single (true) story, construct a consistent character, fix an identity. We are thus defined more by neglected possibilities than by realized ones." As you get to know your inner negotiators, you'll expand your profile. Then you'll get better outcomes, because you're using strengths and skills you've never put to good use before. The Performance Gap you've come to accept for years will start to close before your eyes.

Missing Team Members Perform Those New Skills

We all have parts of ourselves that we see, and parts that we don't. We've let some of them into our profile. We've left others out.

Why should you care?

Because at the end of the day, if you want to get better results in your life, you need to change what you're saying and doing now that leads to those outcomes. To create lasting change at work and at home, you need to recruit those members of your inner team who are absent or underutilized.

Said another way, each of the inner negotiators performs certain functions. They specialize in different skill sets. *You fall into the Performance Gap again and again because you can't do skills that belong to negotiators you've left behind.*

Over time, as you become more familiar with deactivated sides of you, you'll be amazed at how quickly you can master the skills that belong to the inner negotiators you've newly taken on board.

Inner Negotiators Are Personal, *and* Universal

We've talked so far about inner negotiators you can't see. But what about the ones you *do* know about? Most of you can think of one or two voices you're familiar with, for example:

The Judge	The Artist
The Achiever	The Healer
The Caretaker	The Survivor
The Rebel	The Inventor
The Problem-Solver	The Destroyer
The Gambler	The Rescuer
The Crisis Manager	The Mystic
The Seducer	The Failure
The Teacher	The Explorer
The Skeptic	The Activist

In the privacy of your own mind, your internal negotiators seem idiosyncratic and very personal. After all, they know all of your secrets.

To some extent, they are uniquely your own. Your inner cast of characters reflects what makes you distinctive. That includes things like your role in your family, the place you grew up, your ethnic culture, or your religious upbringing. It also includes things other people can't see—your hurts, your loves, your experiments and mistakes, your personal triumphs and your private traumas. All of these experiences shape the constellation of voices on your inner team.

At the same time, we share some universal forces with common functions, "characters" who populate our human story. They evoke related themes for many people. Noted psychologist Carl Jung talked about these as "archetypes" that belong to what he called the "collective unconscious." That means no one needs to teach you the essence of these images—they're inborn like your DNA.

In other words, you don't need to "learn" how to pump your heart in your body—you're born knowing how to make your heart beat. Jung said you also don't need to learn about core elements of the human experience. You're born with recognition of archetypes, like Mother and Father, Hero and Villain, Ruler and Servant, Wise Elder and Fool.

We've come a long way since Jung. Tremendous work has built on his ideas, such as the pioneering work of Robert Moore and Douglas Gillette, whose book *King, Warrior, Magician, Lover* sharpened our understanding of Jung. Thinkers like Carol Pearson and Caroline Myss have written extensively on archetypes. Other experts created ways of bringing them to life through experience, like my friend and colleague Cliff Barry, who designed a system he calls Shadow Work, and Hal and Sidra Stone, who originated Voice Dialogue. Gestalt. Big Mind. The list goes on.

Across the research, you'll find some thinkers have moved away from the idea of inborn archetypes. They believe we create personified images out of our life experiences, but they still connect us to the larger human story. They discuss related concepts with fancy-sounding names, like imagoes, introjects, schemas, or personal myths.

I don't know whether we come into the world recognizing these patterns, or we learn about them during our lives. What I can tell you is this:

- by the time we reach adulthood, these archetypes or imagoes are alive and well in all of us

- they shape us in ways we can't easily see without working at it
- they play a significant role in why we fall into the Performance Gap
- with a bit of help, we can see clearly how they influence us and drive our experiences
- once we recognize how they're working, we can shift their form and create entirely new possibilities in our leadership and our lives.

Meet the Big Four

Leading mythologist Joseph Campbell described each of us as "a hero with a thousand faces." I think mastering a thousand faces sounds a bit daunting. If you have *all of these* different sides of you, how can you even begin to get a hold on them?

To help people develop as leaders and close their Performance Gap, I focus on a small set of those hundreds of faces. I call the group **The Big Four** (see Figure 2.1).

They are:

- your **Dreamer**
- your **Thinker**
- your **Lover**
- your **Warrior**

To be sure, any four of Campbell's "thousand" can't capture every facet of who you are. Not even close. But that's not the goal here.

THE BIG FOUR

| THINKER | DREAMER |
| WARRIOR | LOVER |

FIGURE 2.1

What the Big Four cover is the basic ground you need to succeed at work and at home. By themselves they won't get you to "self-mastery." On the flip side, you can't get to self-mastery without understanding them. The Big Four are universal, and relevant to the way you function every day. They're also most likely to trip you up if you don't see them coming.

Since I consult to a lot of businesses, I sometimes describe the Big Four as a leadership team, occupying your internal executive suite:

The Chief Executive Officer: CEO, or Dreamer
The Chief Financial Officer: CFO, or Thinker
The Vice President of Human Resources: The VP of HR,
          or Lover
The Chief Operating Officer: COO, or Warrior.

Sitting around a conference room table, these leaders would bring their own expertise and priorities to the conversation. If anyone missed the meeting, the team would make decisions that lacked a perspective vital to the company's success.

Without the CEO, they could miss the bold vision that's essential to an innovative strategy. No CFO, and the budget collapses. Without HR, the right people don't get hired or developed. If the COO's absent, it's all talk and no action (see Table 2.2).

The "Executives" in Your Suite	Function and Role
Your Inner CEO or Dreamer	**Creates possibilities** Sets strategic vision, gives direction
Your Inner CFO or Thinker	**Clarifies perspectives** Analyzes data, manages risk
Your Inner VP of HR or Lover	**Cares about people** Feels emotions, manages relationships
Your Inner COO or Warrior	**Catalyzes performance** Takes action, reaches goals

TABLE 2.2

A business will find itself in trouble if it doesn't envision possibilities, can't appreciate a 360-degree perspective, fails to care for its people, or turns in lackluster performance. This is true for you, too.

Linking the inner negotiators to the working world helps clarify the voices they express. It also points to their respective domains of skill and expertise. However, this helps only to a point. The Big Four represent much more than professional titles.

Wanting, thinking, feeling, and doing—these are part of the shared human experience. The Big Four represent your capacity to dream about the future, to analyze and solve problems, to build relationships with people, and to take effective action. How people *express* the Big Four varies by culture. But the basic functions cross boundaries.

Together the Big Four Lead to Optimal Performance

Whether you're leading a team or running a household, the sides of you expressed by these inner negotiators help you succeed in different ways.

- Sometimes you roll up your sleeves and keep working until you finish your memo for a client. Or you cross-check every name on the list and every table assignment before your family reunion, to make sure no one gets left out, or seated next to the *wrong* cousin. Maybe your business partner calls and asks you to fly to Paris for a one-day meeting—on your daughter's birthday.

Here, you want your **Warrior** in the lead.

- Sometimes you have a family member with special needs—an older parent who can't live alone anymore, or a sibling who's confided in you about struggling with addiction. There's a lot to figure out, like how to pay for assisted living, or how to help your sibling get into recovery while respecting his or her privacy. At work you make judgment calls all the time: about contract terms and conditions; how to comply with regulations; making fair work schedules that divide weekends and holidays among the staff; whether to lower your prices; to name a few.

Here, you need your **Thinker** at the helm.

- Sometimes you have the chance to land a valuable new client. To get their business, you need to show that you really understand their business issue and why it matters to them to fix it now. You only have one shot to build rapport and earn their trust. At home you need strong listening skills, too, if you're talking to your sister whose spouse just walked out, or your co-chair of the annual All-School Dinner who wants to step down.

Here, you want your **Lover** out in front.

- Still at other times you need all of your imagination, to plan the most memorable fiftieth-birthday party for your best friend, or design the best costumes ever for the Pirates and Princesses Parade. You need vision to come up with your third career after you "retire." And a story to tell yourself and your family about why the upcoming move is going to be a grand adventure. At work you need to picture the future: to innovate the products and services that people will want a few years down the line; to hire and develop talent today that you'll need tomorrow; to inspire your workforce; to refine your strategic direction.

Here, you should call on your **Dreamer** first.

Become an Equal Opportunity Employer

Ideally, *you have the Big Four operating within you in balance.* Then you can call on each one when the time is right. In reality, very few of us have easy access to all four. In any given situation, all four inner negotiators are available to us in theory. But we're unlikely to make a real choice that considers all of them. We become increasingly skillful as we call on more of them, and learn to use more of them, comfortably and effectively (see Figure 2.3).

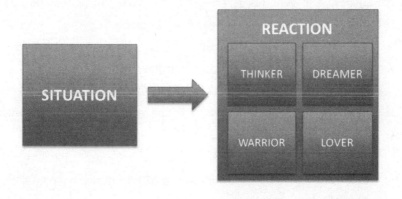

FIGURE 2.3

As we'll explore more in the next chapter, we tend to use one or two of the Big Four a lot—they're lead characters in our profile. We mostly ignore the other ones—they may not figure in our profile at all. Self-mastery involves a process of gathering all four of them together, and practicing how to use their strengths to balance each other.

As I've given talks and taught seminars around the world on this material, people grasp fairly quickly *the idea* of integrating all parts of themselves into their everyday interactions—the inspirational Dreamer; the analytical Thinker; the emotional Lover; and the practical Warrior. As we've talked about a lot in this chapter, what's much harder to get *is how this works in practice*. People wonder, "How do each of the Big Four work inside of me?"

Trust Me, You Have the Big Four Inside of You

The Big Four can be hard to see in yourself. Like these audiences, you might think to yourself, "Emotional Lover? Not me. Ask my employees." Or "Analytical Thinker? Tell that to my husband: he thinks I'm nuts because I read the horoscopes."

I once worked with a rocket scientist who told me he "never feels anything." I told him I found that hard to believe.

"Really," he told me. "I don't have *any* feelings."

I remained skeptical.

"Are you married?" I asked.

"Yes, for twenty-eight years."

"How did you know you wanted to propose if you have no feelings?" I asked.

"That's easy," he said. "Because she was the girl of my dreams, and I knew I would go crazy if I couldn't be with her."

You might not recognize the Big Four in yourself right away. But they're in there.

The Big Four *and You*

For some of you, the way you relate to the Big Four is unmistakable. For others, you're just starting to think about it: Which of the Big Four have I embraced? Have I left any behind? Am I able to balance them to make good choices and take effective action in my life? Which one do I need to develop the most?

It's hard to give you a good answer to those questions in a book. If you want a richer picture of your profile, you can take the survey at www.winningfromwithin.com. Just click on "My Big Four Profile." For now, let's put a toe in the water with a quick exercise. This might jump-start your reflections—but don't put too much weight on what you find.

Profile Quiz: *Getting a Snapshot*

Table 2.4 shows an exchange between two spouses. First, read the comment from "your spouse." Then read the four possible responses. As you read the choices, imagine that *you* are the spouse who needs to respond, and ask yourself:

1.   If this is me, which sample reply will I give first?
2.   Do any of them strike me as "clearly" the most helpful?
3.   Do any of them strike me as something I would never say?

In real life, your response might combine several of these elements. And in real life, these comments might not capture the *wording* you'd choose. For the purpose of this exercise, focus on *the approach* more than the exact words, and pick one you might take as your opening reply.

> Your spouse says: "I really need a vacation. I know we're broke. But I'm burned out and exhausted. I need to recharge my batteries."
>
> **Your opening response is one of the following:**
>
> **ONE:** "Sounds great. I can see us on a blanket on the beach with drinks in our hands. Shining sun. Lapping waves. Cool breeze. Perfect."
>
> **TWO:** "I think we're over our budget. I don't know if there's any surplus we can spend. If we estimate the cost of a long weekend, we can compare the expense to our savings, and then determine what we can afford."
>
> **THREE:** "I'm sorry to hear you're so exhausted. Tell me more: what's going on with you?"
>
> **FOUR:** "Well, if you work a bunch of overtime in the next few weeks, and we only eat at home, we can pay down the credit cards. But if we can't lower the debt dramatically, we can't go."
>
> ---
>
> **TABLE 2.4**

Which response sounds the most like where you would start? Do you like any of them the best? Do you reject any of them outright? Can you identify which negotiator is speaking?

In the first case, you hear the voice of the Dreamer, immediately envisioning the vacation and inspired by the picture of the beach. In the second comment, the Thinker comes through, inclined to look at the numbers and make a rational assessment. In the third reply, the spouse embodies the Lover, empathizing and reaching out to hear more. The fourth response reflects the stance of the Warrior, considering what actions to take toward the goal. The Warrior is also ready to draw the line and say no if needed.

Chances are that you reacted more positively to one or two of these responses. If that's right, you might think more about those inner negotiators, and whether you favor them over the others in real life. To explore a little more, ask yourself what positive results you get from using those voices frequently. Likewise, think about what possible negative impact you might be getting from doing that.

For instance, if you gravitate naturally to the Dreamer, you might be great at inspiring your teams. On the flip side, if you're quick to offer your vision at every team meeting, it's possible you're not leaving enough room for others to share *their* vision with the group.

It's also possible that you reacted negatively to one or two of these approaches. You can ask the same questions of yourself. What benefits am I getting by rejecting this voice? What possible negative impact does it have on me or my life that I'm doing that?

So, for example, let's say you really didn't like the voice of the Warrior. Maybe you found it harsh and unfeeling. Maybe you thought the request deserved more brainstorming and problem-solving before jumping to a conclusion.

In your life, you might find good reasons to stay away from this practical, tough-love approach. Maybe you pride yourself on the way your kids always come to you when they need someone to listen. Or you value your reputation in the state bar association as a lawyer who prefers to collaborate. These are great outcomes you're getting.

At the same time, if you reject the Warrior nine times out of ten, what are you giving up? Maybe those same kids who love to talk to you will turn to other people when they need the cold, hard truth. They don't trust your feedback, because they know you're always "supportive." Those same colleagues might not refer clients to you. Deep down they value a lawyer who'll fight. They question whether you'll go the distance if a lawsuit turns ugly.

Every profile has its trade-offs.

If you really wanted to go on that vacation, take care of your spouse, and protect your family's financial health, you'd be well served to draw on *all of the Big Four*—at the right time and in the right way. Putting that potential into practice is what closing the Performance Gap is all about.

Are Mother and Father the Same?

For our purposes, we're not going into detail about variations among archetypes between men and women. Let me acknowledge that differences exist, just like researchers have found some differences in the brains of men and women. Despite not engaging the topic deeply, I'd be remiss not to touch on the gender aspect of inner negotiators at all. If you're interested, I recommend classic works in this area by Carol Gilligan, Jean Shinoda Bolen, Robert Bly, and Sam Keen. I also suggest you review research from UCLA on different survival responses of women and men.

In my work introducing archetypes to clients from nearly every professional discipline, I can say that gender difference has played a smaller role than this vast area of research would suggest. Let me offer one example.

Do you remember Susan Boyle? She came out of nowhere and

captured the world's attention by singing on television. How did this middle-aged, frumpish lady sing one song on *Britain's Got Talent* and become an international superstar overnight?

I'd say it's because Susan Boyle is both an ordinary woman and a timeless archetype. Don't we all want people to look beyond our outer blemishes to discover our inner beauty and hidden gifts? Aren't we all like the frog waiting to be kissed, so everyone can see us rise and stand fully in our nobility?

I've witnessed the drive that Susan Boyle taps into—to feel seen and appreciated—in men and women in equal measure. Both men and women also have a part inside that's drawn to self-destruct. Both are capable of acting The Loyal Friend, and The Betraying Spouse. Both can play The Tyrant, The Martyr, The Victim, or The Savior. Both can play The Virgin, The Whore, or The Saint. Both at times feel needy and powerless; both carry amazing strength and resilience.

Yes, the development journeys of heroes and heroines include different obstacles and unique milestones. At the same time, fundamentally, we're all human. That's the perspective I'm taking as we continue our basic exploration.

CHAPTER 3

Work with Your Big Four

I asked myself, "What is the myth you are living?"
and found that I did not know.
So . . . I took it upon myself
To get to know "my" myth,
And I regarded this
As the task of tasks. . . .

—CARL JUNG

During the economic collapse of 2008, I worked with a leadership group at a large manufacturer. The highlight of the weeklong training session was a visit to the group by their CEO. The group looked forward to the speech, expecting some insight into the company's current position in the downturn and future corporate strategy. Instead, when the CEO came to speak, he shared the personal journey he'd been on since the recession began.

"What I have come to realize this past year," the top executive told the audience, "is that I need to cope with myself—and with what I call my 'evil twin.' In meetings, I sometimes lead with the 'Good Andrew,' and sometimes with the 'Bad Andrew.'" Under the intense pressure of the financial crisis, the CEO explained, there was a higher tendency than usual for "Bad Andrew" to take over. "Bad Andrew" did things like lose his temper, cut people off, or blame and shame members of the team.

The CEO had come to see that "Bad Andrew" could wreak havoc on his top team. In these very tough times, it was more important than ever for him to bring "Good Andrew" forward. "Good Andrew" listened to people, gave them the benefit of the doubt, and instilled hope and energy into the team.

At the heart of his message to this group of leaders was an appeal to recognize what he called their "good" and "bad" sides. He asked them to try hard to bring their "good" sides to work, particularly while everyone felt the squeeze of the recession.

In your day-to-day life—when you're not reading this book—you probably give little thought to your different sides. When you do think about them, you might muse along the same lines as this CEO. You like your good Dr. Jekyll self, and dislike your bad Mr. Hyde.

Let me tell you something. This is not the way to go if you want to close your Performance Gap, or get better outcomes in your leadership and your life.

Judging Your Big Four Gets in Your Way

By the end of this book, I hope you don't think about parts of yourself as good and bad. At least not as a general theory about who you are. I don't think anyone can escape this binary thinking all the time. But it stinks as a way of life.

I know it's tempting to love what seems good about you, like your generosity. Then you can despise what feels truly awful about you. For me, that includes my neediness, my weakness (dare I say it, my vulnerability). I'm guessing you know a part of yourself that you'd like to take a hike and not come back. Ever. That's your version of "Bad Andrew."

The problem is that when you judge a part of yourself like that, you conclude you're best off by getting rid of it. And that's the opposite of what's going to help you generate more success and deeper satisfaction. Psychologist Robert Johnson put this well in his book *Living Your Unlived Life*: "Becoming whole is a game in which you get rid of nothing; you cannot do without these diverse energies any more than you can do without one of the physical organs that make up your body. You need to draw upon everything that is available to you." There's also the practical dynamic expressed succinctly by Carl Jung himself: "what you resist persists."

You can *certainly* change the way you express parts of yourself. You can recover from destructive patterns that have hurt you, or other people. You can adapt strategies from your past that don't work anymore, and develop new ones in their place. But those processes relate to transformation and integration, not rejection and elimination.

Let me ask you a question. Which of the following are better, and which are worse: North, South, East, and West? Hard to choose? How about these—which are worth keeping, and which should you throw out: Winter, Spring, Summer, and Fall? I don't mean which season do you *enjoy* more. I mean intrinsically, which of them is better or worse? Which can stay and which need to go?

These aren't meant as trick questions. My hope is that, seeing them in this light, you can appreciate that forces of nature aren't better or worse. They're just part of life. I believe that you and I are like that, too. North, South, East, West. In, Out, Up, Down. Dreamer, Thinker, Lover, Warrior. Forces of nature. Consider the affirming words of Chinese Zen master Wu-men Hui-k'ai:

Ten thousand flowers in the spring, the moon in autumn,
a cool breeze in summer, snow in winter.
If your mind isn't clouded by unnecessary things,
This is the best season of your life.

You will be healthier, more effective, and more helpful to the people and causes you care about, to the extent you let yourself access all of the Big Four and bring them into balance with each other.

Of course, *you do need to use them wisely and well.* You can direct these natural forces in a number of directions, creating a range of results.

- The endless **Dreamer** can bankrupt his family chasing windmills. The Dreamer can also bring a neighborhood together to build a shared vision for reducing violence in their streets.
- The aloof **Thinker** can scar her children by never showing them love. The Thinker can also find solutions to vexing problems that will save lives.
- The callous **Lover** can break your heart. The devoted Lover can bring you a sense of home for the first time in your life.
- The **Warrior** in a relationship can scare you, even hurt you physically. The Warrior can also protect you, taking a vow to never let anything or anyone harmful come near you.

The Big Four can be used to different ends. It's up to you to apply them thoughtfully.

To sum up:

1. You need all of the Big Four to develop and deliver a well-rounded skill set.
2. You'll reject and push away parts of the Big Four that you judge as unworthy.

3. You won't be able to perform the skills that belong to parts you reject.

4. You're better off adapting old strategies into new ones, rather than trying to eliminate parts of yourself that you don't want around anymore.

All for One and One for All

As you know, the Big Four enable your visioning, thinking, feeling, and achieving. They make it possible for you to take four approaches to leading and living: inspirational, analytical, relational, and practical. They each care about different things. They draw on unique strengths. And most important right now, *they enable different skills.*

Table 3.1 provides an overview with more detail.

Negotiator Within	Focus of Attention	Power Source	Skills For
Dreamer	What I want What I don't want	Intuition	Innovation
Thinker	My opinion My ideas	Reason	Analysis
Lover	How we both feel Our level of trust	Emotion	Relationship
Warrior	What task to do What line to draw	Willpower	Accomplishment

TABLE 3.1

In my travels consulting to companies big and small, the skills enabled by the Big Four are the ones I see people getting measured by in their jobs. If you look back at the sample competency grid in chapter 1, you'll see what amount to the Big Four categories. That's no accident.

People are typically evaluated on their capability in these four areas: Vision, Analysis, People, and Execution. Of course, the emphasis varies according to role and responsibility. But time and again, it comes back to the Big Four.

How you're evaluated on these scales impacts a lot, including: getting hired in the first place; selection into high-potentials programs; getting raises and year-end bonuses; winning promotions; landing prized opportunities; keeping your job in a reorganization; and entering and moving up in leadership.

So Much to Do, So Little Time

As you can imagine, your Dreamer, Thinker, Lover, and Warrior can do lots of things. To keep this manageable, I've highlighted three "sweet spots" for each of the Big Four. These seem most valuable for people, both at work and at home (see Figure 3.2).

To close the loop from earlier, you can still decide to judge one of the Big Four, or decide you don't want it around. If you do, be aware that you're likely to hit a wall when you need to perform the skills it enables.

Take Bella, who's closely identified with her Lover side. She thinks Warrior energy is evil (see Figure 3.3). Bella needs to lay people off, but she can't bring herself to schedule the discussions. The company is losing cash every month on extra overhead because Bella can't bear the thought of delivering the bad news.

SWEET SPOTS

THINKER

Apply Facts and Logic
Consider Consequences
Look from All Sides

DREAMER

Generate Your Vision
Dare to Pursue Your Dream
Sense a Path Forward

WARRIOR

Speak Hard Truths
Hold Your Ground
Take Action

LOVER

Connect with Emotions
Build and Maintain Trust
Collaborate with Others

FIGURE 3.2

In theory she's right that Warrior energy *can* be used in harmful ways. But as a natural force it's neutral, and right now, *her inner Warrior is what she needs to do her job.* Having banished her Warrior, she's not only hurting herself, she's harming her organization. It isn't evil to terminate employees when you can't afford to pay their salaries.

Or Jared, highly practical, who embraces *only* the Warrior side of himself. He doesn't think his grant writers will get the application done in time to fund their mission to Rwanda. He hasn't seen the timeline for implementation of Phase One and Phase Two before the pilot program. He doesn't have the budget, which needs to

BELLA'S CURRENT REACTION

THINKER   DREAMER

WARRIOR   LOVER

FIGURE 3.3

spell out exactly how the funds will get allocated and spent. And as far as he can tell, no one has finished the written instruments they need to include with the grant for monitoring and evaluation of the program. Disaster.

Given the situation, Jared sees the need to push even harder. He starts leaving urgent voice mails everywhere he can think to call, demanding documents. He emails the team with an expedited schedule for producing the application, despite not knowing how far along the documents are, or what's required to meet his new deadlines.

Unfortunately, his messages felt to the writers like adding insult to injury. They're professionals. They had every intention of meeting the original schedule. They weren't lacking in deadlines. They'd slowed down because in focusing on each of their individual pieces of the grant, they'd lost the grand vision. All of them cared deeply about the Rwanda project and wanted to see it succeed. They just needed a reminder of the aspirations behind their mission.

Ironically, Jared was drafting the Impact Statement for the executive director to edit. He needed to prepare answers to the questions "What is the change you envision as a result of this program?" and "How you will measure progress toward this change?" He'd written things like this many times, so this section was a no-brainer for him.

Had his Dreamer been truly engaged, he might have thought to circulate his document to the writers. Reading about the potential to change the lives of the people they'd met, and the empowerment of the local community they'd see after the program, would've refueled their motivation. Jared misread their behavior entirely: the slip in momentum reflected a need for him to excite the team, not beat them up.

Trouble was, he'd decided long ago that "soft skills" were useless for getting things done. Telling an inspiring story is a skill that belongs to the Dreamer—a part of himself he drew on almost despite himself when describing the goals of the program. With only his Warrior available for managing the grant writers, he had only Warrior skills to apply (see Figure 3.4). And that was *not* what the doctor ordered.

As I hope is clear by now, you need all of your Big Four available to you, so their respective expertise is there when you need it.

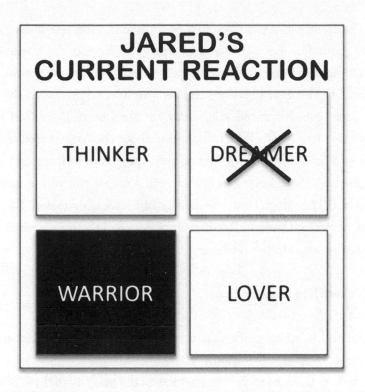

FIGURE 3.4

"All or Nothing" Gets in Your Way, Too

Let's imagine Bella and Jared reached their year-end performance reviews. Bella got feedback about stepping up to the plate. In the face of a difficult but important set of conversations, she'd chosen to avoid them as long as possible. That behavior had directly impacted the bottom line. Jared got a lecture on his blind spot about inspirational leadership.

What did they do with these evaluations?

Bella sent a text to her two best friends. "Review today was not good. I'm too soft. Need to grow up. Business is business." That night she promised herself that starting tomorrow, she would "check her heart at the door" and become a "real" professional.

Jared met his friend Alexander for a drink at Tavern on the Square. Over cocktails he complained about the "stupid feedback." He wondered out loud, "What do these people want from me? We applied for three large grants this year. We got two of them, and one is still pending. That sounds a lot like leadership to me." By the time they'd left the bar, Jared was looking up executive search firms on his phone. He was done.

This Isn't Win, Lose, or Draw

Bella and Jared are stuck. Their reactions look different. But they share an outlook: all-or-nothing.

When Bella hears her feedback, she determines that to follow the advice, she needs to abandon her previous tendency and reverse it completely. She *had* a profile with a High Lover and a Low Warrior. Now she aims to flip her profile the other way, to a Low Lover with a High Warrior.

For Bella, it's up *or* down, left *or* right, Lover *or* Warrior. But that's a false choice. Bella can use both—Lover *and* Warrior—at the right time, in an effective way, for a constructive purpose (see Figure 3.5). Why choose one?

Think of the way parents give kids a time-out. They often affirm the child while at the same time they disapprove of his behavior:

"Sammy, you cannot hit your sister. Tell her you're sorry. . . . Now, you have a time-out for five minutes. You know I love you,

BELLA'S OPTIMAL REACTION

| THINKER | DREAMER |
| WARRIOR | LOVER |

FIGURE 3.5

and you're a good person. But hitting is not allowed. Not in this house, or anywhere else. You go sit on the stairs and think about that. And when you come back, we'll finish making cookies."

Appreciation *and* boundaries. Yes *and* no. Relationship *and* rules. Lover *and* Warrior.

It's Not a Zero-Sum World

Jared sees a similar choice. Give up his style completely, and satisfy his organization. Or stay exactly the same, and leave. "This is me," he told his friend Alexander. "They can take it or leave it." Alexander agreed. "Oh well. It's their loss."

What does Jared think they're telling him? That he *shouldn't care* about meeting deadlines? That *it doesn't matter* if the documentation is complete? Does he really think the executive director wants him to inspire his team *at the cost* of getting grants done well, and winning them? I highly doubt that.

Jared has an opportunity to develop, personally and professionally. He's been asked to expand his repertoire. Only in *his* mind does that mean giving up what he already does well. No one's asking him to trade in his Warrior in exchange for taking on his inner Dreamer. Again, that's a false choice.

Given his track record for winning grants, it would also be a dumb choice. His Warrior is very good at pulling everything together and fulfilling all requirements. He's a good *leader of projects*: he implements well. To go to the next level, Jared needs to retain his excellence in execution, *and* grow capacity in another category on the competency grid: vision.

His Dreamer happens to have some skill. He hits all the right notes when he answers questions about the purpose of the program and the benefits it can provide. Now he needs to bring that visionary Dreamer into his *leadership of his team*.

As long as Jared believes he needs to choose between them, his Warrior will take the day. That's okay, but it will keep him standing in the same Performance Gap he knows all too well—the distance between how *he wants to contribute* to Rwanda, and the *document management* he's doing now.

This is a Gap that Jared can close. Doing that would change his life.

If Jared closed this Performance Gap, he'd feel more fulfilled by playing a more substantive role. He'd earn more money, gaining better financial security. He'd make a bigger difference on the ground for people he cares about, deriving more meaning from his work. He'd develop a reputation for expertise in shaping international missions.

Who knows what doors would open?

The land of opportunity awaits.

But getting there means Jared needs to stop shutting out the information that he has a bit of work to do to grow as a leader. Advice to develop ways to harness his Dreamer's strengths is the farthest thing from "stupid." It's *exactly what he should do* to close his Performance Gap and achieve more of his potential.

It's a Path, Not a PowerPoint Deck

Can Jared snap his fingers and release his vibrant Dreamer power? Can he attend a one-day seminar on Leading with Vision and turn a lifelong pattern around? No, we all know that he can't. Does that mean the change is impossible? Not at all.

This is why people talk about the "path" to self-mastery. It's not a "tool" you gain by attending a webinar. A path is a set of practices, based on the structure of a journey, designed to help you move forward.

Of course, as anyone who's ever tried to follow a path will tell you, "moving forward" is trickier than it sounds. In real life, exploring a developmental path *often feels like you're moving backward.* It can feel like going in circles. Human beings are a messy business. There are no straight lines to heaven.

Like learning anything new, you'll progress faster and more

deeply if you take a class, work with a partner or small group, find a coach or teacher, or engage in an experiential learning program. However, *even if you do all that*, a word to the wise: *Expect the sense that you're moving forward **and** backward*. It happens to everyone.

Also, though you might sense backsliding, you could be right on one level and wrong on another. The inner journey sometimes operates by reverse rules: moving forward *can look and feel like* moving backward. So, while you're busy ruminating that your process "isn't working," somewhere outside the reaches of your perception, you're on the move.

How do I know? Because I've accompanied thousands of people on such journeys. I recognize the highs and lows. I've seen the cycles again and again. I know if you're aiming to "fix" yourself, you'll get frustrated. And I know that if you're open to some surprises—even a few mysteries you can't explain—your possibilities are enormous.

I'd simplify a common experience this way:

- You're going along fine in life, unburdened by your hidden Performance Gap.
- Something happens that puts your Gap on your radar screen—sometimes *big time*.
- You commit to doing something about it.
- You learn about your inner world—perhaps you start a self-exploration with your Big Four.
- You practice a bunch of things at home, and at work. You see a few changes, mostly subtle. Maybe you start to handle a specific interaction differently, and that feels good.
- You're not sure much is happening.

- Then, out of nowhere, you face a significant challenge, maybe one you didn't see coming.

- You surprise yourself by how skillfully and wisely you handle it. Now *that* was different.

- You're amazed that you've closed a Performance Gap that you've repeatedly fallen into *for years*.

- You might not repeat that success all the time. But you gain confidence in your new approach, and you start to integrate it into your core way of operating.

- People around you notice. They start to comment that "you look good" and that "you've changed." Often they can't quite put their finger on it: they ask if you've got a new haircut, or lost some weight. While they're not sure exactly how to **name** what's different, the people around you **will experience** the shifts that have taken place. And **you** know it's not the haircut.

The good news is that if you start down a path, and commit to it, *you will see results in the outside world* of your inner development. Others' perceptions of you will change, and your self-perceptions—your profile—will, too. The way you get there might be different than you'd expect. Or different from what you would've liked. But you'll get there.

There's another reason why I know how these cycles work. I've been down this road more than a few times myself. More times than I can count. I've embraced the Big Four, rejected them, and lived them in every combination. I've had wonderfully successful long-term relationships. I also called off my first marriage with my fiancé one month before our wedding. I've managed money well, and lost a valued role over doubt about my ability to do just that.

I have dreams that I've fulfilled, and others that will never come to pass.

And so it goes. We're human. We succeed. We fail. We try to learn, to grow, and do better next time.

To journey is a fundamental act of living.

I have a little plaque on my desk in Boston. It has an axiom of Hebrew wisdom on it. It says: "It is not upon you to finish the task. But neither are you free to desist from undertaking it." I think there's truth to that. Backward, forward; forward, backward. We'll never "finish." But we can't desist from undertaking it.

CHAPTER 4

Anchor in Your Center

Let the beauty we love be what we do.
There are hundreds of ways to kneel
and kiss the ground.
—Jalaluddin Rumi

As you know, my husband Bernardus is from The Netherlands. So I live in Amsterdam for part of the year.

There are lots of differences between Americans and the Dutch, most of which I discover by breaking unwritten rules of culture that you learn only by violating them. Hard as I try, I can't stop ordering Diet Coke instead of wine or beer with dinner, despite the knowing smiles and the inevitable comment whispered under someone's breath, as if telling a very personal secret: *"She's American."*

For the record, the Dutch don't actually wear those little wooden clogs they sell to tourists. They do have windmills, but they're far more modern than the ones you and I picture when we think of Holland. They also have a custom of enjoying a slice of apple cake when they get together with family or friends. To show solidarity with my new country, I practice that tradition as often as possible.

One aspect of culture I've discovered is that going to the sauna is a big thing in Europe. In Scandinavia, people have saunas *in their homes.* My husband and his friends enjoy the sauna in the classic way. They sit in the heat and sweat for ten minutes. Then, when they're really hot, they jump into a freezing cold pool. Needless to say, this is among the Dutch customs I have *not* embraced.

When I asked Bernardus if he enjoys the feeling of jumping into the freezing cold water, he said, "Of course not. It's like torture."

"Then why do you do it?" I asked.

"It's the feeling you have right after getting out of the freezing cold water," he told me. "My body tingles all over. I get a total clarity of mind. I feel open, calm. I feel free."

Then I got it. *This is their road to center*.

Moving from hot to cold and back again, these sauna-lovers shock their systems to snap out of it, to release the weight of what mindfulness expert Jon Kabat-Zinn calls "the full catastrophe"— the roller coaster of our daily lives. You and I might not choose their method. But all of us need ways to step off the grid, shake off everyday burdens, and get back to solid ground.

We all need routes back to our center of well-being.

Meet Your Inner Board of Directors

So far we've talked about the Big Four, in charge of your Wanting, Thinking, Feeling, and Doing. The Big Four represent different aspects of you: the Inspirational Dreamer, the Analytical Thinker, the Relational Lover, and the Practical Warrior. These four serve as symbols for your inner executive suite: your Dreamer as CEO, your Thinker as CFO, your Lover as the VP of HR, and your Warrior as COO. Now we'll take another step. In the professional world, these leaders would get oversight from a board of directors. Metaphorically speaking, you do, too.

Boards of directors play valuable roles. They bring an independent perspective, enabling them to monitor organizational effectiveness, compliance with the law, and pursuit of the mission.

Boards provide governance at the "big picture" level, guiding the pursuits of performance, good-faith behavior, and improvement over time.

Your team of inner negotiators delivers its highest performance when supervised by a Board as well. Like any group, members of the Big Four are susceptible to conflicts of interest. Your inner Board operates independently, without allegiance to any one of the Big Four over another. Your inner Directors hold the Big Four accountable for staying true to your purpose and values. They also encourage you to keep developing over time.

Opinions vary on the ideal size of a professional board, generally ranging from three to thirty members. People on these boards share a set of responsibilities, and they serve in specific roles as well. In addition to the overall mandate, a board member might sit on the nominating committee, the audit committee, or the compensation committee.

Your inner Board has three Directors. They, too, have a common mandate: they share general oversight of your Big Four. Then each of them has a unique, particular role, which we'll look at in a minute. Your inner Directors aim to keep you grounded, balanced, purposeful, satisfied, and successful.

You Are More Than Your Big Four

While I compared your Big Four to a CEO and other executive officers, I also said those professional titles were limiting. That's why the Winning from Within method uses the Big Four names instead. Likewise, the image of an inner Board of Directors paints a picture of additional roles getting played in your internal world.

And in the same way, that work-related symbol diminishes the real depth involved. So, in this system, I refer to the three members of your inner Board by calling them your Transformers.

As a group, the Transformers operate independent of the Big Four. As their name suggests, they're each a catalyst in the change process. The Transformers exist on a different level than the Big Four, operating at the core of who you are. I call the distinct Transformers your **Lookout**, your **Captain**, and your **Voyager**.

Rather than seeing your Big Four as your core, Winning from Within puts your Transformers at your center, as you see represented in the image that follows (see Figure 4.1).

In common parlance, people talk about what I'm calling the Big Four as belonging to the human ego, or persona. In Western society, we often conflate the ego with our full identity. In other words, perhaps without even realizing it, we start believing that our Big Four constitute all of who we are.

By and large, wisdom traditions take a different view.

Huston Smith is a renowned scholar and a leading voice on philosophical traditions. His specialty is comparative religions, about which he has said, "If we take the world's enduring religions at their best, we discover the distilled wisdom of the human race." In his many books, Smith affirms that this "distilled wisdom" points to deeper dimensions of human nature than the Big Four.

Robert Thurman is another well-known scholar. He's also a professor and an expert on Buddhist philosophy. He calls identification with the ego a "blinding misperception." In his book *Inner Revolution*, Thurman writes that "our operative psychologies teach the habitual ego-centered self is the only one there is, so they reinforce our enslavement to its demands for comfort, stability and consumption." As a group, your Transformers appreciate deeper

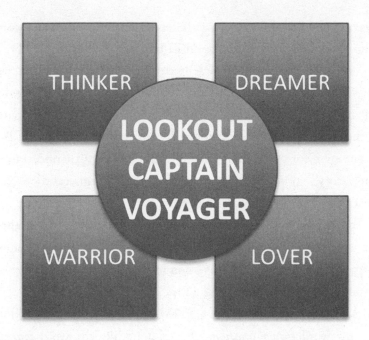

THINKER   DREAMER

LOOKOUT
CAPTAIN
VOYAGER

WARRIOR   LOVER

FIGURE 4.1

dimensions of you, enabling what Thurman calls "freedom from enslavement to the ego as center of the universe."

Putting the Transformers together in one system with the Big Four creates a bridge between our contemporary, action-oriented life and the more introspective teachings of timeless wisdom. It creates an integrated method of "practical wisdom"—a way to apply deeper truths to the choices and interactions we face every day. This more unified way of living and leading brings about outer advancement through inner development, what I'm calling "winning from within."

Your Transformers enable a progression that's been given many names, including individuation, self-actualization, liberation, and awakening from the trance of the small self. Those names come from disciplines not often found in business conversation. But as I've said, we live in unprecedented times. We're looking across boundaries in all sorts of ways for footholds where we can stand in this new world. As one example, VUCA is a term that originated in the military but is heard today in leadership circles. VUCA is an acronym for our current state of affairs: volatility, uncertainty, complexity, and ambiguity. Interdisciplinary conversation is a creative by-product of times like ours.

In the rest of this chapter, I'll introduce you to your three Transformers. I'll give you a few ideas about them, and also apply them to a real-world example. Then in Part Three, we'll look more closely at them, one chapter at a time.

Before we do that, let me acknowledge that some people don't like the word *transformation*. Others don't like the word *journey*. Or the word *change*. You can use any words you want when you think about your development. What matters is that you find a path that works for you, and then you commit to it. The spirit of this idea was described nicely by Michael Bernard Beckwith in his book *Spiritual Liberation*:

> Call it a renewal, redemption, resurrection, transfiguration, or transformation—it doesn't matter. The freedom of discipline means that you agree to free yourself from the limitation of playacting the role assigned to you by society, family, religions, and education, and accept the part that has been written for you since the beginning of time: being your Self.

Transformer One: The Lookout

In 1861, Henry Wadsworth Longfellow penned a poem about a celebrated American figure. His poem, titled "Paul Revere's Ride," opens with these well-known lines:

Listen, my children, and you shall hear
Of the midnight ride of Paul Revere,
On the eighteenth of April, in Seventy-Five;
Hardly a man is now alive
Who remembers that famous day and year.

Longfellow paid tribute to the legendary Paul Revere—possibly the most famous lookout in American history.

A patriot in the American Revolution, Paul Revere was keeping watch on the British military. As any good lookout would do, he created a warning system to alert the colonial militia of approaching British forces. The renowned lookout designed a signal that is well-known to this day. "One if by land, two if by sea" would indicate the British army's choice to approach by land or by crossing the Charles River.

History and legend squabble over the way Revere issued his warning about the movement of the king's troops. American folklore tells it that Revere rode through town, sounding the alarm by calling out his message: *"The British are coming!"* Some accounts suggest he was more subtle. Yet all agree that Revere played a central role in looking out for that lantern signal from the North Church. Revere's role as lookout even included warning Samuel Adams and John Hancock that British troops sought their capture on the night of his famous Midnight Ride. As the battle on Lexington Green ensued, Revere helped Hancock and his family to escape from Lexington.

So, what is a lookout?

As demonstrated ably by Paul Revere, a lookout keeps watch on what's going on, and delivers messages to people who need to take action on the information they get from the lookout. If all goes well, the lookout sends the critical information to those who need it before things go wrong.

One of the members of your internal Board is your *inner Lookout*. As you can imagine, your Lookout keeps an eye on what's going on *with you*. Let's say you're feeling annoyed, and you're drafting a nasty email to your colleague. Before you hit the "send" key, your inner Lookout *sends you* an "instant message" to point out the mess that you'll make by sending it. With that momentary warning, you think better of it, and hit "delete" instead.

Your inner Lookout pays close attention to what's happening inside of you. Specifically, Lookouts watch how your Big Four are doing, and whether any of them is reacting strongly to something going on. Maybe you're at a meeting, listening to a presentation. Your Thinker finds the speaker boring, and misinformed. You have the impulse from your Thinker to interrupt the talk and offer a correction. Thankfully your Lookout is on the job. She sends you an instant message, noting that the presenter is the son of your boss. You decide to daydream instead of take him down.

Your Lookout is transformational because it takes the first step toward *separating you from your Big Four*. Why is that so crucial? Because absent the Lookout's perspective, more often than not we hear directives from our Big Four, and we implement them. One, two: just like that. We feel angry and we make a snide remark. We feel the pull to solve someone's problem, and we offer a solution. We don't consider the limited view that each inner negotiator holds. They issue a command, and we follow suit.

Your Lookout watches the strategies that your Big Four carry around, and sees them for what they are: impulses, suggestions, possibilities that you *might* follow—*or you might not.* They aren't demands. They aren't commandments. *They are expressions of various parts of you*—no less, and no more. It's the voice of the Lookout that whispers to you, "This is *your Warrior talking,* not *you"* or "This is *your Lover feeling these strong emotions,* not *you." This perspective changes everything.*

Transformer Two: The Captain

Wangari Maathai was a Kenyan environmentalist and political activist who founded the Green Belt Movement. She led an extraordinary life and left an enormous legacy. She illustrates the Captain's ability to call on *all of the Big Four,* and the potential for impact when you lead and live that way.

- **With her Dreamer** she had a vision to show the world connections between environmental conservation, human rights, and poverty reduction. She dreamt of safeguarding public lands and improving women's lives. In passionate pursuit of her hopes for a better world, Maathai served on a United Nations panel to advance the Millennium Development Goals, the most successful worldwide antipoverty effort in history. She was the first African woman to win the Nobel Peace Prize.

- **With her Thinker** she studied biological science as well as chemistry, not only earning a master's degree but also becoming the first woman in East Africa to earn a doctorate. Professor Maathai taught veterinary medicine and authored four books. She was awarded honorary degrees from multiple universities and contributed her ideas to global policy debates about climate change.
- **With her Lover** she promoted conservation not only to protect the earth, but also to care for people. She saw how environmental activism could improve the lives of women and children, and devoted her life to their cause. Together with other Nobel laureates Maathai also worked for peace and democracy around the world.
- **With her Warrior** she turned her dreams into a reality. On Earth Day 1977, Maathai launched a one-woman campaign to reforest Kenya. Over the next decades, she used tree planting as a tool for women's empowerment, and delivered an international model for sustainable development. Under her guidance, the Green Belt Movement planted tens of millions of trees in Kenya. Her actions protected the natural world, improved the lives of the people she helped, and changed the prospects of future generations as well.

Clearly, Wangari Maathai was a unique human being, and a notably effective champion of good works. Few of us would ever hope to accomplish things at the scale that she did. Nonetheless, we can all follow her example of drawing out *the full range* of her inner resources and then *putting them to work* to make change in the real world.

While you and I aren't likely to win the Nobel Prize, *we do have a Captain at our center of well-being*. Our Captain understands the sentiment expressed by Clarissa Pinkola Estes when she wrote: "Ours is not the task of fixing the entire world all at once, but of stretching out to mend the part of the world that is within our reach." Following Maathai's example, our inner Captain can call on *every member of our Big Four* to mend the part of the world within our reach.

Put Your Captain at the Helm

Your inner Captain coordinates your Dreamer, Thinker, Lover, and Warrior. Most important, your Captain appreciates that each of the Big Four has its own interests and priorities. Each one represents a part of you that cares about meeting your needs. But they value different things, and they define what you need differently. The Lover seeks to satisfy your drive for relationship. The Warrior looks after your need for protection, and achievement. Each inner negotiator falls prey to something that Anaïs Nin observed: "We see the world not as it is, we see the world as we are."

There's nothing wrong with each of the Big Four advocating for its own worldview. The trouble starts when you can't tell anymore that the voice in your head pushing you one way or another isn't "you" but *is one of them*. By definition, none of the Big Four can take *all of you* and your needs into account. That's not their job. They each have a unique focus and function. Your Captain's role is to hear them out, and then to make an informed choice about your best next move.

Unlike any *one* of the Big Four who will advocate for themselves, what's truly unique about your Captain is the ability to draw on *all of them*, as needed. Think again of Wangari Maathai. We can pretend for a minute that her Thinker loved the academic environment. Left to her own devices, perhaps Professor Maathai would have spent all of her time researching, writing, and teaching. Luckily for the world, she let her Captain steer her ship, drawing out the strengths of all of her Big Four.

Because Captains can call on *any* of the Big Four, they can deploy *all of their strengths* and use *all of their skills*. Remember, each of the Big Four has a unique function, strength, and skill set (see Table 4.6). You gain access to the resources of each one as you gain capability with it. But once you've developed all four, then your Captain can call on *all of them*, unlocking their full range and optimizing your potential for impact.

Inner Team	Strength	Skills For	Provides
Dreamer	Creativity	Innovation	Direction
Thinker	Clarity	Analysis	Reflection
Lover	Compassion	Relationship	Connection
Warrior	Courage	Accomplishment	Protection

TABLE 4.6

Find Your Inner Captain

One of the hallmark passages from competence to mastery is discovery of your inner Captain. It can be a shock to realize that after all of these years, as your inner Dreamer or inner Warrior was calling the shots, a deeper source of wisdom existed inside you. Captains offer a more reliable compass because they consider *both* the vision of the Dreamer *and* the practicality of the Warrior. *Both* the heart of the Lover *and* the logic of the Thinker. ***All at the same time***.

Detecting and engaging with your inner Captain is a bit like the story of Michelangelo creating his sculpture of David. Working with a huge piece of marble, the artist brought forth his timeless statue of the young hero. Michelangelo reportedly said that David was already there, inside the marble block, waiting to be freed. All he needed to do was chip away at everything else.

I teach extended leadership development courses that include exploration of the Transformers. Executives are routinely shocked to discover their inner Captain. Often they've moved through life inhabiting their Thinker, whose favorite strategies tend toward playing The Cynic, The Skeptic, or The Judge. Now they find themselves sitting in a room with thirty people, and they're not judging, not skeptical, not sarcastic. It's a new experience, or perhaps one they haven't felt in a long time.

Often in a weeklong session, sometime around the midpoint, participants notice something's different. They describe feeling more space inside. More vitality. More patience. More goodwill. What I've seen time and again is that otherwise distrustful business people relax and soften when given the chance to come back to their center of well-being. They recover lost hope and resilience. They find stillness. They feel joy.

At the end of one of these programs, a partner in a business, who is also a former Navy SEAL, wrote this to express his insight: "We are born closest to our essence and spend a lifetime masking it in a persona we believe people will accept. This awakened me to my one true self and the notion that within each of us lies an unexplored range to be completely vulnerable and at the same time immensely powerful." Another participant, whom I'll call Winston, is a strategic advisor to the largest health-care systems in the United States. His group got together again roughly a year after they did the leadership program.

Describing the changes he'd experienced, Winston wrote: "The freedom and power that come from living in a place of love has made miracles happen not just for me, but for the most important people I touch." I understand how far-reaching a statement that is, coming from Winston. He'd started the program with hopes of improving his marriage, becoming a better father in his own eyes, and enhancing his impact as a strategic advisor. Discovering his Captain, and learning to treat his Big Four *like passengers* rather than letting them steer the ship, was transformational for him with his family as well as with his clients. In case this isn't clear, I made no edits to either of their comments. I got their permission to share with you what they said, precisely as they'd written it.

Whether you're aware of it or not, your Captain is inside you. You might need to get some distance from the Big Four in order to find him or her. But as you chip away at their loud voices, and remove yourself from their potentially overwhelming pull, you'll find the Captain standing there, patiently waiting for you.

Transformer Three: The Voyager

Sir Richard Branson shares with the world the voyage he's taking through life. The first business for the English supernova was a magazine called *Student*, at the age of sixteen. Adventures with his famous megabrand started with Virgin Records. Next came Virgin Atlantic Airways. Today the English business mogul is well-known as the founder and chairman of Virgin Group of more than four hundred companies. Branson is the fourth-richest citizen of the United Kingdom, according to the Forbes 2012 list of billionaires.

Obviously his enormous wealth affords Branson opportunities that belong to a very small group of people. With that said, Branson consistently models the stance toward life that the Voyager invites all of us to take. The Spanish poet Antonio Machado wrote this message to the Voyager in each of us, and Branson lives it fully:

> *Traveler, your footprints*
> *are the only road, nothing else.*
> *Traveler, there is no road;*
> *you make your own path as you walk.*

Branson embodies the idea of making your own path as you walk.

In one of his current efforts, Branson is busy developing Virgin Galactic. He aims to produce the world's first commercial vehicle into space—what he calls a "spaceline" instead of an "airline." He's also exploring how to travel to the bottom of the ocean. He engages pursuits like these in part because they make him feel alive. Branson has said he wants to live as much of the human experience as he possibly can. "These adventures are physically challenging, and mentally challenging, and technologically challenging, and that is what makes them fascinating." The Voyager in all of us thrives on new experiences, on opportunities to learn, to expand ourselves in directions we haven't traveled before. Like Branson, the Voyager in you takes pleasure in the traveling itself, wherever it leads.

Branson's life story illustrates another aspect of the Voyager, and that is in the way that his profile has evolved and developed over time. Long ago the public knew him as an eccentric dilettante, hosting lavish parties on his privately owned island. Today he's an engaged global citizen, actively mobilizing technology and his formidable resources to contribute to the common good.

As an example, Branson is promoting the Virgin Earth Challenge, a $25 million prize offered to someone who can develop a lasting way to remove greenhouse gases from the atmosphere. Branson also played a formative role in launching the Elders, a group of societal sages who can use their experience and moral authority to address global problems. The Elders was Branson's brainchild, and he helped raised millions of dollars to fund it. These endeavors resulted in part, according to Branson, from his not finding enough meaning in his life during its earlier chapters, when he focused himself on other things, not pressing social issues. His fiery spirit of adventure and his visible development as a person and as a leader make Branson a good symbol for the Voyager that lives in each of us.

Your Voyager Joins You Along the Road of Life

Last summer when I was on Bernardus' sailboat, I saw the Little Dude playing with a rope. When I paid closer attention, I realized he wasn't "playing" at all—he was concentrating quite hard. I walked over to where he was sitting, and saw him closely examining the knot in the rope. I asked him a question, and the answer I got was both simple and remarkable.

"Do you know how to make that?" I asked, pointing to the knot.

"*Not yet*," he replied.

I was struck by his choice of words. In choosing the phrase "not yet" instead of the more typical "no," he signaled an implicit attitude toward his own development. To paraphrase his answer, he basically said, "No, I don't know how to do that TODAY. But I trust that if you ask me again in the future, *then I will know* how to do it." His words reflect a basic stance toward life, one that has faith in his own growth over time.

Though not yet six years old, the Little Dude displayed what researcher Carol Dweck has called the "growth mindset." It means walking through life knowing there's stuff to learn, mistakes are also opportunities, and challenges are more fulfilling than same-old-same-old, even if you're less assured of short-term success. Dweck contrasts that with the "fixed mindset," which says in essence, this is who I am, this is what I've got to work with, I'm doing my best, and please don't expect me to exceed how I'm performing now. Because this is it.

The Voyager is the torchbearer for the growth mindset.

Your Brain Develops as You Grow

Your Voyager supports you to design new strategies for your Big Four, and to experiment with them over time. Gaining flexibility among the strategies available to your inner negotiators will close your Performance Gap. It turns out that as you're trying new things, your brain is following suit by firing neurons in new ways, and blazing new neural trails to reinforce your new patterns.

For a very long time, conventional wisdom said that *only children's brains* form over time. Neuroscientists believed the adult brain didn't change at all.

That was wrong.

It's now widely accepted that *the adult brain does change over time*. Our brains have neuroplasticity, which "refers to the ability of neurons to forge new connections, to blaze new paths through the cortex, to assume new roles." As Jeffrey Schwartz and Sharon Begley continue to explain in their book *The Mind and the Brain*, "in shorthand, neuroplasticity means rewiring of the brain."

Move Toward Lasting Change

Sofia works on a Family Health Team in southeastern Brazil. She's married to Salvador, and mother to Mateus and Lucas. Most days she feels she's fulfilling any two of these roles well, but rarely all three at the same time.

Camila is a friend and colleague from Clínica da Família, the family support center where Sofia works. Camila sent Sofia an email about a conference coming up in Rio de Janeiro. It was a national gathering about new ways to provide health services, with reports from each geographic region. Camila was presenting at the event, and she invited Sofia to come along.

Camila knew that cost would be an issue for her friend. So she offered to share a room with Sofia at the hotel. She also invited her to join a breakfast reception and a dinner for presenters and their guests. That would save money on food.

Sofia's heart sank when she read the email. This was the kind of invitation she hated to get. Because she had no idea how to answer.

In a flash, her head started swimming.

"This is a great chance for me. I want to learn new things. But can I leave the boys *all weekend*? They both have soccer on Saturday. I can't go with Camila and miss their games. But I *would love to go*. I always want to give my best to the families. I could learn a lot from other Family Health Teams. But still. Mateus is *so excited* about the World Cup. Is *my world* more important than his? How can I be so selfish?"

Sofia spent the entire day going back and forth. She felt torn up inside. She knew Camila needed an answer.

With a heavy heart, Sofia finally answered the email.

> To my sweet friend Camila,
>
> Obrigada for your kind invitation. Thank you, too, for your generous offers with the meals and hotel. Right now, I feel that Mateus and Lucas really need me. I don't feel good to leave them alone for the weekend when I'm at work during the week. I hope you have a wonderful conference. I will miss being there.
>
> Beijo and thank you again,
>
> Sofia

When she got into bed, Sofia felt defeated. Yes, she wanted to be there for her family. That was most important. But saying no to the conference left a pit in her stomach. After all, Camila had children, and she was *presenting* at the conference. Sofia wasn't even *going*.

That night Sofia tossed and turned. A familiar refrain rolled around in her mind: "it seems like no matter what I do, I just can't win."

Playing Without a Playbook

Sofia is having a "been there, done that" moment. Why? Because she *has* been there, and *she usually does* just what she's doing now. The problem is she doesn't recognize her own moves.

What's true for Sofia is true for you, too. You won't create lasting change in your leadership and your life until you can spot and name what you're doing. ***You need the playbook for inner negotiation in order to change the game***.

Let's look more closely at the current game.

Life presents us with a situation. In Sofia's case, it's an opportunity to do something for herself. The situation puts a trade-off in play, between her professional development and supporting her family over the weekend.

Confronting this dilemma creates the experience of inner conflict. There isn't an obvious right answer. So no matter which way she goes, she'll feel the loss of what she didn't choose.

In the end, the actual decision may or may not be a good one. But either way, she's left with a sinking feeling that she's missing out and somehow not getting a good outcome. These are sure signs she's in the Performance Gap.

If you ask Sofia how things are going, she'd say it feels awful. She gets an opportunity, feels torn between her different roles and obligations, and deals with inner conflict all day. Then she makes a decision, and feels bad about it.

That's what she sees. Life gives me a situation, and I react (see Figure 4.2).

Sofia's right. There is no way to "win" at this game. Not the way she's playing it.

Leading or living this way is like trying to play a sports match

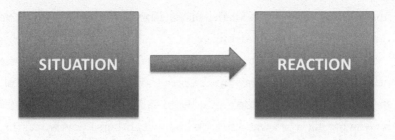

FIGURE 4.2

without a playbook. You want to win the game, but you don't know where to line up on the field, or what to do on any given play. Where are you supposed to go? What should you do? You need to guess, because the fact is, *you don't know what plays you are running*.

This is also like playing without a team captain. Typically a team captain calls the play and the team performs it. The players *don't pick the plays for themselves*.

Right now, Sofia is playing without a playbook because she can't distinguish one play she makes from another. She's also playing without a captain. The Big Four are the players on her team. Since she doesn't have a team captain calling the plays, members of her Big Four are running the show. She might win this way some of the time. But it's not what any of us would call a winning strategy.

How can Sofia start to play a new game? How can she begin to "win from within"? This is where your Transformers come in.

Start Winning from Within

If the Big Four are like players on the field, then the Lookout acts like the sports commentator. He watches the game and reports on it. He knows the details of the plays, as well as the players, so he can narrate the game in detail.

A commentator isn't part of the action. He's not down on the field. He's up in the stands, in the press box, with a full view of all the action. It's not the Lookout's role to call a new play. But he does know what plays he's watching. So he can let others know what's going on, from the fans in the stands to the audience at home. In this metaphor, the Lookout tells the team captain what he's noticing.

In Sofia's situation, her Lookout can tell which of her Big Four are talking, and which are holding back. To the Lookout's discerning eye, the arguments flying back and forth in her head aren't just a jumble like they are to Sofia.

Tuning in to Sofia's inner negotiation, her Lookout notices two voices in her reaction: The Lover, and the Dreamer (see Figure 4.3). From that observation, she can show Sofia who is saying what.

DREAMER: This is a great chance for me. I want to learn new things.

LOVER: But can I leave the kids *all weekend*? They both have soccer on Saturday. I can't go with Camila and miss their games.

DREAMER: But I *would love* to go. I always want to give my best to the families. I could learn a lot from other Family Health Teams.

LOVER: But still. Mateus is *so excited* about the World Cup. Is *my world* more important than his? How can I be so selfish?

For the first time, the disorganized, muddled debate inside Sofia's mind sounds like an inner negotiation between two identifiable inner negotiators. That's a lot better.

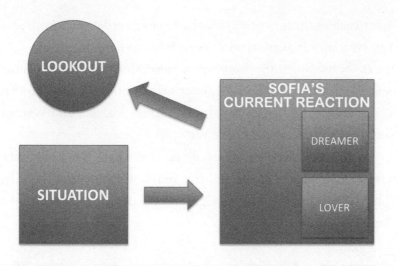

FIGURE 4.3

When you ask Lookouts what's going on, they point out which inner negotiators have the ball, and what each one is doing with it. Identifying their voices and what they're saying to you is a big step forward from the discomfort over messy inner conflict.

Your Lookout can tell you when one inner negotiator takes over, kicking others to the curb. Or when the same two of your Big Four clash over and over, denying you the benefit of what the other two perceive. In other words, your Lookout shows you the negotiation that's taking place inside you, play by play.

Your Lookout has the playbook.

Getting some distance from your Big Four can bring you relief as well as clarity, as one workshop participant told me after we talked about tapping the Lookout when facing a hard decision.

"Normally I'd say to myself, 'I hate this. I'm so confused. I don't know what to do.' It's a blur of noise in my head, pulling me in every direction. It feels a lot better to stand back and notice, my Thinker and my Lover have different views here. I can appreciate what each of them is telling me. But now *I* need to take both perspectives into account when *I* decide what to do."

In Sofia's case, the Lookout noticed that only the Dreamer and Lover were parties to the inner negotiation. Building on that observation, her Captain could see that her Thinker and Warrior weren't at the negotiation table yet at all.

Unlike the Lookout, who only notices what's happening, the Captain can direct the action. So, Sofia's Captain beckoned her Thinker and her Warrior to weigh into the debate. This is how the "conversation" went:

THINKER: Honestly, this isn't a life-or-death decision. If Sofia really wants to go, she should attend the conference. The kids will live without her for one weekend. At the same time, she can find plenty of ways to catch up on the discussions, including meeting Camila for coffee afterward to hear all about it. Her career doesn't depend on this meeting.

Sofia heard the Thinker's comments, and had to agree. Her Dreamer and Lover were raising the stakes. It was *one* weekend, after all. Either way, her decision wasn't going to be life-changing. It was just a choice she needed to make.

Then her Captain asked what the Warrior wanted to add.

WARRIOR: Actually, from where I'm sitting, both of these options sound bad. Sofia is exhausted and drained. Every day she gets the kids off to school, runs to meet with clients, races home to get dinner and homework done, then prepares for sessions she has the next day. If you ask me, Sofia should take time *for herself* that weekend. Maybe spend the day with her sister, do some shopping, go for a walk on the beach. Compared to more professional advancement, or one more weekend doting on her husband and kids, I think doing something for herself is the way to go.

Typically in a situation like this, Sofia would hold an internal debate between her Dreamer and her Lover (though she wouldn't notice it that way), and in the end, her Lover would take the day. She wouldn't stop to ask the Thinker or Warrior for their perspectives. This time, Sofia let her Lookout and her Captain change the game. They got the viewpoints of *all* of the Big Four.

Making New Choices

Your Lookout and your Captain know that each inner negotiator sees the world differently. Like different members of a work team, each has a specialized and valuable point of view. Most of us rarely stop and solicit the views of *all of* the Big Four. We tend to hear from the same one or two. That's our favorite strategy. But like Sofia, if you keep playing the same way, you're going to get the same results time and again.

If you want to create lasting change, the Lookout and the Captain can transform your perspective and your behavior. Your new set of actions produces new outcomes, and that will close your Performance Gap (see Figure 4.4).

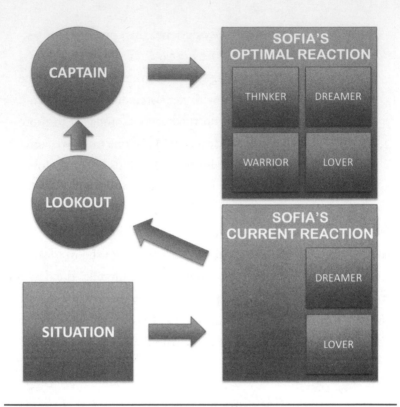

FIGURE 4.4

If you ask Sofia's Lookout or her Captain about what matters about this upcoming conference, they'll say whether she makes a good decision today about whether to attend. They'll also value how she got there. They'd see today as a victory, because she wouldn't usually stop to ask the Thinker or Warrior about their perspectives. Today she did.

From the Voyager's perspective, what matters about today is how it stacks up with the way Sofia handles situations like this in general. Regardless of what she does about this event, the important question involves whether she always puts herself last. Her

Voyager would ask if what she does today reflects *a real choice*, or simply repeats what she does every other time.

This job is harder than it sounds. We put some of our Big Four in the backseat. As time goes by, we forget we put them there. Then we forget we express identities we've *created*—real parts of us to be sure, but only partial expressions of who we are. We design our profiles, and then take them as given. As Parker Palmer wrote in *A Hidden Wholeness*, "Here is the ultimate irony of the divided life: live behind a wall long enough, and the true self you tried to hide from the world disappears from your own view. The wall itself and the world outside it become all that you know."

We get into trouble when the profile we've created becomes our truth. We start using the same strategies time and again. At some point, if we don't engage the Transformers, these strategies start not only to define us but to limit us as well. The Voyager can help.

How does it work?

The Voyager Takes You in New Directions

Wayne came to a workshop that I led several years ago. He was quite a character. He lived and worked in Dallas, and his oversized personality gave new meaning to his state's proud slogan, "Don't Mess with Texas." It wasn't clear what Wayne did for a living. He seemed to advise family-owned businesses, in a line of work he called "Asset Protection." I still don't know what that means. Though I do recall how Wayne introduced himself to the group.

"Hi. I'm Wayne. I'm from Texas. I can't tell you *exactly* what I do, but I *will* tell you that I sleep with two things under my pillow every night. My phone, and my gun."

After an audible pause, he added, "And the stress of this life is nearly killing my wife."

Despite his gruff exterior, I had a soft spot for Wayne from the start. He delighted in joking about "muscle" as a negotiation "weapon" a bit too much. But he was absolutely sincere, and he was clearly looking for something, though he didn't quite know what it was. Ironically, since he described his own profile as All Warrior, All The Time, it was his heart that touched me.

By the end of the week, Wayne appeared a changed man. He was still Wayne, authoritative before opening his mouth. But he'd softened. He'd made contact with other people in the group. He'd discovered that while he did enjoy pressuring people, he also valued connecting with them.

A few weeks later, Wayne sent the following email to the workshop group. Since I've edited this only for length (and changed the names), I got his permission to share his email with you.

> All,
>
> It worked!!! Or should I say "it works"!!!
> Without disclosing confidential information, the main story goes something like this . . .
>
> - Three current owners, 4th generation privately held, low mid-cap company, needed to decide on which one of two individuals was best qualified to take over as President as part of their Business Succession & Continuity Plan.
> - Regardless of who gets the job they will need to buy out all the current owners.

- One of the individuals being considered is "blood" (the son of two of the current owners) and is the top salesman of the company. The second individual is "water" but has been with the company for 25 years, is extremely well liked and respected by all the clients and employees and knows how to run the business inside and out.
- The Owners know who they prefer to take over—"water." They won't say it out loud, out of loyalty to their attorney, who wants them to take "blood." The resistance of the attorney means the Owners are all turtled-up and won't discuss this issue.
- The attorney insists that "blood" (the son) be the next owner regardless of the overwhelming evidence that the son is not capable of the job.
- Using my newly learned Winning from Within information, I "invited" the attorney to a private meeting, quite literally a walk in a nearby park, a neutral location so they could share with me their viewpoint.

Summary as best as I can recall it . . .

ME: Hey, Jack, it's Gallagher.

ATTORNEY: To what do I owe this call to? Did I piss you off again?

ME: No Jack. Let's take a little walk this afternoon at the Arboretum, just you and I.

ATTORNEY: O Hell no!

ME: Come Jack, this is real, no BS, I promise I'll leave my button in the trunk.

Later that day at the park . . .

ME: Jack all I want to know is why on earth do you want "blood" in and "water" out of this deal?

ATTORNEY: I just can't imagine a father not handing over his company to his son after all these years, that's what "legacy" means.

ME: Tell me more. (Side bar—at this point I truly didn't have anything else to say . . . crickets in the night . . .)

ATTORNEY: I know how I felt when my father gave his legal practice, literally handed it over to his partner, and didn't even consider me as a viable option!

ME: Ok?!?!? (totally shocked that we dove that deep in 3 min. into our chat—I figured it worked the first time so I said . . .) Tell me more

ATTORNEY: What the hell do YOU think the owners should do?

ME: Look, I have no clue what the future holds (as I desperately search for "lover" language with a twist of "dreamer" to guide me) what I can tell you is that [dad], [mom] and [partner] are all ok with "water" taking over. In fact based on their last email to you and I, they clearly want "water" to run the business. You're the only one that wants "blood." And because the owners respect your opinion they also want your blessing.

ATTORNEY: I just don't want "blood" to regret me. I don't want him thinking I set him up to fail.

ME: What do you mean?

ATTORNEY: The reality is I think "water" is the best one for the job. Hell, I'm the one that introduced him to the company years ago. I also really pushed the issue to get "blood" a job here too.

ME: Ok so how do you feel about having a conversation with both about what you think before you make your recommendation to the partners?

ATTORNEY: I can do that, I should do that, they need to know that I'm sympathetic, but the reality is that "blood" would run the company into the ground in a matter of 3 years! I really need to step up don't I?

We left the park, shook hands (never had happened) and he thanked me.
Today I got a call from the owners excited to declare their new President. Guess who they picked?
Mr. Water starts his executive transition next month.
Had I gone in as a full Warrior I know I would have not been able to engage this very soft spoken, yet powerful Lover-Type. It was very uncomfortable for me. But great result!!
I need to practice more.

Thanks all!!

Wayne's email illustrates the path of the Voyager.

He already had a good life. He was successful in his business and in love with his wife. But Wayne's profile was limited. He wanted to expand his range—to experience more, to get better outcomes, and to feel more alive. So he went in search of parts of himself he'd buried long ago. Then, in the spirit of the Voyager, he experimented by taking small steps in a new direction.

Notice that Wayne didn't change his profile entirely overnight. He didn't wake up one day after a weeklong workshop and embody the compassionate Lover. He felt awkward and, at times, unsure of what to say.

Yet he did look inside himself for a different source of strength than his typical Warrior courage. He did reach out on a personal level to a colleague, one he'd typically have seen as an adversary. He would've used threats or manipulation before. Now he didn't. Like Wayne, *you* can add new moves to your playbook.

Plenty of people believe that how they behave now is "who they are." It's their personality, or their type on Myers-Briggs. Remember Jared, the grant writer for Rwanda? He got performance feedback to expand his leadership style and immediately engaged a headhunter. Jared told his friend Alexander at the bar, "This is me. They can take it or leave it."

This stance ignores the inner Voyager, the part of you that knows you *can* develop over time, that you *can* change your ways. Your Voyager knows about doors of possibility you can't even imagine from where you're sitting today. Whatever your profile, you *can gain access* to new work opportunities, deeper intimacy in your relationships, and amazing discoveries about your life purpose, by integrating all parts of yourself.

In Part Two, you'll start to get a sense of your favorite strategy for each of the Big Four. That will help you start to put together your current profile, the way you define yourself in terms of where you run high, low, or balanced. Then in Part Three we'll come back to the Transformers in more detail.

PART TWO

Balance Your Profile

CHAPTER 5

Possibilities: See Your Dreamer's Vision

When I dare to be powerful—
to use my strength in the service of my vision,
then it becomes less and less important
whether I am afraid.

—AUDRE LORDE

When I was growing up, my best friend was a girl named Ellie. We spent hours at Ellie's house, dreaming up kingdoms in faraway lands where we could rule as nobles. Our subjects were popular dolls named Barbie and Ken. Ellie's mother's closet provided beautiful "gowns," as well as the all-important blue eye shadow and red lipstick. We were *very* regal princesses.

Sadly for me, Ellie and I didn't live in the same town. We didn't go to the same school. So we couldn't see each other too often.

Of course, back then, a chance to see Ellie meant my parents driving me to her house. That was the only way to see anyone. You actually had to go where they were, and see the person—*in person.*

As Ellie and I grew from little girls into teenagers, we were content to talk on the phone. That was *instead* of seeing each other, since you couldn't *see people* over the phone. We also sat still in the house when we talked. Our phones were attached to the walls.

As I think about that now, I'm sitting in a coffee shop outside of Boston. A mom and her kids are at the table next to me. One of the kids is texting. Another one is playing games on her mother's iPhone. The oldest is catching up with friends on Facebook.

I'm picturing young Ellie and me. What if we'd grabbed Barbie and Ken, and taken a rocket ship time-machine to this coffee shop?

We'd look at each other with wide eyes. We'd wonder with amazement at the seemingly magic gadgets. We'd ask each other two questions:

*"What faraway land **is this**?"* and *"How did we get from **that** land to **this** one?"*

The Dreamer Invents New Possibilities

Human beings have an incredible ability to create.

We make things up all the time.

When we're young, we call it playing. In adolescence, we call it daydreaming. As grown-up professionals, we call it innovating. Design. Disruptive technology. Vision statements. We're adults. We don't play with toys. We're "early adopters" of the newest, fastest, coolest, "smartest" electronics.

At its core, the impulse is the same. We desire. We experiment. We wonder.

Yearning is basic to human nature. We long for love. We aim for success. We wish the economy would improve. We pray for our sick relatives to get well. We want our troops to come home safely, and for soldiers and civilians living in combat zones to stay out of harm's way.

As Dreamers, we continually strive to improve the way we enact our social contract. In 1517, Martin Luther launched the Protestant Reformation by nailing his Ninety-Five Theses onto the door of a Catholic church. Then, for centuries, people gathered in the public square to debate issues and make demands of their governments. We humans are natural change agents, continuing to seek new ways to engage with each other through public discourse. In 2011, strengthening what became known as the "Arab Spring," citizens by the thousands took to the streets in Cairo's Tahrir Square. These men and women longed for a new society. They risked their lives in hopes of a new beginning. They wanted freedom and opportunity.

Like demonstrators in decades past, the Egyptians convened in the public square. But this time something was different. They didn't spread the word by nailing a declaration on the mosque door. They didn't hand out flyers or depend on word of mouth. These activists organized a protest over Facebook, and 350,000 people showed up. They engaged the world in their power struggle by sending photos over Twitter. They toppled a regime by engaging the global community in an entirely new way. Dreamers imagine what's possible for every sector of society. Including how to build society itself.

Dreamers love to push themselves, striving to accomplish what no one's done before. Like Mario Andretti, a legend among all-time greats in auto racing. And another Mario—soccer superstar Mario Balotelli. Or Michelle Kwan, one of the most graceful and competitively successful athletes in the history of figure skating. Testing our limits. Setting new records. Looking for the next frontier. That's what Dreamers do. People already landed on the moon. So *we* want to walk on Mars.

The question remains: How *did* we get here, to this world so remote from the faraway land of Ellie's playroom? How did we start walking down the street and talking on the phone at the same time?

Through the power of visionaries who heeded the call of the Dreamer within.

Think about Swedish entrepreneur Niklas Zennström and his Danish partner, Janus Friis. They're founders of a company they first called Sky Peer-to-Peer. You and I know their revolutionary product as Skype.

Because of these futurists, you can interview job candidates from around the world face-to-face, without anyone leaving their office. And that's just the beginning.

I know a lawyer who led settlement talks over Skype. He looked all the parties in the eye when he put the best offer on the table. That would be unremarkable, except for where the parties were: one in Dubai, one in Lima, and one in New York. You can do personal things over Skype, too, like applaud your kids' haircuts when you say good night. That's very helpful when you're stuck at an airport gate at tuck-in time.

Zennström and Friis are pioneers. Their vision was to create a peer-to-peer communications application that enabled people to talk as they would on the phone, *and see each other at the same time.* From opposite sides of the world. For free.

Ironically, what's *now* amazing about Skype is how utterly *normal* it seems, as if we came into the world able to see each other across the globe. Talking on Skype is like having a cup of coffee at breakfast. It's no big deal.

If you step back for just a minute, you remember what a big deal these advancements *really are*, both for us and for our societies. Innovators create enormous value by turning their dreams into reality. Ask Microsoft, which acquired Skype in May 2011 for $8.5 billion. Or the 663 million users who'd registered with Skype by September of that same year.

Or ask me.

Skype created *a lot* of value for me. It let me sleep at night.

Remember in 2010 when that volcano erupted over Iceland, spreading volcanic ash through the skies of Europe? If you don't recall, *no one could leave Europe.* Planes were grounded. There was no flying with volcanic ash in the jet stream.

Those of us on the European continent were basically quarantined. Some people didn't care. But those of us with roots in North America, who had hopes of getting back someday, definitely did.

During the lockdown, I was visiting in The Netherlands, and contemplating my future move to live there. For the first time, it crossed my mind that I could move there—*and not be able to return.* For roughly ninety years, the volcano's explosion switch had been turned "off." In all that time, no major eruptions.

Now suddenly, the switch had flipped "on."

"What if it stays this way?" I worried. "Could the volcano maintain the ash cloud covering European airspace—*for years?*"

Admittedly this wasn't my most rational moment. But remember, this was Vulnerable Erica time. Logical reasoning isn't her currency.

"When will I see my family and friends again??"

Zennström and Friis came to my rescue.

Skype. There would always be Skype. I'd be okay.

The Dreamer Enables Innovation

In the end, Skype was but one wave in the social media ocean. A tsunami in new technology marked the early years of the new millennium. Silicon Valley overflowed with young Dreamers who birthed new forms of communication, shopping, enjoying music, and more. They put unprecedented capability into the hands of everyday people. Buying plane tickets. Trading stocks. Diagnosing your child's fever.

They also transformed human relationships. People text more than they talk. Invitations became "Evites." If you want information about your cousins' nuptials, visit their wedding website. Between Myspace, Facebook, and LinkedIn, nearly everyone built a presence online.

One by one, industries we took for granted vanished in the face of another Dreamer's vision of how to use the Internet. Email threatened to bankrupt the U.S. Postal Service. Amazon.com wiped out Borders Books. iTunes killed Tower Records. Netflix took Blockbuster Video off the map. The way we look up information changed so completely that students today can't imagine a world without Google or Wikipedia.

All of this groundbreaking innovation was driven by people whose inner Dreamers believed in things the rest us never considered. Inspired by imagination, these Dreamers saw how new technologies could create a whole new world.

Business is a common place for strong Dreamers to shape the future. And not just on the Internet. Coco Chanel pioneered a new kind of fashion for women. Nearly a century later, Sara Blakely started making "body-shaping" garments for women in her home. As a 100 percent owner of her business, Spanx, Blakely became the world's youngest self-made female billionaire.

Recall Narayana Murthy, visionary cofounder of Infosys. With his wife, writer Sudha Murthy, as his Dreamer champion, Murthy architected the huge success in IT outsourcing in India.

And consider the meteoric rise of "Jenny from the Block"—the affectionate term entertainment superstar Jennifer Lopez gave herself to affirm her humble roots. Recognizing the drive of her inner

Dreamer, *Time* magazine wrote, "As the Bronx-born daughter of Puerto Rican immigrants, Lopez . . . has an outsider's hunger and a native's assumption of infinite possibility. She works hard and dreams big."

Indeed she does.

In 2012, *Forbes* magazine ranked J. Lo number one on its Celebrity 100, listing her as the most powerful celebrity in the world. She's also one of the wealthiest, with hundreds of millions of dollars to her name. Not only an entertainer, J. Lo has her own clothing line, multiple fragrances, a past stint on *American Idol*, and her own singing competition show, *Q'Viva*. While she's admittedly unlucky in love, you can't miss the incredible way that J. Lo went after her dreams.

Dreamers also play crucial roles in moving society forward. Like Jawaharlal Nehru, a leader of the independence movement in India, and its first prime minister. In his inaugural speech, he declared proudly that "at the stroke of the midnight hour, when the world sleeps, India will awake to life and freedom." Lech Walesa, a strong Warrior as an activist, brought out his Dreamer to preside over Poland's transformation to a postcommunist state. Luiz Inácio Lula da Silva, widely known as "Lula," fulfilled his hope of lifting millions of people out of poverty as president of Brazil.

Earlier, I compared the Dreamer to a CEO. In a public-service context, visionaries thrive in roles such as president or prime minister, in which they can impact the course of history by realizing their dreams. Former German chancellor Helmut Kohl had a profound vision for unification and cooperation. He became the main architect of a united Germany, as well as a lead player in the creation of the European Union. Soviet statesman Mikhail Gorbachev introduced unprecedented reforms in glasnost and perestroika. Gorbachev and fellow visionary President Ronald Reagan helped to bring an end to the Cold War.

Creative Dreamers gave us *Jurassic Park*, Willy Wonka's chocolate factory, and Pandora, James Cameron's alternative universe in the blockbuster *Avatar*. Dreamers channel beauty, inspiration, and transcendence into the arts, from Alvin Ailey's masterpiece *Revelations* to the ballad from John Lennon that asks us to "imagine all the people, living life in peace."

The Dreamer is everywhere around you.

It is also *within you*.

Dreamer Quiz: *What's Your Favorite Strategy?*

Here's a "quiz" to check out your Dreamer's favorite strategy. Don't take the results too seriously. This is simply meant to give you a place to start reflecting.

Look at the scenario below. Then read the three potential responses. As you read them, ask yourself: "Which of these sounds the most like me?" If you don't click with any of them, think of a person who knows you well. Which option would they say describes you best?

Feel free to jot down any reactions as you read.

Inner Dreamer Scenario

Imagine you've worked for a few years in your field. You're a strong individual contributor at the office.

Out of nowhere you find out the division head isn't coming back from maternity leave. In a scramble, your boss asks if you'll take the role.

What thoughts cross your mind? How do you feel? What will you do?

Option One: Get Out of Town

You think to yourself, "Is this a joke? Me? I could never do that. I have no idea what I'm doing. I need so much more training and experience before I could even imagine taking a role like that. Just thinking about it stresses me out."

You thank your boss for thinking of you but point out that other people are better prepared for that level of responsibility.

One of your peers takes the job.

He stumbles a bit at the beginning. But he finds his footing with support from the team. Lacking the experience to get trapped in the tried-and-true, he creates innovative strategies. He takes the organization in exciting new directions. His reputation soars.

You're left to wonder: "What if?"

Option Two: When Do I Start?

You think to yourself, "Finally!" What a great opportunity to show what you can do.

It's thrilling to imagine how you can change things, to envision what you can build. You know people will be dazzled by your creativity and your passion.

You realize that with this promotion you can probably get a bigger mortgage and a bigger house. You can see the dinner parties now. And maybe a wine cellar in the basement?

You accept the offer immediately.

A few months into the role, you're already seeing results.

You've made bold investments to seed big changes down the road. You also gave a large donation to your college alma mater for scholarships, which makes you feel great. Life is good.

You don't notice that your team is exhausted from burning the candle at both ends. People talk in the hallway about the strain on the budget from what they see as your "gambles" on unlikely prospects. You did get copied by mistake on an email between team members complaining about the long days.

When you lie in bed at night, you're tickled about what's possible. Yet part of you wonders if your team is up to the challenges you've laid down by the terrific opportunities you're giving them.

Option Three: With a Little Help from My Friends

You're intrigued. Is this something you can do?

The scope of this job is beyond anything you've done before. At the same time, you've felt unrecognized in your current role. You have so much potential. It's exciting if a little nerve-racking to imagine saying yes.

You talk with your boss. You offer a picture of how you'd like to change things. You also tell him that you're going to need support. You've never managed this kind of budget or this many people.

You decide to give it a shot, provided he promises to help. With his commitment to stay involved, you accept the new role.

Things start out rocky.

You make some unpopular decisions, and in retrospect, you wouldn't make them again. The learning curve is steep.

Before too long, though, you hit your stride. People give you second chances because they know you're trying. The team is energized by your excitement, even if some of it comes from nerves. The improvements you'd hoped for start falling into place.

You get a bonus at the end of the year, for performance that "exceeded expectations." With extra cash in hand and a raise for next year, you start thinking about a bigger house.

What Would You Do?

So, what would you do with an opportunity like this?

Which of these options appeals to your inner Dreamer?

These situations represent a Dreamer whose favorite strategy is to run low, high, and balanced, in that order.

In Option One, a Low Dreamer lacks not just the vision but the conviction to "go for it." She defers to her more experienced colleagues because she can't imagine rising to this role. Her Dreamer's audacity is frozen by fear and self-doubt.

In Option Two, the Dreamer is running high. She's giddy with possibility, to the point where she's lost sight of practical limitations. This High Dreamer thrives on opportunity, already tasting the spoils of her victory. Overtaken by both vision for the company and personal ambition, she's blind to the way she's taxing her team.

She will be shocked in her performance review to learn that her team finds her difficult and overly demanding.

In Option Three, the Dreamer is more balanced. She has a healthy respect for both her strengths *and* her limitations. She lets herself daydream about what might be possible, and feels excited by the prospect of taking the job. At the same time, she's realistic that this position is a "stretch." She knows she can't succeed alone. She gets her boss' buy-in to provide help. She's balanced in that she is at once bold in her actions, creative in her approach, and intuitively sensitive to her needs as a new leader.

The Dreamer in Daily Life

Your Dreamer might tend to run low, making it hard for you to imagine a different and better future. It might run high, so you're busily filling up whiteboards with one initiative after another. All things being equal, you have the widest range of choice if you find *a balanced way* to relate to the Dreamer, as well as to the other members of the Big Four.

In daily life, you need your Dreamer to create and seize opportunities. To roll the dice because you see potential. To cook up new ways to tell an inspiring story. To paint or write poetry.

With your Dreamer you can do things like:

- set bold fees for your services
- inspire your workforce to become industry leaders
- demolish your kitchen for a renovation
- move out of your home office and rent the first "real" space for your small business

- try an experimental medical treatment
- accept a drop in salary for a job whose mission means the world to you
- join the gym

Your Dreamer knows you get more than one turn at bat. It's the part of you that says "get back on the horse," after you've tried and failed.

Then you can do things like:

- continue pitching your vision to venture capital firms after several turn you down
- set ambitious sales targets for this year when you didn't hit your targets last year
- send out your resume again, and again, and again
- get back on the court after a sports injury
- campaign for legislation you care about, even though the same policy has failed to pass before
- start dating again after a divorce
- build up your savings account, after you emptied it to upgrade the furniture you still had from graduate school

Putting Principles into Practice

One of the principles that the Program on Negotiation at Harvard (PON) drilled into me was to make links between theory and practice. Roger Fisher expressed this lesson in fancy words, saying "good ideas are always operational." What he meant is that explaining a principle to people but leaving them without any sense of "how to do it" is incomplete. Our mission was to generate new approaches that would help people in "the real world."

I remember a conversation I had about fifteen years ago in the PON conference room with William Ury. We were talking about an article I was writing when I told him, "I have twenty-five good ideas" for it.

"Choose the best three, and leave out the rest," he said.

"Why?" I asked. "There are so many interesting things to say. I want to be thorough and accurate."

"Yes, I'm sure you're right. Twenty-five ideas *will* be more thorough, and maybe more accurate. What I've found in my work is that I often need to choose between being *thorough* and being *helpful*. I choose to be helpful. I think you should do the same."

Since that discussion I've learned this lesson firsthand. I still get tempted to share twenty-five ideas. But I've seen for myself that people can't remember or use that many concepts at once. William was right. Three ideas work well. Like my teacher and friend, I choose to be helpful.

Given that, starting here with the Dreamer, and in each chapter in Part Two, I'll highlight three "sweet spots" of each inner negotiator. As you can tell from the story above, those three won't tell you the *whole* story of the Big Four. Instead, the three points of focus will help you *develop the strength of your inner negotiators* and *expand your choice of strategies*.

Dreamer Sweet Spots

Pablo Picasso said, "Every child is an artist. The problem is how to remain an artist once he grows up." The Dreamer's power source is **intuition**, and his strongest muscle is **creativity**. The Balanced

Dreamer provides *direction*, and specializes in the skills you need for *innovation*.

The Dreamer's sweet spots enable you to:

1. **Generate Your Vision**
2. **Dare to Pursue Your Dream**
3. **Sense a Path Forward**

The Dreamer's inner resources include audacity, imagination, passion, and hope.

Let's see how these work in practice.

Generate Your Vision

People often come to my workshops knowing they have a Performance Gap they want to close: what they're getting now is *not* what they want. That's a fine place to start. Working with your inner Dreamer will help you transition your vision from what you *don't want* to what you actually *do want* to bring into your life.

Figure Out What You Want

Jordan came to a weekend workshop I ran that focused only on developing your inner Dreamer. Given the topic, people came to the class specifically because they felt blocked in figuring out what they wanted, or they didn't know how to go after it. It was a two-day Dreamer Boot Camp.

By his own description, Jordan's life was going along fine. He managed a restaurant, had two healthy young children and a stable marriage. His parents and siblings all lived nearby, and they got together every Sunday. His family had good friends in the local church, where his kids sang in the choir. Life was good.

When he introduced himself, he told the group, "My problem is that I don't have any dreams."

At a Dreamer weekend, lots of people feel the way Jordan does. They say they don't want anything, or they can't "think of" anything to want. When I hear things like that, I imagine that the person in front of me *does* have some dreams. The "problem" is that *they can't hear* what their inner Dreamer is trying to tell them.

In other words, if you ask them a direct question like "What excites you about the future?" you'll probably get an answer like "I really don't know." That's an honest answer. But it's not coming from their Dreamer. You've asked their Thinker a question that only their Dreamer can answer. Their Thinker is telling the truth: he doesn't know. *But the Dreamer likely does.*

I open these weekends with a lesson I learned from my friend and colleague Marcia Wieder, who created Dream University. She tells people they can start with a sentence like "My dream is to have a dream." In Winning from Within terms, that's a good way for inner Thinkers to let their inner Dreamers know their input is welcome.

The key in situations like Jordan's, when you can't "think of" what you want, is to stop expecting your Thinker to come up with your vision, and start asking your Dreamer. When you shift into your Dreamer's perspective, you'll find wisdom about your hopes and aspirations waiting for you.

It turned out that Jordan *did* have something he wanted. He dreamt of opening *his own* restaurant. We also discovered that Jordan's Thinker had a lot to say to him about his hopes for the future, things like:

"That's not realistic."

"It's a total waste of money."

"You don't know what you're doing."

"You will fail."

To move forward, Jordan needed to *negotiate with his Thinker*, and *broker a deal* between these two members of his inner team. That's a very different approach than beating himself up for *not having any dreams*. On the contrary, it's noticing that *he does have a dream*. But like the Supreme Court justice who couldn't bring himself to talk to his wife about his ties, *something inside of Jordan is getting in his way*.

To pursue his ambitions, Jordan needed to turn toward his Thinker, who was causing an impasse. It started by Jordan finding a new way to relate to his Thinker. He found out that his Thinker didn't object to his *specific* dream at all. It wasn't about the restaurant. His Thinker *was trying to protect him* by raising doubts in his mind. These doubts were coming up because *that's what Jordan's Thinker does*. It generates doubt. In every situation.

Jordan realized that "doubting" was a favorite strategy of his Thinker. He also saw for the first time that *the purpose* of the doubting *for the Thinker* was to shield him from getting hurt. With these insights, Jordan negotiated this agreement: his Dreamer could start taking steps forward, *provided* he checked in with the Thinker along the way. Jordan promised to confirm to the Thinker that he wasn't getting hurt, and to hear any concerns on the Thinker's mind as things progressed. With this new arrangement in place, Jordan left the weekend prepared to look for a business loan.

You can imagine my smile when I got an email inviting me to the Grand Opening of "Jordan's Bar and Grille."

Check If Team Members Are Blocking Your Dreamer

Before Jordan negotiated for his Dreamer to take any concrete steps, notice that he paused to explore what was up with his Thinker.

Why was he so negative? Why wouldn't he let Jordan take a shot? Jordan needed to know that in order to move ahead.

You can loosen the grip that your inner negotiators have on you by appreciating what they're trying to accomplish. Very often, like Jordan's Thinker, they're trying to help you. That might seem hard to believe, particularly if they're wreaking havoc in your life. In your life now, it might not feel helpful *at all*. Quite the opposite. You might blame this inner negotiator for the Performance Gap that holds you back in your life.

Creating more effective strategies will come about by *negotiating* with your Big Four, not by trying to ignore them, or eliminating them from your life. Just imagine for a minute that it's true—your inner team does what they do because they're trying to help. *And* they're operating on outdated information. At some point, their strategy likely *did* help. *But they haven't noticed that times have changed.*

For you to start making new choices in your leadership and your life, you need to *update their database* about your current situations. You can tell them that you appreciate their intention to help but their old strategy is now getting in your way. When they understand what you need from them *in your life today*, they can start to adapt.

Dreamers and Thinkers Can Do Great Things Together

In Jordan's life, his Dreamer and his Thinker were at odds. One was blocking the other. But that's not a given. All members of your inner team can work together for a common goal, if you learn how to negotiate with them and harness their respective strengths.

I met a woman named Inge at a seminar I taught in Germany. She combined her Thinker and Dreamer to great effect. Originally trained as an architect, Inge now works as a town planner in Hamburg.

Inge told me that when she sits down to design a new neighborhood she needs to start with the facts. Her Thinker gathers information: How many people are involved? What kind of housing is needed? She collects the details required for things like commercial zones and parking.

Then, eventually, she needs to consider: *How will we do it?*

Earlier in her career, Inge would've moved straight from gathering these facts to sketching a plan. "I've done it that way," she told me, "but it's very rational, so I made very conventional structures. The crane moves along the track, putting up the flat, and the next one exactly the same."

As I listened, I imagined row after row of identical buildings, without color or personality. Just slabs of gray concrete. Then Inge added, "You can get them up quickly, but you wouldn't want to live there."

"Why not?" I asked.

"Because these places are not alive, they are dead."

How does Inge plan a new neighborhood where people *do* want to live?

She still starts by gathering all the facts she can find. But then her Dreamer negotiates with her Thinker, asking it to step back for a bit so she can muse on the plot of land. "You put the facts into the back of the head, because now you need a vision."

I asked her to explain.

"I start to get an image in my mind. I see a slope, a hill, at first it's a rough picture. I start to imagine the hill, and I see some green, and then houses on the hill." Then she starts sketching. "I grab the pencil I love most, and see what happens. I fill in details as I fix my picture onto the paper. And then I see—*yes*—we will put the houses on this hill."

Soon Inge starts to see a dynamic drawing. The green takes shape into a park where people walk their dogs, and kids ride bikes.

Homes on the hill are different shapes, all designed for larger families. She adds a tree-lined street with smaller houses for singles or couples in their first home.

"Yes," Inge tells me, "*here* people can live."

Before too long, her inner Thinker negotiates back into the process. Inge feels her Thinker's tug to account for limits and requirements. "Now you come back to the facts at the back of your mind," she told me. "You have what you imagined on the paper, *and* the facts. Now you find out what's possible, and what's not possible."

I couldn't resist asking, "If you start with the facts, *and* end with the facts, why not just work with the facts?"

"You *can* if you want a place where people can *sleep* and *eat*. But not if you want to make a place where people want to *live*."

Inge integrates both Dreamer and Thinker to get optimal results. She uses her Thinker's strength of clarity to assess practicalities and constraints. She draws on her Dreamer's creativity to muse about the spaces she's designing. Inge practices the wisdom of Charles Schwab, founder of the huge financial services firm that carries his name. Schwab said, "A man to carry on a successful business must have imagination. He must see things as in a vision, a dream of the whole thing." Inge doesn't choose between her Dreamer and her Thinker. She gets the best of both by using them as a team.

Tell an Inspiring Story

To realize their visions, Dreamers often need to enlist followers. Particularly if you're aiming for large-scale change, you need to get other people on board. Painting the picture for other people by telling a great story is one of the Dreamer's skills. People often ask me about leading without authority. "I could make this department fly," they tell me, "but I'm not in charge. How can I get people to listen to me?"

Show them a bright future through a compelling story. That excites them about getting there together. In scientific terms, storytelling engages the right brain of the listener, which is more visual, and also the side of the brain that houses their emotional life. Giving information, but not delivering it in a great story, speaks to the left brain, which is more linear and not emotional. One of your Dreamer's sweet spots is generating your vision. That goes hand in hand with telling an inspiring story that brings people on board to support you. Stories about vision should touch the emotions of the person listening, to inspire them.

Consider my client Nick, a VP of operations. Before his year-end performance discussion, he received a written review (see Table 5.1). For every category in the review, he got a rating of "E," "M," or "F," according to this scale:

Exceeds Expectations: You consistently exceed performance standards.
Meets Expectations: You consistently meet performance standards.
Fails Expectations: You consistently fail to meet performance standards. You perform unevenly and need to improve.

TABLE 5.1

Overall, the review was good, a mix of E's and M's. With one glaring exception. In the category of "Inspirational Leadership," Nick got an F.

Next to the F, the comment said, "Nick thinks short-term and doesn't see the bigger picture. He needs to inspire others with a strategic vision. As a leader, we expect him to role model the aspirational tone of the company's change strategy."

I know a lot of professionals like Nick. They nod and acknowledge this exact feedback during their reviews. Then they turn to people like me and ask:

What on earth is "inspirational leadership"?

I came in to help Nick develop skills as an inspirational leader. Without noticing, he'd lost touch with his inner Dreamer. He needed to make contact again.

We started by looking at a recent conversation between Nick and his VP of Human Resources. I wanted him to notice his focus on short-term goals and the bottom line. Not inspiring stuff.

This is Nick's write-up of the discussion.

WHAT I THOUGHT and FELT BUT DIDN'T SAY	WHAT WE ACTUALLY SAID
I'm really worried about the CEO hitting me on the head about cost targets.	
	HR VP: Nick, how are you looking at our people plan this year?
We need to trim some fat from the budget, and fast.	
	Nick: Our business plan calls for 20 percent cost reduction. Let's determine where we

WHAT I THOUGHT and FELT BUT DIDN'T SAY	WHAT WE ACTUALLY SAID
	have redundancy and which people we can let go.
	HR VP: That would impact a lot of people. Maybe there's room for some of them in another part of the business.
These HR people don't know anything. Why do they try to be "business partners" with us?	
	Nick: Well, we need to stay competitive. Keep your eye on the ball. They call it a "bottom line" for a reason.
Did she even read the business plan? Give me a break.	

In this conversation, you can see which negotiators occupy the seats at Nick's inner table. Look back at the left-hand side above. Which voices do you find in his internal dialogue?

I'll tell you what I see.

- First, his Lover expresses worry about the CEO.
- Next his Warrior pipes up, advocating action to trim the budget, as soon as possible.
- Then his Thinker weighs in, bringing Nick's attention to the business plan. The Thinker takes a moment to judge the VP of HR.
- **Where's the Dreamer?** Missing in action.

Nick wants to improve as a leader. He wants to inspire. To do that, he needs access to the part of him who carries vision. That's his Dreamer, and right now, he's the inner negotiator who's absent from the table in Nick's internal world.

In the coaching session I asked Nick, "What would your Dreamer be musing about, if he were listening to the conversation about the people plan?" He wrote it down on the left side of the page:

WHAT MY DREAMER MIGHT THINK and FEEL

How is the industry evolving? What kind of expertise will we need in the future?

I continued.

"And if your Dreamer were musing on that, what would you say to the VP of HR? Can you write it down on the other side?"

This is what his Dreamer could say.

WHAT MY DREAMER COULD SAY

Nick: Well, given where we think the industry's going, we need to rethink the people profile. We need to move from a low-skills, low-customer-touch profile to a high-touch, customer-focused approach.

Progress. We took another step.

The next question I asked was a little extreme, but it was part of an exercise. "What would happen if the Dreamer took over the inner negotiation *completely*? If he pushed the other three out of the way, so he could improvise and talk about the future with no cares at all about real-world constraints?"

This isn't advisable as an approach to dealing with people for real. Balance is the name of the game in the real world. When you're working on developing one of the Big Four, though, it often helps to take big stretches. When you're in a learning context, like a workshop or a coaching session as Nick is, experiments help you to expand your range. Just be thoughtful about the difference between the "practice environments" and the situations where what you say and do have real-world consequences.

Here's his practice dialogue, with his Dreamer on a roll:

WHAT MY DREAMER MIGHT THINK and FEEL	WHAT MY DREAMER COULD SAY
	VP of HR: Nick, how are you looking at our people plan this year?
Production in our sector isn't moving overseas yet, but we need to be ahead of the curve!	
	Nick: In five years we'll have all operations in Asia. Next year we should open our first factory in Shanghai.

WHAT MY DREAMER MIGHT THINK and FEEL	WHAT MY DREAMER COULD SAY
	The year after we should hire a full R&D department there.
	VP of HR: That seems like a very fast timeline, don't you think?
Oh, come on, see the possibilities!	
	Nick: Use your imagination! China is the future. We need a *strategic* approach to our people plan. I'd set all eyes on Shanghai.
	VP of HR: We can look into the Asia opportunity, but we've got loads of ties to our local markets here. We should understand the impact of nonlocal product development and production.
Yeah, whatever. *I'm excited!*	
	Nick: Now that we're talking about this, maybe I should move my family to China for a few years. I wonder if my kids are taking Chinese in school. Maybe **I** should start studying Chinese?!

Finally, after "playing" both roles, Nick is able to dial the High Dreamer back to become a Balanced Dreamer, looking ahead, setting a vision, and bearing in mind what can realistically be achieved.

This is what happened at the next real meeting.

WHAT I THOUGHT and FELT BUT DIDN'T SAY	WHAT WE ACTUALLY SAID
	VP of HR: Nick, how are you looking at our people plan this year?
I thought about this, and wonder if it'll inspire you as it did me.	**Nick:** In my view, we're going to move production and R&D to Shanghai in the next five years. What does that mean for the capabilities we're going to keep here?
	VP of HR: Good question. I think we have a lot of strong technical skill. But we don't have the leadership skills we're going to need as things are changing so fast.
Right. And the technical skills aren't needed here anymore. What we do need	

WHAT I THOUGHT and FELT BUT DIDN'T SAY	WHAT WE ACTUALLY SAID
is people who understand our customers. First, we have a short-term cost issue, though.	
	Nick: Our business plan also calls for a 20 percent reduction. At the same time, we need to think strategically about the people decisions to make sure we're building the right teams here and abroad for the future.
	VP of HR: I agree.
	Nick: Can you start making a plan for short-term FTE cuts [full-time equivalents] while making sure we keep bench strength in leadership, and marketing and sales?

When your inner Dreamer is balanced, you can shoot for the stars *and* keep your feet on the ground.

Dare to Pursue Your Dream

You know the adage "If you can't stand the heat, get out of the kitchen." It sounds a warning bell. Some people steer clear of their dreams because they fear getting burned. What can you do if you feel like that, but you also want to dream big? You know that putting yourself up front comes with certain pressures and trials. Can you *learn* to take the heat?

You bet you can.

The first step in that direction is going in with your eyes open. You're a lightning rod when you stand in front, whether you're pushing your family to create new routines, or leading a political protest. Putting yourself there gives you unique opportunities. And yes, at times it carries risks.

Expect Naysayers, and Follow Your Passion

My parents are good examples of how to feel the heat and stay in the kitchen.

Thinking again of those visits to Ellie's house, I recall it was often my father, David, who drove me there. In fact, my father drove me most places—not just to school, but to ballet lessons, to piano, and to Little League practice.

My father was a parenting pioneer. Long before men and women shared child-rearing responsibilities, my dad was changing diapers, packing school lunches, and doing carpool.

I remember playing at Ellie's house once when her mom commented on my pretty new shoes. I thanked her and happened to mention that my dad had bought them with me.

"He did *what*?" her mother asked me, incredulous.

"He took me to buy my new shoes."

Ellie's mom was in a state of shock.

Then she burst out laughing.

"*David* took you to buy shoes? *At the shoe store?*" she asked, still laughing. "I don't think *my husband* knows where our children's *feet* are. He *definitely* doesn't know where *a shoe store* is!"

My dad was ahead of his time.

Meanwhile, where was my mother? Why wasn't she taking me for new shoes?

Well, she had four young children, had just finished her Ph.D., and had a full-time teaching load in New York City. You could count on one hand the number of women in our small town who had children *and* jobs outside the house. Another vanguard ahead of her time.

It worked for them, and it worked for us. There was a problem, though. Their approach to raising a family was not well liked by their friends and neighbors. The other mothers in town didn't look kindly on the "working mother" whose husband picked up her children from school. Likewise, the men in my family never understood my father.

"What kind of man *is* he?" an uncle would ask. "Why can't he just let *their mother* feed them?"

You bet, they felt the heat.

But they also felt empowered by their vision.

They believed in equality between the sexes (in the language of the time) and wanted to expand traditional gender roles. Sometimes they felt hurt by the judgments of their neighbors. But they were energized by the desire to role-model a marriage of equal partners for their daughters.

As the medieval philosopher and theologian Meister Eckhart wrote, "Wisdom consists in doing the next thing you have to do, doing it with your whole heart, and finding delight in doing it." My parents followed their own path with their whole hearts, with joy. That's how they felt the heat and kept on cooking.

In a twist of irony, one of my sisters chose the opposite path. She got a great education: Princeton followed by Cornell. Then she was a Fulbright scholar.

She also met a terrific guy, got married, and had five children. Since my second nephew was born nearly fourteen years ago, my sister has been a *very* happy stay-at-home mom. She loves motherhood. She's *great* at it.

Of course, it got under our mother's skin that "her own daughter" would stay at home and "waste her education" by not "fulfilling her potential" out in the world. My sister then had to accept our mother's judgment, and still follow the beat of *her* own drummer.

Like our mother before her, my sister dared to dream her own vision, and live it. She is there, day in and day out, raising her children every step of the way. She fulfills her potential by tailoring her "mothering" to each of five different children. This is no small feat. Each one is a unique person, with his or her own strengths and needs.

Like our mother before her, my sister role-models for *her* children that you can figure out your own path. Then, no matter what other people say, it's in your hands to live your dream.

Expect Setbacks Along the Way

You hear lots of stories about "overnight sensations" and nearly magical turns from "rags to riches." When you dig a little deeper, you generally learn that it didn't feel magical along the way, and it didn't happen overnight. Part of daring to dream means holding firm to your hopes—even in the face of disappointments, obstacles, and outright rejections.

The story of J. K. Rowling is a good example. Today she's sold more than 400 million copies of the Harry Potter books. She's author to the bestselling book series in history. Yet the manuscript for her first book—*Harry Potter and the Philosopher's Stone*—was submitted to *twelve* publishing houses, and *rejected by them all*. Imagine the force of her passion and faith in that book to continue. Today Rowling is one of Britain's wealthiest citizens. Yet before *Harry* she lived in poverty, describing herself as one small step away from homelessness. Big dreams aren't for the fainthearted.

The Dreamer's audacity isn't only about cooking up bold visions. It's also about nerve, and the guts it takes to hang in there until the world sees *what you see* in your dream. Basketball sensation Jeremy Lin stayed true to *his* Dreamer's longing, despite one setback after another. He was undrafted out of college, rarely played in his rookie season, and got assigned to the NBA Development League (D-League, or minor league) *three times*.

To our eyes, Lin popped up "out of nowhere" to lead a winning streak for the New York Knicks. He was so successful when he finally joined their starting lineup, Lin became a global phenomenon, fondly known as *Linsanity*. Virtually a benchwarmer before his rise to stardom, Lin signed a three-year contract with the Houston Rockets in 2012 for $25.1 million.

In the public eye, it took about two weeks for Lin to change from an unknown athlete to an international basketball hero. But in truth, he'd been playing since his youth, throughout high school and college, and had longed for years to get a "break" in the big leagues.

As life would have it, Lin's very next season, and his first with the Rockets on that pricey contract, was rocky. He had a few great games. But only a few. So his Dreamer returned to the challenge of holding center when people doubt him, and waiting for his next chance to prove he's got what it takes.

In a completely different context, people often say the civil rights movement "started" the day in 1955 when Rosa Parks refused to give up her seat on a segregated bus. But movement organizers say that moment was years in the making. The bus boycott, including the search for the right legal case to take to the courts, was planned long before Rosa Parks entered the scene.

To accomplish great things in your life takes more than envisioning what you want, or even daring to go after it. Like Rowling and Lin, you need to want it enough that *you'll keep going after it*, even when things aren't going your way.

Set Your Aspirations High

Theodor Herzl famously said, "If you will it, it is no dream." His message tells us to aim high and believe that anything's possible if we set our eyes on the prize. All of that talk about naysayers and setbacks is preparation for going in with your eyes open, and then going for it with everything you've got.

After people do something remarkable, especially if they do it at scale, in our minds they change from being someone like us. They become "that famous economist" or "that amazing woman who got a new law passed." Actually, before they went after their dream, they were a person just like you or me.

Take Khan Academy. This is an educational website, set up by Salman Khan. It aims to provide a high-quality education through videos to anyone, for free. Khan Academy has delivered 240 million lessons to users around the world, making Salman Khan an education maverick. But how did it start? Did Khan know all his life that he'd be a great innovator? Did he know of his unique destiny to turn global education on its head? *Was he a lifelong Dreamer?*

Absolutely not.

He was a nice, well-educated guy, who was helping his cousin with algebra. Since he was tutoring her remotely across the country and others wanted to join, Khan thought using YouTube would be an efficient way to teach math. Only along the way did the vision emerge to create a free, global university. Then he saw the potential for what was possible: he'd landed on a practical way to educate a vast number of people at very low cost. Done well, his vision could eliminate economic barriers to a quality education. He also opened vast new possibilities for teachers in classrooms. They started to experiment with ways to use his videos, such as freeing students to learn at their own pace by replacing one lecture given to a full class with students choosing the level of content they are ready for when they pick their own video.

By now Khan Academy is a worldwide education phenomenon. Khan himself is recognized as an innovative genius. But it's important to remember that before his enterprise took off, he was a good person living his life, going to work, loving his wife, and not particularly seeing himself as a pioneer of anything. Something got rolling, and *then he started to dream big.* As he felt the response to his early videos, *his aspirations grew even larger, and wider.* Khan embraced the surprising turn of events: what had started as a friendly way to help a family member could possibly revolutionize education around the world.

Khan's story should remind you that big dreams are not reserved for some other, special group of people. You have a visionary Dreamer inside of you. That Dreamer can cook up wonderful things if you believe in it. You can hold yourself back by telling yourself what you want is out of reach. Or that it isn't important. "It's just my silly dream, after all." But remember the wise words from Herzl: If you will it, it is no dream.

Sense a Path Forward

The hardest thing for many people about drawing out their inner Dreamer is the habit of falling back on their thinking skills. As we talked about in Jordan's situation, you don't need to choose between your Thinker and your Dreamer. You want to make room for both of them.

Dreamers excel at sensing your next steps as you figure out where you're going and how to get there. As you saw throughout Nick's dialogues, Dreamers look at things *strategically* rather than *tactically*. They look down the road. Dreamers care more about where you'll be five years from now than at the end of this quarter.

They also call on intuition to inform the choices they make. Like Dr. Jonas Salk, the medical researcher who discovered the polio vaccine. Salk conducted his research on the vaccine for more than seven years, running the most elaborate field trials to date in history. About his enormous and far-reaching experiments he said, "Intuition will tell the thinking mind where to look next."

Embracing your Dreamer doesn't mean you should check your prudent Thinker at the door. As Ronald Reagan loved to say, "Trust, but verify." In fact, you start balancing your Big Four when you see that intuition and deduction are partners, not adversaries. Consider Albert Einstein, the Nobel Prize–winning physicist. Einstein had a superlative scientific and mathematical mind: he articulated the theory of relativity. Yet Einstein himself said that "the only real valuable thing is intuition." Partners. Not adversaries.

Intuition Says Follow Your Nose

Jane Goodall is the world's leading expert on chimpanzees. When she was young, Goodall found her way to Tanzania. Originally she had no degree, and no formal training. So when she started spending time with chimps, Goodall wasn't following the protocols of standard research methods.

Under scientific guidelines, Goodall should have numbered her research subjects. That provided the necessary objectivity. But she didn't know the rules, so she related to the animals in her own way. Intuitively she gave them names. Watching the chimps she knew as Fifi, Mike, Gigi, and David Greybeard, she observed them to have unique personalities and social relationships that were unknown at the time.

Other primatologists criticized her for getting emotionally involved with her subjects. Yet her deviation from conventional methods is precisely what enabled her amazing discoveries. Had she constrained herself rather than following her gut, we might still not know about the links between chimps and human behavior. Instead, she showcased the humanity of our animal cousins.

Eventually, Goodall went to Cambridge and earned her Ph.D. Yet throughout her career, she followed her gut sense and her innate love of animals. Even after her scientific training was complete, this willingness to value her intuition set her apart.

People define intuition in different ways. Scholars use fancy words to talk about it. The idea of tacit knowledge, for example, refers to what we know in a "pre-logical" phase, before we understand something rationally. Tacit knowledge is made of what we perceive through our senses directly. In a landmark work, *The Process of Education*, Jerome Bruner defined intuition as "the intellectual technique of arriving at plausible but tentative formulations without going through the analytical steps by which such formulations would be found to be valid or invalid conclusions." That is a mouthful. But Bruner was a forerunner in supporting intuitive intelligence along with analytical thinking. You and I are more likely to recognize intuition when we experience it, such as when we tell a friend, "I'm not sure why, but I have a bad feeling about this."

I've found that at life's profound moments, opening myself to *a sense* of what to do or say, rather than trying to think it through, is often the best thing I can do. That's one simple way to understand what intuition means. Let me give you an example.

I shared with you in the Introduction that my mother died of a stroke. It was a massive hemorrhage in her brain that took her life within forty-eight hours. Thankfully I made it to the hospital to sit with her before she passed away.

When I got there, the nurse explained that my mother had lost functioning in most of her brain. "Think of her like a little girl, around two years old," she said. "That's the level of comprehension she has now. You can talk to her if you want. But she won't understand you. Her language center is totally shot."

I sat down next to the hospital bed and took my mother's hand. It was perfectly manicured, since she got her nails done every Friday morning at the same place for the last twenty-five years. It was Saturday night, and it was late. Those polished nails on her soft hand were so very familiar.

I was talking to my mother, but I couldn't block out what the nurse had said. I wanted to communicate my love. Yet I had to admit to myself that given the state of her brain, my words were useless. They were meaningless sounds, if not noise.

Without thinking, I started humming the song we sing at the Friday night table, when we begin dinner on the Sabbath. I learned this song, "Shalom Aleichem," from my mother, who no doubt learned it from her mother. Like me, she'd heard this tune since she first came into the world, and every Friday night of her childhood. Just naturally, or perhaps intuitively, I sang this tune to her while I stroked her hand.

All of a sudden, I looked up, and there was a tear streaming down her cheek. A little tear of recognition, a tear of contact. That tear told me some part of her was still there, even if it was two years old. She knew the music, she heard my voice. She didn't have language anymore, but that tear said to me, "I know you're here, and I love you, too."

Not a minute later, that same nurse came in.

"Don't worry, honey," she said. "She's not crying. Probably a little piece of dust in the tear duct. Something's irritating her eyes. Don't worry. It doesn't mean anything."

Dust in her tear duct? Doesn't mean anything?

I suddenly wondered: Did she recognize the song? Could she hear me singing to her? Could she feel that I was there?

Of course, I'll never know what "really" happened in that hospital room. And it doesn't "technically" matter. I had a sense of making contact with my mother when she wasn't conscious anymore.

I felt connected through the music. Maybe *both* explanations hold some truth. Perhaps there *was* a piece of dust in her tear duct, *and* she heard and recognized the tune. I don't know. And I don't need to choose.

Maybe you've had moments like this, when you sensed something but you couldn't explain it. Maybe someone gave you a logical explanation, but like me, you had an uncanny sense that you knew something else about what had happened.

My take on instances like these is to allow ourselves to know what we know, even when we can't prove it. At least in moments like mine, when nothing was at stake besides what that tear meant to me. No one will lose their job or their home if I'm wrong. I accept the wisdom of Chinese Taoist master Lao-Tzu, who said, "A good artist lets his intuition lead him wherever it wants. A good scientist has freed himself of concepts and keeps his mind open to what is."

To be clear, that doesn't mean I think intuition's usefulness is limited to personal life, or to private moments. With the information overload we face in the workplace, our Dreamer's intuition is a great asset in professional life. As John Naisbitt, author of *Megatrends*, said, "Intuition becomes increasingly valuable in the new information society precisely because there is so much data." Thankfully, as human beings we're blessed with a range of strengths and skills. Like me with interpreting my mother's tear, we don't need to choose.

We've now looked in more detail at the inner Dreamer, exploring the strengths, sweet spots, and some favorite strategies. In the next chapter, we'll do the same for another member of the Big Four, your Thinker.

Below is a short set of reflection questions. Feel free to read them now, or at your leisure.

Reflection Questions

- Do the Dreamer's worldview and sweet spots come easily to you? Is it challenging for you to see how the Dreamer operates in you?

- How do you relate to creativity, audacity, imagination, passion, and hope?

- How do you use your Dreamer's power of intuition?

- When have you let your Dreamer pursue a big dream? When have you held your Dreamer back? What did you learn from these experiences?

- What does your Dreamer want these days: for you, for the people you care about, for your organization, or for the world? What pictures emerge if you give the full force of your Dreamer's imagination to these hopes and visions?

- What are you noticing about your Dreamer's common strategies? Does your Dreamer step out in front of the rest of your Big Four? Does your Dreamer tend to get left behind? What happens when your Dreamer takes over, or gets shut out?

- How can you experiment to foster better balance among your Big Four?

CHAPTER 6

Perspectives: Understand Your Thinker's Insight

The real voyage of discovery consists not in seeking
new lands but in seeing with new eyes.

—MARCEL PROUST

We began exploring the Big Four with the Dreamer, because closing your Performance Gap starts with knowing where you want to go. It's a skill to know what you want, and it takes inner strength to go for it. Once you know what you want, you're ready to bring in the analysis of your inner Thinker.

Why do that?

Because Dreamers who chase after their vision without the reasoning of the Thinker can aim for results they'll never achieve. I heard a telling example of this when I ran a one-day seminar for real estate brokers.

The brokers complained that home sellers often want to set their asking price by the amount of money they'd like to get for their house.

"I want a million dollars," they say.

"That's nice," the brokers think to themselves.

And then they take out their data: selling prices for comparable properties, actual deals for other houses on the same street, industry trends that show how the market is faring in that neighborhood.

"Sellers don't care what we tell them," the brokers told me. "They already have their eye on the new mansion they want to buy, and all the data in the world doesn't convince them they won't get what they want for their house."

When asking prices are set by an inner Dreamer without input from the Thinker, houses sit on the market for a long time.

"They get mad at us for not moving their property more quickly," brokers said. "Inevitably, when we bring the asking price down to the range of the comps [comparable sales], we sell the house. Of course, we could've done that from the beginning. People just can't let go of the number they want, even if all the data we have says they aren't going to get that offer."

The Thinker Likes Information and Ideas

Cogito ergo sum. Je pense, donc je suis. I think, therefore I am.

René Descartes gave us these famous words in 1637, in his *Discourse on Method.* Our existence rests on more than our inner Thinker. But our capacity to think and to reflect is central to what makes human beings remarkable.

Our unique cognitive capacity has inspired philosophers and artists from time immemorial. Socrates told us that "an unexamined life is not worth living." He was pointing to a deeper level of contemplation than we engage in day-to-day, one that invites us to think carefully about our choices, our actions, and our lives. This call to live by our rational faculties led generations of ancient Greeks to explore the depths of rationality. Plato, Socrates' prize student, examined the idea of the perfect society as one ruled by reason. Plato's own student, Aristotle, based a philosophy of living on the understanding that humans are "rational animals." Since we are rational by nature, he said, living a good life requires us to live thoughtfully.

At the turn of the twentieth century, Auguste Rodin put his respect for the intellect into physical form. *Le Penseur*, or *The Thinker*, is a renowned bronze statue that pays homage to the beauty as well as the importance of the human mind.

Great minds have always pursued an understanding of our place in the cosmos. The Buddha, for example, was a scientist of the mind, illuminating what he understood as the nature of reality. Throughout history, sages have handed down teachings about the natural order of things. Confucius in *The Analects*. Lao-Tzu in the *Tao Te Ching*. The Upanishads. The Sutras. The Bhagavad Gita. Biblical exegesis and far-reaching commentary come from places around the world: Constantinople, Dharamsala, Jerusalem, Rome, Mecca, to name a few.

Thinking Is Fundamental to Who We Are

Marie Curie turned a page in scientific history with her work on radioactivity. The movie *A Beautiful Mind* captures the story of mathematician John Nash, who articulated game theory. John Maynard Keynes' ideas were so influential that to this day there is a school of thought known as "Keynesian economics."

Like Keynes, Thinkers take bits of information and connect the dots, forming theories about how things work. Supply and demand. LEAN manufacturing. Eating disorders. The autism spectrum. Too Big to Fail. Thinkers give names to things so we can understand them, talk about them, and take action to address them.

You can write off theory as best left to academics in the "ivory tower." Yet, as social psychologist Kurt Lewin commented, "There's nothing so practical as a good theory." Just ask Richard Saul Wurman, the original founder of the global conference powerhouse TED, whose driving mission is to spread "ideas worth sharing."

Sigmund Freud opened the world of the psyche by naming the unconscious. Ralph Ellison articulated the "underground" condition of African-Americans in his novel *Invisible Man*. Betty Friedan highlighted the need for American housewives to find more fulfilling roles. She called their predicament the "problem that has no name." Howard Gardner opened our eyes to multiple intelligences. Mihaly Csikszentmihalyi explained the state of "flow," which later became part of a movement for "positive psychology." And on it goes.

Thinkers Give Us Helpful Answers

Without the research and clarity of the Thinker, we're left with nameless phenomena that can be vastly misunderstood. Then we act badly, or fail to act at all. You may know parents who regret scolding their kids for not concentrating on homework after they learned their child had dyslexia or attention deficit disorder.

Life is rough going without explanations.

On the flipside, harnessing the Thinker's clarity creates a lot of value. Look at Warren Buffett, often called "the Oracle of Omaha." The chairman and CEO of Berkshire Hathaway, Buffett is well known for his investing model, and for generating vast wealth through smart investment choices. Buffett is also a novel thinker about philanthropy. He practices substantial giving as a paradigm, asking other affluent people to embrace his philosophy.

Speaking to a different segment of the market, personal finance expert Suze Orman helps people understand how to manage their financial lives. Orman uses her Thinker skillfully to provide basic economic education. She explains such things as reducing debt and controlling spending in a style that everyone can follow. As I've discovered as a writer, it takes a lot of hard thinking to present complex ideas in an accessible, practical way.

If the CFO represents the Thinker in a corporate setting, then in the public sector Thinkers may be likened to policy makers. Thinkers write rules and regulations to guide society. They make legal arguments to judges, who use *their* inner Thinkers to interpret the law. One way to view American history is through the lens of Thinkers who opined from the bench: Earl Warren, Thurgood Marshall, Antonin Scalia, Ruth Bader Ginsburg, Sandra Day O'Connor, and William Rehnquist, to name a few.

Outside of courtrooms, Thinkers engage with large-scale policy questions as well. How to reduce poverty in Africa? How to prevent acts of terror? How to stop more ice from melting in the Arctic? How to create jobs and improve the economy? How to stop bloody civil wars?

There are no magic bullets. Challenges like these require nuanced problem definition, systems thinking, methods for testing hypotheses, and statistical analysis. The good news is that Thinkers are built for just these kinds of activities.

We need our inner Thinker to make sense of things. To understand the law of gravity. To decide which school to attend. To evaluate our employees at the end of the year. To help a dear friend choose the right surgeon. To do our taxes.

We think when we read two proposals, compare them, and pick one. Or when we make a list of the questions we have for our doctor. When we write a recommendation. Prepare a proposal to bring before the town council. Or put together a list of referral sources and helpful state agencies when someone needs support.

We deliberate before answering thorny questions from our kids. We do the math before we pay the bill. We figure out our opinion before we blog about it. We make charts and lists to find some way on earth to get everything done.

Thinker Quiz: *What's Your Favorite Strategy?*

As we did for the Dreamer, let's take a "quiz" to learn about your Thinker's favorite strategy. Remember, your favorite strategy isn't the one you "like" most. It's the one your Thinker uses most often.

At some point in your life, your Thinker's favorite strategy of running low, high, or balanced got you good results. Maybe it still does. Or maybe it doesn't, and this is at the root of your particular Performance Gap. This quiz will help you tell.

As before, read the situation below and the three options. Notice which one feels most like you. You might also note if any them leads to you think "I would never act like *that*."

Inner Thinker Scenario

You're at a team meeting with a group of colleagues. You each have twenty minutes to give an overview of your progress since the last meeting.

You're responsible for a complex set of issues, and you've burned the midnight oil to consolidate the results for this progress review. A few minutes into your presentation, someone interrupts you. "That's wrong," they say. "Your numbers are wrong."

"What?" you ask.

He says it again: "Your numbers are *wrong*."

What do you think? What do you feel? What will you say?

Option One: It's My Mistake, Not Theirs

You're thrown by the interruption. All of a sudden you feel confused. The numbers seemed right last night when you checked them one last time. Could they be wrong? What if the assumptions built into the calculations were wrong? You didn't actually test *those*.

You start to sweat. Uncertainty and doubt rise in your mind as you scramble to redo the math in your head. "I'm sorry," you say. "I thought the report was ready. It sounds like I should run the numbers again."

You go back to your seat flustered, at a loss about what happened.

Option Two: It's Their Mistake, Not Mine

"I'm sorry. I don't think I heard you correctly," you say. "Did you just say my numbers were wrong?" You can't believe the nerve of this guy to question your results. Who is he kidding? You think to yourself—*to state the obvious*—your numbers are *not* wrong. Your numbers are never wrong. Besides, you're the one with all the data. You did the benchmarking. You ran the analysis. You wonder how much data to put on the table so everyone is clear that—in fact—*his assessment is wrong, not yours.*

You clear your throat to mask your annoyance. "Well, actually, they're correct. However, if you'd like to run the numbers yourself, be my guest. I promise you'll come up with the same result that I'm presenting here." During ten more minutes of back-and-forth, you stand firmly and mostly calmly by your report.

Option Three: A Mistake? We're All Human

You're surprised. You did all the research. You ran the numbers several times. Then again, you're human. Everyone makes mistakes.

You ask him to clarify what he means about the numbers. You feel a bit defensive, but you want to understand why he's pushing back on your report. You listen to his critique, unsure of whether or not you agree. With mixed feelings given all the work you've done on this, you agree to run the numbers again.

To close the conversation you tell him, "I'll look into this and make sure we take your view into account. Wherever we land, I still think this analysis is an important piece of the answer."

Which of these reactions seems most like you?

How you react gives you a hint about your Thinker's favorite strategy.

In Option One, a Thinker running low puts more stock in her colleague's assertions than her own. Quick to doubt her calculations and her basic assumptions, she's easily derailed. She lacks faith in her facts, and is easily confused about her thinking.

In Option Two, this High Thinker may as well be saying, "You're an idiot, do the math!" He is clearer in his convictions than the Low Thinker, which is good, but his arrogance may work against him in persuading others. If, in fact, the error *is* his, he'll have a tough time convincing others the next time something like this happens.

In Option Three, a Balanced Thinker stays true to herself without attacking her colleague for his dissenting opinion. She doesn't submit blindly like the Low Thinker did. Yet she doesn't act self-righteously like the High Thinker, either.

While she acknowledges an error is possible, she maintains that her contribution is still an important part of the puzzle. The Balanced Thinker is neither self-doubting nor self-righteous. Instead, she combines her intellect with patience and prudence.

The Thinker in Daily Life

In daily life, there's a lot to think about. Things to learn. Trade-offs to consider. Assessments to make. You need a strong inner Thinker to figure it all out.

With a Balanced Thinker, you can do things like:

- Write a well-defined project plan with milestones, a sensible budget, and clear measures of success
- Research available deductions for your tax return
- Comment on a blog entry to present a different point of view
- Study all summer so you can pass your entry exams
- Make sense of unexpected results from your lab experiment
- Develop strong arguments in defense of your client's position
- Compare your performance to benchmarks in the market and to your shareholders' expectations

- Consider the trade-offs between working at the office with the long commute or working at home with all the distractions
- Run an effective postmortem session after a failed project, to learn as much as you can about what went wrong
- Decide who to propose to the school board as possible candidates for the upcoming elections
- Review your work travel for the next few months, and design a viable plan for child care
- Look into options for summer plans, factoring in the activities, program costs, educational benefits, and scheduling needs of the whole family

Putting Principles into Practice

Thinker Sweet Spots

The Lakota are indigenous people from the American Great Plains, and part of a confederation of Sioux tribes. This comes from their tradition: "No one was quick with a question, no matter how important, and no one was pressed for an answer. A pause giving time for thought was the truly courteous way of beginning and conducting a conversation." The Thinker's power source is *reason*, and her strongest muscle is *clarity*. The Balanced Thinker provides *reflection*, and specializes in the skills you need for conducting *analysis*.

The Thinker's sweet spots enable you to:

1. **Apply Facts and Logic**
2. **Consider Consequences**
3. **Look from All Sides**

The Thinker's inner resources include prudence, humility, curiosity, and patience.

Let's see how these work in practice.

Apply Facts and Logic

Kenneth Feinberg is an attorney who specializes in mediation and dispute resolution. His ability to analyze information clearly in the midst of high-stakes emotions has enabled him to adjudicate thousands of high-profile cases, many of them in wrenching circumstances.

Consider the daunting task of heading the 9/11 Victims Compensation Fund, when he found himself seated across the table from thousands of family members who'd lost loved ones on that terrible day. It was Feinberg's job to determine the compensation they were entitled to receive, for lost wages and suffering brought about by the tragic event. Families were angry. Hurting. Their feelings were raw. Many wanted someone to blame for their pain.

Initially, Feinberg's reserve in determining an appropriate amount of money for each family was interpreted as unfeeling. "It's a brutal, cold, thing to do," he admitted to a reporter. "Anybody who looks at this program and expects that by cutting a U.S. Treasury check, you are going to make 9/11 families happy, is vastly misunderstanding what's going on."

While they didn't find him warm, they did consider his appraisals fair—or *fair enough* not to pursue further action. Out of more than five thousand cases brought before him, only seventy-three of the families opted to reject his offer of compensation and litigate instead.

People like Kenneth Feinberg can juggle an enormous range of facts and variables in complex situations. If your Thinker runs low, it can feel challenging to manage a much smaller number of facts, or to apply logical reasoning to your experiences.

I remember a woman who came to my summer program at Harvard. She was on the brink of leaving her marriage. She said her husband didn't understand her. She was at the end of her rope.

We looked at her dialogue as a group. Here's how it started:

WIFE: I can't stand this anymore.

HUSBAND: You can't stand what?

WIFE: I can't stand the fighting, yelling, you treating me like I'm stupid. I can't take it anymore.

HUSBAND: What are you talking about? Is this because I asked you to take back the shirt you bought me? I didn't like it, and the price was absurd. Why would you pay that much?

WIFE: I'm sick of this. I'm not an idiot.

HUSBAND: Who said you were an idiot? I said I didn't like the shirt.

WIFE: This is ridiculous. I'm not taking this anymore.

HUSBAND: What's ridiculous?

WIFE: All of it.

HUSBAND: All of what?

The dialogue continued this way for another page. The woman, Kate, told our group she was fed up with her husband. "Can you believe this? I tell him *all the time* why I'm not happy, and he *still* doesn't get it."

Well, I had to admit it. I didn't get it, either.

I could tell she was unhappy, and she was *done* with the way things were. But I couldn't tell *what exactly* she wasn't taking anymore. Do *you* know what leaves Kate feeling "treated like an idiot"? I don't. And neither does her husband. If she wants to change the situation, bringing in her Thinker will help.

Spell Out Examples with Detail

At her inner negotiation table, this woman's Lover has all the cards. Her Thinker has long since folded and stopped playing the game. Kate says she doesn't see the point of explaining herself, because "if he cared about me, he'd know what I mean."

That's too bad.

Because her inner Thinker can make clear arguments and offer evidence.

I suggested that she let her Thinker play the next hand.

"What if you give him concrete examples of what's not working for you. Do you think that would make a difference?" I asked.

"Why should I have to spell it out for him?" she asked me.

"Because you want him to understand you," I said.

It turns out that if you want people to know what you're talking about, much of the time you actually need to tell them. If your Thinker runs low as Kate's does, and even more if your Lover runs high like hers, this seems unjust. You wonder, "What isn't clear? What more do I need to say? And why is it *my fault* that he doesn't get it?"

Actually, this isn't about fault. It's about closing your Performance Gap. At this rate, this woman isn't getting the result she wants. She doesn't want a divorce. She wants a husband who understands her. Her Thinker can help.

In the workshop, we tried an exercise where her Thinker negotiated with her Lover for a chance to speak directly to her husband. Her Thinker wanted to give him tangible information to explain how she felt. Her Lover agreed to try.

So, in the class, her Thinker had a turn to speak out loud. This is what she said.

> KATE'S THINKER: Remember when we took the whole family out to dinner, and the waiter handed me the check? I started looking it over, and you pulled it away from me. Then *you* looked at it and gave your credit card. What do you think—that I can't add? I felt stupid, especially in front of your parents.
>
> Or when we went to get a new coffeepot, I picked one out, and you put it back on the shelf. You came back with a different one, and gave me a lecture about why I didn't pick a good brand. You assumed you knew more about it than I did. I wanted the one I picked because it was on sale. I knew the brand—it was good enough for me. When you take something out of my hands and replace it, without even asking why I took it in the first place, I'm thinking you must *really* think I'm an idiot.
>
> And the night of the car accident. I skidded on black ice and dented the car. When I came home you asked me if I'd gotten the snow tires put on the car, and I said no. Then you yelled at me like I was a little child, saying how stupid it was to drive in a storm without snow tires. I agree, I should have changed the tires. But when

you talk to me in that tone of voice, it sounds like you're scolding a five-year-old. I understand that you're upset if I hurt the car. But please speak to me like an adult.

In this exercise, her Thinker gave her husband what he needed. Concrete examples. Information. Interactions he can remember.

Of course, he might dispute her interpretations.

But he can finally *understand* her impressions.

At least now they're in the same conversation.

Negotiating with yourself means letting your Big Four consider which of them is in the best position to get the result you want. In this case, her Lover needed to step back and let her Thinker make her case.

Admittedly this approach doesn't feel as satisfying to her inner Lover. She knows Pascal's famous words, that "the heart has its reasons that reason knows not of." Fair enough. At the same time, since she wants to influence her husband, her Thinker is most likely to get her points across. That shift in roles within her inner team will create a new dynamic, one that has potential to foster real change in how they communicate. That won't solve all of their problems. But it does give them a place to begin.

Savor the Spice of Life

For the woman we just talked about, letting her Thinker engage more with facts and logic will open doors. However, if your Thinker runs high, too much attention on rationality creates a risk. You can live your whole life and miss all the magic. High Thinkers need to watch out, so they don't miss *deeper* significance because they're too busy calculating statistically significant results.

Life is messy. Things don't always add up. Your advice can be technically correct but leave people feeling cold. In truth, living in your head all the time can leave *you* feeling cold. You wake up one day in the world of Pink Floyd, feeling "comfortably numb." Some of the best parts of life happen when you let your inner Thinker take a rest.

I remember growing up and following the same Thanksgiving traditions every year. Rain or shine, we'd start the day by going to the high school football game. Back at home, we'd catch the end of Macy's Thanksgiving Day Parade on television, then settle in for the annual showing of *Miracle on 34th Street*.

In this black-and-white movie classic, a bearded old man named Kris Kringle comes to New York and asserts that he is Santa Claus. Because he's a very convincing Santa, he lands the coveted spot of playing him at Macy's department store. Children in the film believe Kris really *is* Santa. Of course, the adults know that Santa doesn't exist.

Kris is so certain of his identity that he's seen as insane and sent to trial to determine the truth of his claim. His attorney is tickled when he finds a way to force the court to accept Kris as Santa Claus, knowing he's pulled off a grand ruse to affirm the crazy old man.

In the last scene, we see the wish fulfilled of a little girl who had asked Kris for her dream house. There it is: the house of her dreams, with an open front door. The young girl rushes in to see "her" house. Lo and behold, leaning against a wall inside, we see a walking stick that matches the very cane Kris Kringle uses. Now we're left to wonder: *Was he the real Santa Claus after all?*

All my life, I've loved this closing scene. Every year, I waited with bated breath to see that cane mysteriously show up against the wall in the dream house. Despite my serious education, I wanted that cane to mean *it really was* Santa who granted her wish.

Logical? No. Just sweet.

Physicist and Nobel laureate Erwin Schrödinger understood the need for High Thinkers to step outside of the objective world in order to find ultimate meaning in their lives. He said:

"The scientific picture of the real world around me is very deficient. It gives a lot of factual information, puts all our experience in a magnificently consistent order, but it is ghastly silent about all and sundry that is really near to our heart, that really matters to us . . . we do not belong to the material world that science constructs for us."

If your identity becomes aligned with your Thinker alone, you might get the right answers but miss the point of the questions. It's fine to let your Thinker be first among equals. But make sure that facts and logic don't squeeze out the other members of your Big Four. Their respective interests provide a crucial balance for you.

Consider Consequences

Remember champion cyclist Lance Armstrong? He won the Tour de France an amazing seven times. He was a folk hero, beating testicular cancer and raising millions for cancer research. But in the end, his titles were revoked and he was banned forever from competitive cycling for using performance-enhancing drugs. In addition to violating the rules and spirit of fair competition, Armstrong broke faith with the public by giving adamant denials for years, only to admit to his actions later. Did he think all of this would never come to light?

What about Larry Summers? As president of Harvard University, Summers said publicly that biological differences in the sexes could help explain why so few women become professional scientists or engineers. He did this—suggesting that girls are innately, *genetically* incapable of competing with boys in math and science—while speaking at a conference called, "Diversifying the Science and Engineering Workforce: Women, Underrepresented Minorities, and their S. & E. Careers." Did he consider the likely fallout from doing that?

Then there's Rielle Hunter and John Edwards. They were having a baby together in secret while he ran for president of the United States. Good plan.

We read stories like these and we ask ourselves: *What were they thinking???*

Well, they weren't thinking.

They put their Thinker in a box, and shoved that box onto a high shelf in a dark closet. Had they tapped their inner Thinker, they might've considered the inevitable consequences. Instead, they followed something else. Call it impulse, drive, lust, need, addiction, greed. Maybe the thrill of playing the provocateur? Whatever it is, it's not the judgment of a Balanced Thinker.

We'd like to think that people who do irrational things have nothing to do with us. Famous and infamous people seem to exhibit action untempered by the voice of reason nearly every day. We're not like that, right?

Actually, **we all do things that make no rational sense**. While *our* mistakes generally don't make international news, we're all capable of losing our minds. In fact, experts in behavioral economics like Dan Ariely show us that we're "predictably irrational." All of us. In multiple ways.

It's wrong to assume that if you reason your way through facts and data, then you'll make purely rational decisions. Paradoxically, you can engage your Thinker to catch the *other* influences on how you're making evaluations. With its eyes open, your Thinker can spot the potential influence of decision biases before you fall prey to them. One valuable way to do that is to stop and ask yourself about the implications of what you're planning to say or do.

You don't have a crystal ball. But *you can* make educated guesses about the dominoes you're about to knock over. Recall times you've thought to yourself *after the fact*, "Well, I guess I could have seen that coming, had I stopped to think about it." Instead of getting blindsided later, you're better off developing the Thinker habit of *considering consequences in advance.*

Stop and Ask Yourself: What Is Likely to Happen?

Rachel is employed by the Agency for Health Care Research and Quality, a state office that addresses public health and safety issues. She described a situation in which her agency director, Bram, kept pushing her to take on new commitments, even though she told him repeatedly that she didn't have time.

DESCRIPTION:

Bram came in today AGAIN to push me to review proposals for the anti-bullying campaign. The state just released funds for new initiatives in this area, after a highly publicized incident between two young teens. I'm frustrated because Bram won't make time to interview people for the At-Risk Youth position. Instead of filling it, he thinks he can force me to do two full-time jobs.

BRAM: You need to review these proposals for the upcoming campaign to prevent bullying.

ME: Actually, Bram, I have more than I can handle now. My plate is full.

BRAM:	Surely you can find time to review a few proposals. I'm concerned that only *some* of them address cyber-bullying. The others deal with in-person bullying, but those aren't going to work, since the recent incident involved nasty gossip on social media sites.
ME:	You and I have already talked about my workload. There's too much going on for me to start something new. You should find someone to fill the open At-Risk Youth position. They could do things like this.
BRAM:	Rachel, it would be a real shame to miss this opportunity for these new state funds. I'm sure you don't want that to happen.
ME:	I don't know what to say. I don't have *one spare minute*, Bram.
BRAM:	Well, I'd appreciate your input on these proposals. We don't want to miss this opportunity. They're on my desk.
ME:	[*Strained smile. Says nothing.*]

Bram might leave Rachel's office feeling like the victor. He knew what he wanted, and he didn't back down. Managers often make this mistake, believing that their Warrior can stand out front, and they can pressure direct reports to get things done. But Bram's Warrior fails to notice something important: nowhere in this conversation did Rachel *agree* to review the proposals.

Bram's Low Thinker isn't factoring *the likely impact on Rachel* of feeling pushed around. His Thinker also doesn't consider that she might be telling the truth, and she just doesn't have time to do this. A Balanced Thinker would have challenged Bram's Warrior to think about these things.

So, what *are* the likely consequences of Bram's behavior? Do you imagine Rachel running down the hall to get the packet of proposals? Surely not. People in Rachel's shoes tend to choose from among three options, none of which is good for Bram. But *all of which are fairly predictable*, if he stopped to think about it.

1. **Minimal Compliance:** She breezes through the pages in a flash, and drops Bram an email saying "reviewed the proposals. Wouldn't take any of them." And then she goes back to her regular job.

2. **Passive Aggression:** She goes down the hall and gets the stack of proposals. Then she lets them sit on her desk until someone else comes looking for them. A month later.

3. **Aggression:** She brings them home to read over the weekend, and "accidentally" leaves them on the subway train.

In virtually no scenario is Rachel going to drop her current responsibilities, race to Bram's office, review the proposals carefully, and then miss deadlines for projects she values, and which were already in place before Bram came to see her.

On top of not making a viable plan for these proposals, Bram's Warrior has forfeited the holy grail of managers: employee engagement. A Balanced Thinker would have asked Rachel about her commitments, and then *prioritized with Rachel* about ways to get everything done.

Look from All Sides

Bram is suffering the effects of a Low Thinker. Some of you tend toward the other end of the spectrum, with a Thinker who runs high. If you're like the High Thinkers I know, you might struggle with one of the Balanced Thinker's sweet spots, which is looking from all sides.

Granted, the High Thinkers I work with are more like Super-High Thinkers. They have amazing intellectual horsepower. They dissect issues and synthesize information with incredible speed. They make difficult decisions every five minutes. And they're working on some of the world's most vexing problems. They feel smart. Because they are smart. However, they're susceptible to one of the High Thinker's booby traps.

Arrogance.

Some High Thinkers cross the line from confidence to hubris. Sometimes hubris flourishes into full-blown self-righteousness. That's when my Helper Alarms go off, because I see people headed for their Performance Gap. It's nearly guaranteed. And they can't see it coming. Ironically, their grandiosity gets in the way of seeing their grandiosity.

Remember You Could Be Wrong

I sat next to a little boy at a dinner recently. He turned to ask me a question.

"Why do your feet get cold before a big presentation?"

I thought about what he might have overheard.

"Oh," I said with a smile. "Your feet don't *literally* get cold. That's an expression about getting nervous. People say 'I got cold feet.' But they don't mean their toes actually started to *feel cold*."

I thought that settled the matter. It didn't.

"No, no," he told me. "*You* don't understand. When people get nervous, their feet *do* get really, *really* cold. Sometimes they can't continue until they get warmer socks."

He seemed *quite sure* about the whole "cold feet" thing. So I deferred.

"Okay," I conceded. "Maybe I have it wrong."

I had to smile after this exchange. *Not* because little kids are so cute. But because as adults *we still think like they do.* We get an idea in our heads. We decide we're right. And that's the end of it. You can tell me why I'm wrong. But I'll tell you right back why you don't get it. I saw this in high relief a few years ago, when I was asked to work with Karl. He was a German partner of a global firm, working at the time in India.

Karl was in a breakdown with the CEO of his largest client. The client said Karl wasn't listening to him. Karl was beside himself that his client wouldn't accept his recommendations. Karl was so sure of his report that all he could do when he met with his client was tell him why he was wrong. The CEO had been an industry leader for decades. Apparently that had no relevance for Karl. So the CEO was on the verge of firing him.

When I met with him, Karl told me about his pitched battles with the CEO. Both men *insisted* they were right. After getting some context, I asked Karl, "Is it *possible* that you're missing something?"

He made it plain.

"No."

"Could the CEO have a valid perspective that's different from yours, maybe a separate piece of the same puzzle?" I asked.

"No."

"Are you interested in trying to understand his objections to your advice?"

"Listen. I have two Ph.D.'s in this area, and I literally wrote the book on this. There is nothing about this subject that I don't understand. The only thing I don't know is how to get my client to recognize that he's wrong."

I wasn't able to help Karl. At the time I didn't know how to reach Super-High Thinkers. Not one as convinced as Karl that *he couldn't possibly* be missing something.

Looking back, it's entirely possible that Karl's solution was a good one. Maybe even the only reasonable one. But the "rightness" of his answer didn't solve his problem. And it didn't help his client. Because in the end, the CEO did fire Karl. And then he implemented his own solution. Karl may have had it right on the merits, but he lost the client, *and* the CEO made a poor choice for his company. Everyone lost.

Keep Your Pride in Check

Something related happened to Jamie Dimon, CEO of JPMorgan Chase. Let me set the context. A while back, supersized risks by Wall Street banks were constrained by regulations known as Glass-Steagall. In the boom years, Glass-Steagall was repealed, giving banks free rein. When the global financial crisis hit, it became clear that repealing the safeguards was problematic. The banks, then called "too big to fail," had jeopardized the world economy and now required bailouts from the U.S. government.

To prevent a repeat of the banks' bad behavior, discussion renewed around regulating them. Former Federal Reserve chairman Paul Volcker led the effort, proposing what became known as the Volcker Rule. The theory went that under the rule, banks could still prosper, while not toppling the global markets and harming millions of consumers.

Jamie Dimon led the charge to lobby Congress to reject the Volcker Rule. He gave interviews with a swagger, scorning attempts to reform Wall Street. He declared with condescension that Paul Volcker "doesn't understand capital markets."

In the midst of expending all this energy fighting against regulatory safeguards, Dimon disclosed $2 billion in trading losses. This was just weeks after saying concerns about the trading were a "tempest in a teapot." His situation was exactly the kind of breakdown that Volcker's rule aimed to prevent. In a further irony, it was the loophole that Dimon helped create that enabled the $2 billion mistake. Over the months that followed, that number continued to rise steadily into the tens of billions. In the end, Dimon went on national television to admit "I was dead wrong" to dismiss concerns.

On one level, Dimon's Thinker failed by letting self-interest push away what already appeared as common sense. Around the world, people like Hong Kong's global finance expert Andrew Sheng were voicing the clear need to regulate the financial services sector. The system had failed, at an enormous social cost. This was hardly a well-kept secret. In the documentary *Inside Job*, about the financial crisis, Sheng described the far-reaching debacle: "Why should a financial engineer be paid four to a hundred times more than a real engineer? A real engineer builds bridges. A financial engineer builds dreams, and when those dreams turn out to be nightmares, other people pay for them." Dimon's Thinker should've reasoned along with the emerging global consensus.

On a deeper level, though, Dimon's Thinker failed more profoundly by losing touch with his humility. Like Karl and Jamie Dimon, High Thinkers often feel—and act—like they're superior to other people. A Balanced Thinker knows you can be smart *and* respectful, heeding wisdom like that of Thomas à Kempis in *The Imitation of Christ*:

The more you know and the better you understand, the more severely will you be judged, unless your life is also the more holy. Do not be proud, therefore, because of your learning or skill. Rather, fear because of the talent given you. If you think you know many things and understand them well enough, realize at the same time that there is much you do not know.

Rabbi Abraham Joshua Heschel, a leading Jewish philosopher of the twentieth century, offered a similar teaching. "Important and precious as the development of our intellectual faculties is, the cultivation of a sensitive conscience is indispensable." A prime example of applying this philosophy in business is the leadership of Kazuo Inamori, founder of Kyocera Corporation, creator of DDI (later KDDI), and a hugely successful entrepreneur.

Throughout his career, Inamori insisted on corporate cultures based on doing right by employees and by society. In a case study written about him and taught at Harvard Business School, Inamori recounts talking with his first team at Kyocera.

The only thing I could offer to them was my commitment that I am going to do the right thing as a human being. . . . They responded, "What is the right thing to do as human beings?" I responded that the right thing to do as a human being are the things that your parents and teachers told you that were right and the things which are inherently right to everyone.

Rooting his businesses in this management philosophy became Inamori's signature.

Years later, the Japanese government asked Inamori to lead Japan

Airlines when it fell into bankruptcy. After he succeeded in turning things around, Inamori talked about the effort required to persuade High Thinkers at JAL to embrace these fundamental principles. In 2013, by then chairman emeritus of JAL, Inamori spoke at the British embassy in Tokyo about the airline's reconstruction.

> Many of JAL's executives were intelligent people who graduated from prestigious universities. In the beginning, they appeared to be uncomfortable learning elementary principles such as "Always be humble," "Accumulate tedious efforts," and "Pursue what is right as a human being." Some were opposed to learning, saying "These are such obvious things. Why do we have to learn such things now?"
>
> This is what I said to those people. "You show contempt by saying these are such childish lessons. You may know about them, however, you certainly do not adhere to them or practice them. You may have much knowledge in many areas, but you do not have the slightest idea of pursuing what is right as a human being, which is the most fundamental concept. This is the reason that led JAL to bankruptcy.

Wise business leaders know that harnessing their intellect in business doesn't mean checking their humanity at the door. As with all of the Big Four, the Thinker contributes best in tandem with the rest of the inner team.

Find the Merit in Other Perspectives

Thinkers can struggle to recognize the value in other approaches to leading and living. Strong Lovers, for example, often find themselves on opposite sides from Thinkers. The High Lover rejects the rational approach of the Thinker. High Lovers feel like Thinkers "don't get it." Of course, High Thinkers *don't* get all the "drama" and emotional intensity that Lovers carry around. Thinkers prefer the lyrics of rock icon Tina Turner, who belted out the question that's often on their minds: *What's love got to do with it?* Perhaps *because* their outlooks are so different, these two inner negotiators need each other for stability and perspective.

I learned this the hard way.

Years ago I had a colleague I'll call Tom who never wanted to sign contracts with our clients. He got angry that I even suggested it. Tom said contracts would turn the engagements we did for clients into "transactions" instead of "relationships." He insisted that we use what he called "a gentleman's agreement": we give our word, we shake on it, the deal is done.

To my eyes, Tom was driven by an inner Lover running high. Because my Thinker was the loudest voice in my head at the time, Tom found me brittle, cold, and naïve about what it takes to build enduring, trust-based relationships. He lived in fear that I would blow up client opportunities by insisting we commit to things in writing.

Meanwhile, with my Thinker in high gear, I judged *him* as naïve. As a lawyer by training, I couldn't believe he wanted to perform long-term consulting engagements without contracts. This made no sense. From my High Thinker's point of view, his Lover was foolish to believe everything would go swimmingly without ever needing to look back at what had been agreed, *in writing*.

I suspect that Tom thought I had "trust issues." To my Thinker, this had nothing to do with trust. It was about managing risk. Plenty of people act in good faith and remember things differently. And some people *don't* act in good faith. That's why we write contracts. I lived in fear of clients not paying us because they "remembered" things differently, or worse, a disparity between "recollections" of an agreement serious enough to land us in court.

Like Tom and me, strong inner Lovers and strong inner Thinkers are uneasy bedfellows, even within the Big Four of the same person. Looking back now, I see how both perspectives are necessary. Tom's Lover was right that we wanted close partnerships with our clients. My attitude could've signaled that I preferred arm's-length relationships. At the same time, my Thinker was right to want to record the meeting of the minds. On a few occasions, the ability to look back to the terms in a contract was essential. In one case, the lack of a written contract proved disastrous.

The tension between Tom and me taught me to make more room for my inner Lover in contract negotiations. I don't haggle anymore over small points. My inner Lover keeps my eye on the ball of the long-term relationship above and beyond any one particular project. I do still sign contracts for the work I do, but I worry less about getting paid for every piece of help I provide. As it turns out, I also *enjoy* my relationships with clients a lot more now. In that way Tom was right. My Thinker was taking a transactional approach. And now I strike a better balance.

We've talked about the Dreamer, and now the Thinker. In the next chapter, we'll look at another inner negotiator in the Big Four, the Lover. Following is another short set of reflection questions.

Reflection Questions

- Do the Thinker's worldview and sweet spots come easily to you? Is it challenging for you to see how the Thinker operates in you?

- How do you relate to clarity, prudence, humility, curiosity, and patience?

- How do you use your Thinker's power of reason?

- When have you let your Thinker consider implications, consequences, and levels of risk before making a move? When have you disregarded your Thinker's preference to consider things carefully? What did you learn from these experiences?

- What beliefs or opinions is your Thinker holding strongly these days? What are some alternative or even opposing perspectives? What information or analysis could soften your Thinker's certainty that you're correct?

- What are you noticing about your Thinker's common strategies? Does your Thinker step out in front of the rest of your Big Four? Does your Thinker tend to get left behind? What happens when your Thinker takes over, or gets shut out?

- How can you experiment to foster better balance among your Big Four?

CHAPTER 7

People: Feel Your Lover's Heart

Our life is made of love,
and to love no longer is to live no longer.

—GEORGE SAND

Where the Dreamer muses about vision, and the Thinker analyzes ideas, your Lover values relationships. As you would imagine from its name, the Lover carries your emotions and connects you with other people. If you're the person in your family who hosts on holidays, or lets everyone know when a family member gets sick, you can guess your Lover is on the case.

The Lover is about forging relationships. Think of Diana, the "People's Princess." Or Magic Johnson, Los Angeles Lakers point guard and member of the Dream Team that won Olympic gold. He was a great champion on the court. He was also a uniquely joyful, unselfish, and lovable player. He even became friends with his former bitter rival, Larry Bird. Lovers often produce greatness through partnership with other people. Watson and Crick. Woodward and Bernstein. Simon and Garfunkel. Venus and Serena.

A signature of the inner Lover is the drive to nurture and tend. It's the impulse you feel to leave work on time because your dog is alone at home. To buy organic vegetables from a local farm to care for the natural environment. Or to sponsor the student who rings your doorbell in their fund-raiser for school.

The Lover Cares About People

When we hear the word *lover*, most of us think first of romantic love. The kind of love we vow to each other, "in sickness and in health, in good times and in bad, for as long as we both shall live." The need for loving partners goes back to the Garden of Eden. In Genesis, we're told that Adam is alone, without a proper mate. For the first time in the creation story, God says this is "lo tov"—not good. It's "good" once Adam and Eve get together.

This form of devotion evokes passion and poetry from the Lover. As it says in the Song of Songs, "Rise up, my love, my beautiful one, and come away . . . for your love is more delightful than wine." Shakespeare's Romeo declared, "Life's not worth living without Juliet."

In 1607, Emperor Shah Jahan was fifteen years old when he was betrothed to his fourteen-year-old future bride. He had a few wives in his lifetime. But it was this woman who became his true love. He gave her the name Mumtaz Mahal, meaning "Jewel of the Palace." Mumtaz Mahal died in 1631 while giving birth to their fourteenth child. Shah Jahan built the Taj Mahal in her honor. It took twenty-two years, and twenty-two thousand workers. An ode to his beloved, the Taj Mahal is one of the seven Wonders of the World.

Abelard and Heloise. Cleopatra and Mark Antony. Jacob and Rachel. Odysseus and Penelope. Rama and Sita. Napoleon and Josephine. Ginger Rogers and Fred Astaire. Ellen DeGeneres and Portia de Rossi. Jay-Z and Beyoncé. Barack and Michelle.

Love is timeless.

Romantic love, and with it sexual intimacy, plays an important role in our lives. Our inner Lover encompasses all of that, but also plays a *much* broader role. As you know, love is felt and expressed in many relationships. Both literature and popular culture have long celebrated the love in personal bonds of friendship, as just one example.

Tom Sawyer and Huck Finn. Don Quixote and Sancho Panza. Laurel and Hardy. Lucy Ricardo and Ethel Mertz. Celie and Shug in *The Color Purple*. Dr. Watson and Sherlock Holmes. Thelma and Louise. Jerry Seinfeld and George Costanza. And we can't forget the television comedy that aired for ten seasons. It was *all about* the camaraderie among *Friends*.

Indeed, the Lover is expressed in myriad roles that we play: friend, parent, coach, mentor, philanthropist, advisor, carpooler, humanitarian, confidant, blood donor, volunteer, caregiver, teacher, sister and brother, son and daughter, *and on it goes*.

If your Lover leads your inner team, you might devote your life to helping other people. Like mega-philanthropist George Soros, who's spent decades funding initiatives around the globe. Or Marian Wright Edelman, founder and president of the Children's Defense Fund. You might set new standards for treating employees well, like Indian aviation pioneer J. R. D. Tata. The humanitarian and business icon felt the social responsibility of leaders to serve society at large, acting from a sense of fellowship with his people. Or you might reach out broadly like Rick Warren, senior pastor of Saddleback Church. Warren's ministry emphasizes teachings like "Love the Lord your God with all your heart" and "Love your neighbor as yourself."

In times of crisis, elected officials tap their inner Lover to connect with their constituents. New Jersey governor Chris Christie embodied the essence of the Lover when he toured his state after Hurricane Sandy. The state was in ruins. People were devastated. Governor Christie visited citizens with his heart open. He gave a seemingly endless number of hugs to strangers. He showed people he was there for them. Rudy Giuliani did the same as mayor of New York City, when he addressed New Yorkers in the aftermath of September 11, 2001. His heart was broken. And he let it show.

The Lover specializes in the "people skills" that are central to leading on the international or national level. Consider the complexity of relationships that Christine Lagarde needs to manage successfully. She's the managing director of the International Monetary Fund, an institution with 188 member countries. Or the challenges facing Peng Liyuan. Formerly a beloved performing artist of national acclaim, she's now wife to the president of the People's Republic of China. Through warmth, sincerity, accessibility, and style, she aims to show the world the human side of China. While those in the West refer to her as China's First Lady, her own people frequently call her *Guo Mu*, or "Nation's Mother."

Lovers notice how it feels to work for you, and what it's like to live with you. They value authentic communication, and they listen as well as they talk. Those of you with strong inner Lovers care about the morale of the team. You feel sad when other people get bad news. You let the world touch you.

Your Lover carries a basic interest in other people. So if you access your Lover easily, you're likely to enjoy a rich web of affiliations and friendships. You accept that vulnerability is a necessary part of building intimacy. You know how to give, and how to receive.

At the office, strong Lovers take the lead on employee engagement. They keep their eyes out for high potentials, and they care about developing talent. These are people who flag what *you're doing well* when they give you feedback, along with your "developmental opportunities." They will work the system behind the scenes to help get you promoted or elected as a new partner.

When your inner Lover's heart is open, you let other people help you. Those supporters provide fuel for your excitement—or prop up your flagging will—so you can reach the top of the mountain. They also help you deliver results by holding you accountable. This Lover wisdom stands behind daily meetings at Alcoholics Anonymous, and weekly weigh-ins at Weight Watchers. We need each other to accomplish great things.

Our inner Lover enables us to provide help and support to other people. To sit in a hospital waiting room with a friend while she waits for test results. To take a buddy out for a drink when his girlfriend moves out. To read a draft of a co-worker's assignment before they hand it in. To build and maintain a high-performing team. To get out of silos and work *together*.

We draw on our inner Lover to join in solidarity. To wish each other luck before a big game. To sit together in the living room watching election returns, in collective excitement that our candidate will win the day. To applaud our alma mater when we show up at school reunions. To stand side by side in our community after hearing terrible news.

We share love when we cheer together for our national team. When we help a friend fix his laptop, because we're his unofficial IT consultant. When we toast the law school graduates in our office because they passed the bar exam. When we celebrate an anniversary. We love when we apologize. And when we forgive.

Lover Quiz: *What's Your Favorite Strategy?*

As you've done in previous chapters, review the short scenario below. See which of the three options fits best for you.

Inner Lover Scenario

You sit on the Events Committee for your company. You're with your team to decide who'll attend the national meeting later this year. Going to the annual gathering is a "perk" of the job: it's held at a sunny resort in some impressive city; it's lots of fun; and you get to network like crazy.

Like last year, the economy is hitting the company hard. The message from management is clear: unlike the twenty people who've gone in the past from each region, this year the committee can select only five. The committee chair asks if you'll notify the fifteen people who expect tickets that they aren't invited to the national meeting. You say "sure."

What are you thinking? What are you feeling? What will you do?

Option One: As Easy as 1, 2, 3

The committee moves ahead to the next agenda item. You pull out your handheld and text an instant message to the potential invitees to the national meeting: "Due to the weak economy, we're unable to send you to the national meeting this year." You hit "send" and bring your attention back to the current topic under discussion. Having done the job you were asked to do, you don't give this task another thought.

Option Two: Heartbreak Hotel

You go back to your office with a heavy heart. The people will be so disappointed. You know the economy is putting pressure on everyone. At the same time, you feel like management doesn't appreciate the impact of including people—or in this case, *excluding* them—from national company events. People work hard all year, and they look forward to attending the big conference. Telling people they aren't invited is about the same as saying "you don't matter to us." You're worried about how to send the message while still communicating that the company values each of the people.

You consider sitting down with each of the fifteen people to talk about the situation. But then you have a better idea. Instead of telling them that they're **not invited** to the national meeting, you'll tell them that they **are invited** to a special office gathering, to be held just this year, to celebrate the efforts of your regional office. You feel relieved and excited as you think about ways to deliver this *positive* message.

You decide to host the meeting at your house. In your home the atmosphere will feel personal, like a party. People will feel recognized and appreciated for the hard work they do all year. You get to work designing the invitations.

Option Three: Make Lemons into Lemonade

You regret having to deliver this update to your troops. They've worked *really* hard this year, going above and beyond. It just doesn't seem right that they won't be able to attend the big conference. Everyone's been looking forward to it all year. You have so much going on right now . . . your to-do list is as long as your arm. It would be so much quicker—and less painful—to just shoot them a message with the bad news. You grab your handheld . . . and then pause. You respect these people. You *like* most of them, and you know they like you. Getting an email with this news will feel like a slap in the face, even if *it is* quicker and easier for you.

You decide to break the news at the weekly meeting held in your office. You'll send your intern out for coffee and muffins, as a little-pick-me-up. You know bringing snacks to the meeting doesn't make up for their missing the conference. But small gestures like that show that you're sorry to disappoint them, and that you care.

What Would You Do?

In the first option, this Low Lover sees it as his responsibility to deliver the information: no more, no less. For him, it's just another thing to cross off the to-do list. It doesn't occur to him that there are people with feelings and expectations on the receiving end of his text.

In the second case, this High Lover goes overboard in her compassion for her team, blurring the lines between what's business and what's personal by throwing a party at her home. While her empathy is admirable, there's a good chance her team will be confused by the largesse of her gesture. There's no money for the conference, but there's money for a party, complete with invitations? That seems like an expensive apology in a cost-conscious environment.

The Balanced Lover in the third option realizes that *how* she communicates is just as important as *what* she says. Unlike the Low Lover, she resists the temptation to avoid the confrontation by sending a text, despite the fact that it would be quicker and easier for her, too. And unlike the extreme gesture of the High Lover, the Balanced Lover comes up with the idea for a fun, unexpected treat. The team will enjoy it in the coziness of her office during their weekly meeting, making it both special and appropriate to a work environment.

The Lover in Daily Life

Because the Big Four are a team, you can't really work on any one of them exclusively. At the same time, it helps to look at the unique strengths and functions one at a time as you're getting your mind around how they work.

With your Lover you can do things like:

- stay home with your child who's too sick to go to school
- show a new colleague the ropes
- ask your longtime client to give your junior partner a shot
- help your aging parents so they can continue to live in their current home
- stay up late wrapping holiday gifts
- gain sensitive information from your patient
- help your spouse connect to the Internet even though you've explained it five times
- develop and retain top talent
- sit together with your soon-to-be-ex-spouse, to tell your kids that you're separating, but you *both* love them

- call your siblings to remind them to change the clocks back
- rally other renters to approach the landlord together
- foster cross-selling between service lines
- rebuild goodwill after making a mistake
- keep up morale when your company goes through a reorganization

Your Lover also enables you to receive love, like when you:

- read words of appreciation on a birthday card and *let them sink in*
- get tough feedback from your boss and know he means to help
- accept a team member's offer to deal with your angry client, so you're off the hook
- let friends cook for your family in the aftermath of a death
- accept financial help from your parents so you can get a mortgage
- let a peer give you credit for a shared customer, so you can hit your sales target

Putting Principles into Practice

Lover Sweet Spots

Renowned composer and bandleader Duke Ellington said, "I merely took the energy it takes to pout and wrote some blues."

The Lover's power source is *emotion*, and his strongest muscle is *compassion*. The Balanced Lover provides *connection*, and specializes in the skills you need for *relationship*.

The Lover's sweet spots enable you to:

1. **Connect with Emotions**
2. **Collaborate with Others**
3. **Build and Maintain Trust**

The Lover's inner resources include openness, generosity, empathy, and acceptance.

Let's see how these work in practice.

Connect with Emotions

At a meeting in London, an executive named Nigel shared this story with me. He asked if I had any insight into what happened.

"I'd taken my client out to dinner. Out of nowhere, he looked me straight in the eye and asked, 'Nigel, do you care about me?' I didn't understand the question. But I answered yes."

His client didn't let it end there.

"I know you care about solving my business problem. But I'm asking if you care *about me*. In other words, *if I got fired from this job*, would you still call? Would you *still care* about me *then*?"

Nigel was silent. He didn't know what to say. He told me later the conversation was dumbfounding. Why would Nigel call his client if he didn't have his job anymore? Why would the client *want* Nigel to call? What would they talk about? What's the point of calling if not to discuss the problem they were working together to solve?

If your inner Lover moves through life in low gear, these are reasonable questions. For you, like Nigel, the client's questions may sound strange—or just irrelevant. Your role is to focus on the challenge at hand, and get results. Performance is the point. Relationship isn't much on your radar screen.

You're not alone.

Both men and women have inner Lovers who run low. On the whole, it's often men who've been taught since a young age to push their emotions away. Research on male adult development shows how social norms contribute to emotional mismanagement and limited empathy skills.

Psychologist Paul Dunion has spent decades exploring the process of adult maturation, including founding a group called Boys to Men. In his book *Dare to Grow Up*, Dunion writes about the systematic ways men are taught to numb themselves and ignore their emotions. "The waters of their emotional lives dry up, leaving them parched by the loss of what they truly love."

I've seen firsthand what Dunion describes when I lead learning programs for senior leaders. By and large the people in these groups are men. Like Nigel, they've earned their reputations on powerhouse IQ, the reliability of their quantitative analysis, and their ability to generate shareholder returns. Now they find themselves hitting an unexpected barrier to achieving their highest aspirations: expectations of intimacy in business relationships.

A Wall Street investment banker explained it to me this way: "Clients are pushing back on us. They tell us they're leaving to go to another advisory firm. When we ask why, they say things like 'I trust your advice, but I don't trust *you*.'"

The fact is that in today's world, credible Thinkers, no matter how brilliant, will hit a wall if they can't connect on a human level. It's a bit of a bait-and-switch, really, after years of being directed to achieve compulsively. These Low Lovers accepted long ago what Dunion calls the cultural mandate of manhood: habits of isolation, rejection of emotion and intuition, and focus on the outer world to the exclusion of the interior one.

This isn't the case, by the way, everywhere in the world. I did a leadership program in Argentina, for instance, where the men were very expressive emotionally. They grew up with different norms. In most groups I run with a global mix, though, the Low Lover fills the room.

In fairness, people whose Lover ran high tended historically toward "helping professions." Vocations like teaching or social work. In the past, a stance like Nigel's would work just fine in business-related settings.

That was then. This is now.

In today's world, every serious professional is expected to bring *some* level of emotional intelligence to their work. Managers expect it. Clients demand it. That requires Lover capabilities. Fair or not, there's no escaping the new reality: *relationships matter everywhere.* You don't need to become Mother Teresa. But you do need to show there's a beating heart in there somewhere.

Making space at your inner table for your Lover might also save your life. Emotions get rerouted through the body. They show up as back pain, ulcers, migraines, even heart attacks. Some oncologists believe some cancers result in part from unexpressed grief or anger. Stifling emotion over long periods of time can lead to depression. On top of that, people use things like alcohol and painkillers to escape from feeling their emotions. If taking the edge off turns into addiction, then substances like these can wreak havoc in your life. How you deal with your inner Lover directly impacts your physical, mental, financial, and social health.

Bringing some attention to your heartache is another way of saving your life. I've heard leaders say things like, "I went back to work the day after my miscarriage. I never let myself feel the loss. I still need to grieve for that child." They express feelings that appear seemingly out of nowhere, like a flash of lightning on a clear day. "I just realized why my wife fell out of love with me. I stopped being the guy she fell in love with. But I'm *still* that guy. I hope she'll give me another chance."

Emotions also open the door for reclaiming what gives you peace and joy. As a college professor said at the end of a program, "When I go home I'm going to pick up my guitar again. I miss my guitar."

These are my favorite parts of running seminars, when we engage with the deeper dimensions of leadership. It's the moment when the walls come down, the fear has melted, and suddenly everyone realizes they can actually be themselves. For real. The level of excitement, relief, humor, affection, and innocent joy touches everyone. Sometimes it's life-changing.

It brings me back to a novel I read in college by Zora Neale Hurston, *Their Eyes Were Watching God*. She has a character, Janie, who's been beaten down by life, and—like many of these professionals—goes through her days in a highly guarded inner fortress. In a certain moment, Janie realizes she's okay: she's not alone, she's safe, and she's loved. Hurston's words describe what I feel like I'm witnessing in these moments of transformation, from crossed arms to open hands, from fear to trust, from numb isolation to genuine community and fellowship. Hurston writes about Janie something that I see in front of my eyes, that "her soul crawled out from its hiding place."

For every reason, the working world needs to make room for the inner Lover as part of a balanced, dynamic inner team. It's not a coincidence that new life comes from Lovers. When you're cut off from your inner Lover, you abandon your own beating heart, the source and sustenance of your aliveness.

People Are Not Corporations

In a controversial decision, the United States Supreme Court held in 2010 in the *Citizens United* case that the First Amendment rights of a company deserve the same protection as that of any other "citizen." In principle, they said, corporations are people.

Whatever you think about that decision—and its implications for campaign financing—you want to make sure you don't live by the opposite principle. Simply put, people are not corporations.

If your Lover runs low like Nigel's, you might struggle to relate to people in a natural way. Maybe you don't look up when people sit down next to you, or say hello when you pass them in the hallway. Developing your Lover's strengths and sweet spots will help you pivot to the next level, in your profession as well as in your personal life.

As we've said, Low Lovers run into trouble with emotions. This happens in both directions: they *don't express their own emotions* well, and they *don't express empathy* with other people well, either. Langdon is a freelance writer who brought the next dialogue to a workshop I led. You'll see both of these dynamics, this time in a personal context. This conversation took place as he caught up with his wife at the end of the day.

WHAT I THOUGHT and FELT BUT DIDN'T SAY	WHAT WE ACTUALLY SAID
	My Wife: I had a terrible day at work. My manager is on my back, and I don't think the new project is going to work out.

WHAT I THOUGHT and FELT BUT DIDN'T SAY	WHAT WE ACTUALLY SAID
	Me: Oh?
	My Wife: And I found out the others have been talking behind my back, saying I don't belong leading the team. They *completely* fail to see how I am carrying this whole thing!
Oh, today's drama.	
	Me: Sounds like a problem.
	My Wife: You would think they'd respect me after all I've done for them.
She's always the victim.	
	Me: It's time for you to talk to the Big Boss. I've told you that before. As for me and my day, I've made some great progress today.
	My Wife: I've told you a million times that I don't want to become the "problem child" in the office. Running for help isn't going to help me. I can't believe they're talking about me behind my back.

WHAT I THOUGHT and FELT BUT DIDN'T SAY	WHAT WE ACTUALLY SAID
Blah blah blah . . . Here we go again. Do you want to hear about my day?	
	Me: Do you want to hear about my day?
	My Wife: I'm in the middle of telling you something very important. Can't you just listen for one minute?
I don't believe this! I'm so sick of this!	
	Me: [*Silence.*]

At home and at work, for men and for women, connecting with emotions in an authentic and appropriate way remains a big challenge.

This isn't a permanent state of affairs, by the way. In "emerging leaders" programs with men and women in their thirties, emotional life stands alongside intellectual life as a given. These younger professionals carry different expectations from the generations before them. One factor in this shift is that these women expect men to act like full partners, including sharing their feelings, empathizing, and, down the road, nurturing kids. Since these men grew up dating these women, they entered the world of relationship by expressing emotions and creating intimacy from the beginning. Their Lover capabilities are often well intact.

At the other end of the spectrum, if your Lover's favorite strategy is to run high, you can become overly emotional. You can create unnecessary drama, or force closeness where it's not invited.

I'm reminded of Tamar, a colleague who was proposing a large project to a potential client. All signs were positive. So Tamar flew out to spend the day with the decision-maker, a woman named Catherine, known to friends in the industry as "Cookie."

Tamar's Lover nearly always ran high. As usual, she felt she'd made "an instant connection" to her prospective client. By the end of the day they were trading tips about spas and yoga teachers. Tamar had hinted at the idea of attending a yoga retreat together.

When she got home, Tamar sent a follow-up email.

> Dear Cookie. Thought we had a great meeting. Can't wait to spend more time together.

She signed the email "T" for Tamar.

Later that day, Tamar sent Catherine another email. This time she sent a recommendation for a physical therapist, for the back pain Catherine had mentioned, offering to make an introduction, or to go with her to see him next time she was in town.

Catherine didn't return Tamar's emails.

Unsure of what was happening, Tamar figured she should reach out. She emailed again.

> Dear Cookie. Haven't heard back from you. Assume you're totally swamped. Looking so forward to re-connecting and taking the world by storm! Warmest best wishes, T.

No answer.

The deal collapsed.

Tamar was totally confused. She and Cookie had *such* a strong connection. Tamar found Cookie's behavior *so* inexplicable that she had to know what went wrong. In the past, Catherine had worked with Tamar's friend Raj, so she asked Raj to investigate. Raj had dinner with Catherine and came back with a report.

"I'm sorry to tell you this, but she found you 'inappropriate.' Ironically, she liked the proposal a lot. But she said you pushed way too far, way too fast. She wasn't looking for a new best friend. She wanted a high-quality service provider."

The discussion with Raj was a painful but instructive "aha" moment for Tamar. She acknowledged that she relied on her personal "click" with potential clients as the basis for her business deals. She often sent recommendations in her follow-up from meetings, from restaurants to places for a great massage. And, yes, she did look for ways to "befriend" clients as quickly as possible. This time it had undercut her credibility and cost her a major contract.

From then on, she signed her emails with "Tamar."

Openness to others is a valuable Lover skill, when used in a balanced way. Taken too far, it can bring the opposite result, distancing people and souring a relationship. Well placed, it creates trust and rapport.

Collaborate with Others

Lovers get satisfaction from relationships because they enjoy other people. They thrive on community. But they also know you can harness relationships *to make things happen*. Sometimes the drive to collaborate is tactical: you'll get things done more quickly if you work with other people. Other times it's your standards of excellence. Partnering with other people increases the chances you'll make the best decisions, and catch mistakes. Sometimes you reach out for survival, like handing your newborn infant to a friend so you can take a shower. No man is an island.

Get Things Done Together

My sister Heather is a marathon runner. Before the big day, she gets ready by running with Team in Training, a fund-raising group for the Leukemia & Lymphoma Society. During months of training, when her alarm goes off at five in the morning, and rain is bearing down outside, she doesn't jump at the chance to run fifteen miles.

Left to her own devices, she might roll over and go back to sleep. But when you train with a team, you can't stay in bed. People are counting on you. That fellowship gets her out of bed and out the door. The connection between relationships and results is even more apparent on Marathon Day. Heather is also a pediatric oncology social worker. She works with children with cancer and their families. Fighting blood cancer isn't an idea for her: it's personal.

The marathon is 26.2 miles through the San Francisco hills. Oh, man. "I don't know if I'd finish if I ran for myself," Heather once told me. "But I don't worry. I think about the families, and the kids going for their treatment. I'm running for them—and that will get me across the finish line."

For my sister, relationships enable her to run a marathon, *literally*. For the rest of us, life often feels like running a marathon. The hills. The distance. The emotional stamina we need to persist. Like Heather's Team in Training, we need to help each other face the rain and then keep going.

Notice That Working Together Creates Value

Relationships are both an end unto themselves, and also a means to an end: *relationships create enormous value.* You can see that easily in business partnerships. Think of Bill Hewlett and Dave Packard. They started designing gadgets in a garage outside of Packard's house. In 2010, Hewlett-Packard—known around the world as HP—employed more than 320,000 people and reported more than $126 billion in revenue. Or Sergey Brin and Larry Page, who became friends spending time in their college dorm room. The pair was fascinated by how the Internet could determine how often a research paper was cited in other papers, leading them to a new "search engine" that they called Google.

Like HP and Google, partnerships improve our world. Like luxury designers Domenico Dolce and Stefano Gabbana. Through their company, Dolce & Gabbana, they create fashion with a distinct flair, reflecting their love of southern Italy. And Oprah Winfrey and Gayle King. This Wonder Duo brings coaching and advice to millions of people in a vast range of media. Taking on serious topics to educate the public, Winfrey and King relish their relationship, showing us how to engage with real problems and keep each other going along the way.

And we do need to mention those wonderful human beings—Ben Cohen and Jerry Greenfield—who brought us chocolate chip cookie dough ice cream. In 2000, Unilever bought Ben & Jerry's for $326 million. Not a bad result for two guys who became friends in seventh grade and decided to learn together about the ice cream business. I'm happy to say that supermarkets sell Ben & Jerry's in The Netherlands. So in moments of homesickness, I can run out and buy a pint.

Of course, the Lover's ability to forge partnerships creates many kinds of value. Look at the impact of Dr. Paul Farmer, Ophelia

Dahl, and their cofounders of Partners in Health. PIH started in the 1980s with a few colleagues working in a makeshift medical clinic in rural Haiti. Farmer and Dahl now help provide state-of-the-art medical services as well as hope to millions of sick and poor people in ten different countries. From Malawi to Mexico, the forging of long-term relationships gives their work meaning and is core to their strategy.

In an article in the *Atlantic* marking PIH's twenty-fifth anniversary, Dahl commented on the power of partnerships for improving global health. "Be it transforming a sick person to a well person, or a parking lot into a clinic—the transformations became amplified as we grew our partnerships. You see that most NGOs work alone—when there are thousands of NGOs in Haiti—and simply forming partnerships, connecting to local and national government, makes things much, much more efficient." Working in places with 200,000 residents and not one doctor, PIH relies on partnerships with local groups in rural villages, people they train on the ground as doctors, foundations who support them, and high-quality teaching hospitals in the United States.

Indeed, the ability to collaborate is often the make-or-break variable in value creation. When mergers and acquisitions fail, the most likely culprit isn't a poor business model: *it's the inability to align the people.* On the flip side are institutions such as NIBR, the Novartis Institutes for BioMedical Research, where successful industry-academia collaborations lay the groundwork for life-changing discoveries.

In an interview, NIBR president Mark Fishman said, "We're looking for projects that will change the practice of medicine." Fishman praised the scientist-to-scientist relationships, saying that "working with academia is extremely important for us: it expands our horizons and acts as a quality control." In matters of life and death, or in deals worth millions of dollars, it's the Lover capacity to partner and work well with different people that makes the crucial difference.

Accept That It Takes Two to Tango

Eleni directs a business operations unit that provides fiscal, HR, and IT support throughout the office. As the provider of shared services, Eleni's "center of excellence" touches every part of the organization, which includes fifteen divisions. Over the last few years, her office has worked hard, in her words, "to transform the culture from one of internal competition and divisional self-reliance to one of collaboration and cross-division teamwork." She's seen real progress, which is why she got angry with Atul when he challenged her plans. This is the case that Eleni brought to a leadership program.

DESCRIPTION:

As part of our culture transformation, the office decided to implement a formal retirement ceremony honoring any member of the office, regardless of which division they work in, indicating that the office values every person at every level and in every division. Employees have expressed appreciation and enjoyment for the opportunity to celebrate with others from across the organization.

ATUL: I *don't* want a retirement party. Please do *not* throw me a stupid party.

ELENI: Atul, you know it's the office tradition now, and it's important for the office to honor you for your service.

ATUL: The best way to honor me is to respect my wishes.

ELENI: I do respect your wishes, but I want you to respect the office and my point of view as well. If we don't have the party, everyone will think badly of the leadership. Besides, it's important for those who are left behind to be able to say goodbye and show their respect for you publicly.

ATUL (*loud enough so people in adjoining offices can hear*): You don't care about me. If you did, you would respect my wishes.

ELENI (*also getting angry*): Look, the last two people who retired from this unit said they didn't want a party when it turns out they really did. They both were very grateful and happy afterward. If I had listened to them I would have broken the tradition *and* ended up making them feel bad.

ATUL (*still angry and loud*): They were the kind of people to say one thing and pretend to be modest when they really craved attention. You know I'm not like that. I really am a behind-the-scenes person, and making me go through a reception would be torture for me. In fact, if you have a reception I won't go.

ELENI (*still angry but speaking very quietly*): I respect you and your wishes, which is why I am so angry with you right now. You have really put me in a no-win situation.

ATUL: If you care about me at all you won't have that party.

When Eleni spoke in the group about this, she was passionate about the culture transformation. She expressed pride at how far they'd come toward living their new values, like teamwork and valuing each person. I have no doubt that Eleni believed in this vision and wanted to role-model it for her staff.

Yet she was a bit off track.

I asked Eleni what she was thinking during this conversation, and she said her thought was "Oh, we're going to have this thing— even if Atul doesn't show up! My team and I have worked *too hard* to build our reputation and a culture of respect in this office to let this sour person ruin it."

While Eleni truly believes that she's motivated by her inner Lover, in fact her Warrior is in the lead here. Not unlike Bram, when he kept pushing Rachel to review proposals for the anti-bullying campaign. Remember that the Warrior provides protection. What is her Warrior protecting?

It seems like her Warrior feels protective of the office culture she's worked hard to create. Yet the authenticity of that culture transformation rests on *actually valuing each person*—not listing it on the "New Office Values" chart on the wall. As you read between the lines, Eleni's Warrior seems more focused on protecting her reputation than on truly honoring Atul, her departing staff member.

Eleni's Lover needs to negotiate with her Warrior to get a seat back at the table. To practice what she preaches, Eleni needs to *listen* to Atul, and take him seriously. When her Lover starts taking in what Atul needs, then the two of them can look for a creative solution. A good outcome will honor Atul in a way that works for him, maintain the spirit of the culture transformation, and protect Eleni's reputation as well.

On the flip side, not every relationship is meant to be, or lasts forever. Sometimes the best thing to do is let go. For High Lovers, that's a lot easier said than done. Like the song first recorded by Neil Sedaka says, breaking up is hard to do.

In the traditional negotiation context, we approach the decision of whether to reach an agreement, or walk away from the table, as a rational one. We teach people to assess the value of the best option on the table, and then compare it to the value of their best alternative—a term of art called your BATNA: your Best Alternative To a Negotiated Agreement. In theory, best practice is simple: compare your best option to your best alternative, and then take the one that's better. It's hard to argue with that advice. It makes so much sense.

As I'm nearing two decades as a teacher and a practitioner in the field, I can tell you the problem with that very reasonable advice. Walking away from a live human being, whether you've been married for ten years, run a business together, or attended the same weekly yoga class, doesn't pull on your inner Thinker. From ending a relationship, to turning down an offer, walking away cuts to the core of the Lover's heart. If your Lover runs low, you can exit when the time comes. But for the High Lover, the notion that you could simply compare apples to apples, and based on that assessment you could stay or go, doesn't exist in their reality.

I'll give you an example.

Malvikha is a certified personal trainer and a certified sports massage therapist. She thrives on motivating people, and helping them to accomplish their fitness-related goals. She recently decided to pursue a nutrition certification. Since she couldn't work full-time and go to school, she enrolled for some courses at a local nutrition program and set up a comfortable environment in her house to train private clients.

Overall, things worked out well. She found a number of clients fairly quickly, and her flexible schedule gave her enough time to study. The problem was in the "back office." Malvikha had hired her friend Preeti as her bookkeeper. She found out that while Preeti was a lovely person, she was an incompetent bookkeeper. Malvikha was spending more time fixing Preeti's spreadsheets than if she'd done them herself in the first place.

Her friends pushed Malvikha to let Preeti go, and get someone else. The current setup was bad in every way: Malvikha was spending money she didn't really have to pay Preeti, and her bookkeeper wasn't saving her time to spend on school. She wasn't maintaining a proper system, so she worried about making mistakes in her next tax return. By every objective measure, Malvikha needed to walk away.

For a Balanced Lover, situations like this can feel awkward, but they're manageable. For a High Lover like Malvikha, they're a dead end. No matter what her friends said, she had a retort:

"But she's *such* a nice person."

"But she *really* needs the money."

"But she trying *so hard*."

"But she'll *hate* me."

It was a classic High Lover dilemma. Malvikha acknowledged that she "should" get a new bookkeeper. "But I can't fire Preeti. **She's my friend.**"

Like Malvikha, High Lovers prioritize relationships over getting what they legitimately need. That makes it very tough to walk away. They're caught in a two-sided emotional bind that dissuades them from cutting things off. They don't want to hurt other people. That's rule number one. But they also don't want to suffer themselves. Remember, High Lovers feel their emotions intensely.

Part of what keeps Malvikha from firing Preeti is avoidance of the guilt and inner turmoil she will face if she does. Balanced Lovers understand that you should never be callous with other people, or blatantly disregard their feelings. And—that general principle *also applies to you*. Balanced Lovers are well rounded, able to care for other people as well as for themselves.

Build and Maintain Trust

In leadership and in life, trust is one of the essentials that lives in the Lover's domain. Trust can't be seen with the eyes, but it can definitely be felt. You know when trust starts to form in a new relationship. You feel it when trust gets broken, when it's repaired, and when it gets lost. How do you build and maintain trust with others?

It starts with building rapport. Making contact. Finding a point of affiliation with each other. In my experience, if you want that initial rapport to evolve into real trust, you need to put yourself out there a little, in a genuine way. You don't need to tell your deepest secrets. But learning how to disclose *something* about yourself—ideally something that matters to you—is part and parcel of earning trust.

In this area as much as any other, the operating principle of Winning from Within applies: what you experience on the inside will lead directly to what you create on the outside. If you want to earn people's trust, then start acting in trustworthy ways. If you want them to think that you care about them, then find a way to soften the walls that keep you from your emotional life, *so you can feel a sense of caring* for them.

Balanced Lovers know that for a relationship to work, the trust needs to be sincere. Often, Low Lovers go through the motions of the right behaviors and then they're surprised when people don't really trust them. I saw a great example of this distinction last year, expressed by one of my students.

In the negotiation course at Harvard Law School, we require the students to keep a daily journal of their insights from the day. They turn it in at the end of each week. We have cross-registrants in the class, and last year I had a student from Harvard Business School. I asked him if I could share an excerpt from his journal with you anonymously, and he said yes. This is a direct quote from what he wrote:

> I previously believed that my interpersonal communication at the outset of a negotiation was one of my strong suits. It helped me build rapport which I could later utilize to claim an unfair share of the value near the end of the negotiation.

He went on to write that he'd received feedback from his peers that "much of my rapport building comes across unauthentic and disingenuous," and he wondered why. He pondered what he could do to "appear more natural and genuine."

His confusion points to an essential truth about building and maintaining trust. He won't progress by trying to "appear" more genuine. That backfires. Building rapport as he did, to set the stage to take advantage of people later, isn't actually building rapport. It's theater, at best. Fostering trust means you don't aspire to "appear" natural, but rather to "feel" natural.

You might not see yourself in the attitude of his journal entry. Maybe it sounds extreme. But actually, I get into discussions on this topic quite often. People tell me they *already do* treat others well, but "it doesn't work." As my client Javier said to me, "They still complain that I'm not listening. Or they say 'I feel like you're not present.' What do they want from me?" His question was a sincere one.

Javier was frustrated because he was doing everything he'd learned in a daylong training on listening skills. He told me that he looks people in the eye, repeats back what they say, and makes sure to ask at least a few questions. These techniques are straight out of his Active Listening Operating Manual.

Why aren't they working?

Because you can't bluff trust.

Actually, I'll admit that you can bluff it a little, or for a little while. But then the gig is up. The curtain is pulled. And the Wizard is discovered to be just a man with a microphone. This is the point that Javier is missing. "Doing" active listening behavior, when you're ***not genuinely open***, means ***you're not actually listening***. People have an uncanny radar about this: they know you're faking it. And here's the funny thing. They *don't actually care* if you repeat their words back. They care whether or not *you care*. ***That is what they want from you.***

If you relate at all to my student, or to Javier, then you want to negotiate with yourself to make some room for your Lover to show up for real. See what I mean in the start to the meeting below, between Jermaine and Quincy. Jermaine's inner Warrior is filling his mind. He wants action, today.

WHAT I THOUGHT and FELT BUT DIDN'T SAY	WHAT WE ACTUALLY SAID
I need to get something done with this group. *Now.*	**Jermaine:** I really hope we move ahead and keep this group focused on action.

WHAT I THOUGHT and FELT BUT DIDN'T SAY	WHAT WE ACTUALLY SAID
	Quincy: Yes, but building relationships is also important.
Oh, shoot, here we go again. *Process, process, process. What a WASTE OF TIME.*	
	Jermaine: Yes, I agree, but too often we meet and only update each other. This isn't the best way to spend our time.
	Quincy: [*Silent, looks away.*]

If Jermaine notices that he's shut Quincy down, he might back-track in his words. He might suggest a five-minute check-in about everybody's vacation. Still, the voice in his head will tell him in no uncertain terms that this is a complete waste of time. If Jermaine needs Quincy in order to get things done, he has a problem. Because Quincy knows the difference between being humored and being understood.

There's no magic phrase that Jermaine can say to Quincy to get out of this moment. There's only an actual rebalancing of his inner Warrior and Lover that will make this better. It's not a zero-sum game, either. Jermaine's inner Warrior doesn't need to give up on getting things done today. What he needs to do is negotiate with Jermaine's inner Lover, and make a deal.

If he's smart, Jermaine's inner Lover will deal with the Warrior on his own terms. The Warrior wants to get things done. So Jermaine's Lover can point out to his Warrior that by engaging Quincy *sincerely* on what matters to him—in this case, relationship-building—he's much more likely to get on board for the Warrior's action agenda. Seeing the sense of that argument, the inner Warrior might chill out for a few minutes while Jermaine's inner Lover *actually tries to get to know Quincy better.* When Quincy feels that his priorities matter to Jermaine, he's far more likely to reciprocate by focusing on what Jermaine values.

In a later journal entry, my business school student wrote the following:

> I wish I had an easy answer to correct this error but I don't believe there is one. Rapport is something that cannot be forced; it should develop naturally. It's true that charismatic individuals may have better luck at establishing rapport quicker and more efficiently, but again, that's not something one can fake. I don't know the solution to this issue other than working to be more natural and authentic and look for genuine common interests which can build initial bonds.

In my comment on that entry, I wrote, "Yes, that's it exactly."

Earn Your Own Trust

If your Lover runs high, you likely take good care of other people. For you, it's natural and right to put other people's needs, feelings, or ambitions, ahead of your own. If two of you are working late at the office, *you're* the one who'll say, "Go ahead home. I'll finish things here." Not because you wouldn't *love* to call it a day. But as you see it, *one of you* has to stay and finish. So your High Lover figures, "Why should *I* get to go home while my colleague is stuck at the office? That's not fair."

As you think back, you might notice that over the years, this Lover perspective has given you plenty of late nights at the office, finishing projects *by yourself,* when you sent other people home. Generosity is a beautiful Lover quality. But when you always put yourself second, you're failing to earn trust in a significant way: **you aren't trustworthy to yourself.** In practice, High Lovers often need their inner Warrior or Dreamer to step forward to protect them— *from themselves.*

Juliette is a mother in my neighborhood. She used to invite other mothers and their young kids over to her house to make art. Juliette had a master's in fine arts but had chosen to stay home while her kids were little. This seemed like a fun way to stay connected with her painting while her children were young.

News spread throughout the town, and soon Juliette had nearly daily "classes" in her living room. She didn't charge anything: she just loved the joy in the little faces over the masterpieces the kids made.

The art classes had another effect. A real community developed among the women who were raising their kids at home. Many of them had higher-education degrees. A bunch had led high-power careers before choosing to stay home to raise their children full-time. While none of them would have made time for themselves to meet a friend on a weekly basis, the art classes gave a perfect platform for them to spend quality time with other women while still prioritizing their kids. Everything seemed to work perfectly.

One day, a new mother came to the class. She'd heard about Juliette. She understood these really were "classes" with substantive instruction. Far from dropping kids on the floor with finger paint, Juliette was *teaching* them about art. Word on the street was that Juliette was also wonderful with kids, including the ones who had challenges to learn. At the end of the session, the visitor approached Juliette.

"First, let me introduce myself. My name is Dr. Ford, and I work in pediatrics at St. Elizabeth's Hospital. I saw your class today—you're terrific. We need someone just like you to join our team at the hospital. We have kids who are inpatient for weeks at a time. In most cases, their bodies needs treatment, but their minds are razor sharp. They're bored and restless. We've gotten a gift to fund a position for a teacher of fine arts, to offer classes during the day, aimed at various levels that are age-appropriate to the kids. Could I meet you for lunch to tell you more about it? I think you'd be perfect."

Juliette stood for a minute in a state of shock. When she finally gathered herself together, she thanked Dr. Ford for dropping by, exchanged email addresses, and said she'd get in touch.

Before the door even closed behind Dr. Ford, Juliette's inner Lover was already yelling at her. "How can you even *think* of doing this? These mothers *are like family*. They *need* you. **How will they survive without you?**" As her High Lover's voice became more intense, Juliette started to agree. "I guess I should just turn it down."

This is the precise moment when High Lovers are at risk of betraying themselves. Before Juliette has a chance *to even consider* if this is something she'd like to do, her High Lover is already demanding that she not put herself "above" or "ahead" of the community of mothers that she's fostered.

Thankfully, in this case, her inner negotiators were working as a team. Juliette's inner Dreamer stepped in.

"Juliette, what do **you** want?"

Juliette hadn't thought to ask herself that.

"This is *your* life. A job like this is **exactly** why you got your master's in the first place. *And*, your kids are in school now. They aren't even home with you anymore. You should go for this!"

If your Lover runs high like Juliette's, situations like this feel wrenching. Your inner Dreamer wants you to pursue *your dreams.* Yet your High Lover holds you back, begging you to put other people and their feelings ahead of your own aspirations. If you follow the High Lover's priorities every time, you'll have a well-traveled path of self-neglect. To my mind, this dynamic relates to whether you're trustworthy to yourself. Can you trust your Lover to care about you, or will he or she only take care of other people?

If you've tied your profile completely to your inner Lover, then your identity as a "giver" might trump everything else. You might reflect on why *everyone else* deserves to benefit from your generous nature, but you don't. Christopher Germer explores this in a wonderful book, *The Mindful Path to Self-Compassion.* He writes:

> If you're used to beating yourself up during periods of sadness or loneliness, if you hide from the world when you make a mistake, or if you obsess over how you could have prevented the mistake to begin with, self-compassion may seem like a radical idea. But why should you deny yourself the same tenderness and warmth you extend to others who are suffering?

If your Lover runs high like Juliette's, you can always come back to the basic wisdom teaching: you should love thy neighbor as thyself. Those simple words tell us that it's valid and important *to love ourselves,* as well as we love everyone else.

We've met the Dreamer, the Thinker, and the Lover. Now we'll add the last inner negotiator to the mix of the Big Four, the Warrior. As before, below are some reflection questions for you.

Reflection Questions

- Do the Lover's worldview and sweet spots come easily to you? Is it challenging for you to see how the Lover operates in you?

- How do you relate to compassion, openness, generosity, empathy, and acceptance?

- How do you use your Lover's power of emotion?

- When have you let your Lover build and maintain deep trust with someone? When have you blocked your Lover from getting "too close" to someone? What did you learn from these experiences?

- In what relationships does your Lover feel a pull to invest these days, such as: with clients, colleagues, staff, your mentor or mentee, or with your boss? With students, friends, your spouse or romantic partner? With your parents, children, or siblings? With your community, professional network, with a group or club where you belong? What would your Lover express, ask, do, or stop doing to invest in these relationships, if you gave the green light?

- What are you noticing about your Lover's common strategies? Does your Lover step out in front of the rest of your Big Four? Does your Lover tend to get left behind?

- What happens when your Lover takes over, or gets shut out? How can you experiment to foster better balance among your Big Four?

CHAPTER 8

Performance: Carry Your Warrior's Sword and Shield

Don't wait for a Gandhi, don't wait for a King,
don't wait for a Mandela.
You are your own Mandela, you are your own Gandhi,
you are your own King.
—LEYMAH GBOWEE

While the Dreamer aspires, the Thinker analyzes, and the Lover connects, the Warrior gets the deal signed, sealed, and delivered. The Warrior is fundamentally about claiming your power, and using it carefully, consciously, and ethically.

With a Balanced Warrior, you won't trample over other people. You won't submit blindly to them either. Balanced Warriors don't fight without a reason. They act in the service of Dreamers' values and visions, fighting for principles like liberty, democracy, and human dignity.

Members of the armed forces can embody the classical Warrior as they defend the safety, security, and ideals of their people. That takes the courage and sense of duty that fuel the Warrior. As you'll see during most of this chapter, the Warrior *also* plays a vital role in civilian life. The inner Warrior emboldens you to stand up and speak out. To tell the hard truth. To do the right thing. Your Warrior pushes you forward to realize your goals and fulfill your commitments. It's your Warrior who steps up to protect you and the people you love.

Warriors Take Action

When we hear the word *warrior*, many of us think of well-known fighters from history. Attila the Hun. Julius Caesar. Alexander the Great. Joan of Arc. Napoleon Bonaparte. George Washington. And of course, David, who notoriously slew Goliath. We also conjure famous Warrior groups, like the Vikings, the Zulu, the Amazons, the Samurai. Not all Warriors want to fight in the traditional sense. The Shaolin monks, for example, who developed kung fu, avoided fighting whenever possible.

Political dissidents draw on Warrior fortitude to speak out, lead the opposition, and withstand attacks. Mahatma Gandhi famously won independence for India through nonviolent tools of protest, actions like boycotts, hunger strikes, and the Salt March to the sea. "Nonviolence is the greatest force at the disposal of mankind," Gandhi said. "It is mightier than the mightiest weapon of destruction devised by the ingenuity of man." Think of Aung San Suu Kyi, known by many in her native country as "the Lady." She withstood house arrest for fifteen years to fight for democratic principles in her society. She was offered freedom if she left the country, but she refused in order to maintain her stand for true political freedom.

Balanced Warriors fight to defend core human values. Like Galileo, the Italian astronomer who fought for the truth that the earth revolved around the sun. Or Miep and Jan Gies, who risked their lives to hide the family of Anne Frank during the Nazi occupation of The Netherlands. And Vaclav Havel, an intellectual-turned-politician who used his writing to lead a resistance movement that called for a free Czechoslovakia. These Warriors took a wide range of action to protect ideals and people they cared about.

Your Warrior Is a Protector

I discovered my inner Warrior in second grade.

My family lived in a tailored suburb of New Jersey, populated by New York City professionals raising their kids near parks and good schools. The town was safe and quaint, if homogeneous. In this small community, the kids went to school together from kindergarten through eighth grade.

When I returned from summer break to begin second grade, I found a new child in the class. A family from India had moved to town over the summer, and Pranita now joined our ranks.

Much to my surprise and grave discomfort, my peers did not welcome this new student, the first nonwhite person in our class. In fact, Pranita became the target of significant teasing and pranks. Kids took her lunch and hid her pencils. On a regular basis, when she sat down, someone would approach her and tell her to move. She would always ask to stay, but the other child would insist, claiming she had taken his or her seat.

Pranita often defended herself, affirming that the place was hers. But the exchange always came to the same retort: *"Does it have your name on it?"* Lacking a response to this question, Pranita routinely gave up and moved.

Watching these dynamics filled my seven-year-old body with moral outrage. The daughter of civil rights activists, I needed to do *something*. My inner Warrior kicked into action.

One day, our teacher fell ill, and we had the extra dose of chaos brought into a classroom by a "substitute" teacher. Under these conditions, the usual joking at Pranita's expense became taunting. I knew I had to draw the line.

Knowing what was coming later, I took a thick black marker in my hand. Turning to the back of a wooden chair, I engraved the letters P-R-A-N-I-T-A onto the seat. I invited Pranita to come sit with me on her new secret personal throne.

A class bully promptly approached us and told Pranita to move. As always, when she said it was her place, he charged, *"Does it have your name on it?"*

At this I moved into action, eagerly springing from my seat to turn her chair around. I showed everyone the label, and announced proudly "Yes, in fact, it *does* have her name on it. It is *her* seat, and you may not ask her to give it up ever again."

The substitute was unimpressed with my act of civil disobedience. She sent me to the principal's office for defacing school property. That night my parents took me out for ice cream and congratulated me for standing up for what is right.

The Warrior Delivers Results

Warriors are defined by their personal power and their ability to take action. Remember Anita Hill, who alleged that U.S. Supreme Court nominee Clarence Thomas had sexually harassed her when he was her professional supervisor? Thomas was confirmed and took a seat on the Court. But Hill's testimony shed a bright light on the issue of sexual harassment in the workplace.

Margaret Thatcher and Golda Meir were known as "Iron Ladies" for their toughness and strong-willed leadership. Decades later, South Korea's president Park Geun-hye earned the same moniker. During her inauguration, Park took a hard line toward her dangerous neighbor to the north. "I will not tolerate any action that threatens the lives of our people and the security of our nation," she warned. As a candidate, she'd spoken of hope for a new, unified Korean peninsula. But as president, Park vowed that provocation from Pyongyang would not stand. When an American journalist asked her about taking military action against North Korea if attacked, her message was clear: "We will make them pay."

Luis Moreno Ocampo is a Warrior for justice, serving as the first prosecutor for the International Criminal Court. Before he called war criminals to account for genocide at the ICC, Ocampo prosecuted human rights abuses in his native Argentina. In the Trial of the Juntas, he brought charges against senior military officials of a former dictatorial government. The prosecution largely succeeded in proving the crimes against the people of Argentina, such as the forced "disappearance" of thousands of people.

Some Warrior leaders give their lives in the struggle for peace, like Anwar Sadat, Benazir Bhutto, and Yitzhak Rabin. Other fighters risk their lives despite being private citizens. Like fifteen-year-old Pakistani student Malala Yousafzai, known to many people simply as Malala.

In early 2009, at the age of eleven, Malala began publishing a blog in which she described her oppressive life under Taliban rule. She wrote about her dreams for liberating all girls through education. Written under a nom de plume, the blog was soon after broadcast by the BBC. The following summer, a *New York Times* documentary captured Malala's life on video. On October 9, 2012, Malala was shot in the head and neck while riding on a school bus. Miraculously, she survived. Rather than intimidate her, the attempt on her life fortified her Warrior commitment to the cause of education for girls.

Your inner Warrior enables you to take a stand for issues that matter to you, the way Cristina Saralegui advocates for AIDS education. Discovered as a talented conversationalist, Saralegui got a shot on TV as host of her own program, *The Cristina Show*. Her

Univision Network phenomenon ran for twenty-one years. Saralegui and her wildly popular show received twelve Emmy awards.

Saralegui is nothing if not a mover and a shaker. She repeatedly broke barriers on her TV show, discussing things that had never before been talked about on Spanish-language television, like sex education for teens. She is enormously successful in media and in business, and yet she focuses her fame, wealth, and impressive life force to educate Latinos and Latinas about HIV and AIDS. With her husband, Marcos Avila, Saralegui founded the Arriba la Vida/Up with Life Foundation, to increase awareness and education about AIDS in the Hispanic community.

The business world often attracts High Warriors, like Carl Icahn, king of hostile takeovers, and David Einhorn, notoriously aggressive as a hedge fund manager. Hotel mogul Donald Trump personifies the brutish Warrior-as-businessman in the public mind. He sustained his own reality show, *The Apprentice*, by priming the audience to hear him say those killer words week after week: *You're fired!*

Warriors in business don't hesitate to draw lines in the sand. When she became CEO of Yahoo, Marissa Mayer swiftly moved to ban telecommuting, telling her employees to show up at the office or quit. She defended the policy in the name of the synergies generated in hallway discussions. But Silicon Valley was shocked by what looked like disregard for the needs of working parents for flexibility.

Warrior Quiz: *What's Your Favorite Strategy?*

As with the Dreamer, Thinker, and Lover, your inner Warrior has a favorite strategy, and has your best interests in mind—as far as *he* is concerned. At some point in your life and/or career, your Warrior decided that running low, high, or balanced got the best results for you.

As a reminder: You may not like the results you get from your Warrior's favorite strategy. In fact, there's a chance this approach is a cause of your Performance Gap. Figuring that out is a good place to start.

Here's the Warrior quiz to get a hint about your favorite Warrior strategy.

Inner Warrior Scenario

You work in a large public sector organization. Your mission is to serve the common good. Many foundations, as well as the federal government, give you a lot of money. As a result, watchdog groups monitor you closely: allegations of misconduct would appear on YouTube in a heartbeat.

One day, the executive director asks you to sign a form allowing him to use the group's official car and driver over the weekend for his daughter's wedding. You pause for a minute, hoping he is kidding. But he isn't.

What thoughts cross your mind? What do you say? What happens next?

Option One: This Is a Nightmare

You think to yourself, *"I can't believe he is asking me this. He knows it violates company policy, and he knows I can't say no to him, since he's the executive director. What a disaster."*

Then you say, "Okay. Please make sure it's back by Sunday night."

You spend the weekend hating yourself for agreeing to something you think is wrong, and praying that you don't get caught. You scheme about taking the form to the shredder when no one is looking, and buying the silence of the driver with a drink on Monday night after work.

Option Two: You've Got to Be Kidding

You think to yourself, *"You can't be serious. Your daughter's wedding? If you want to go on CNN and defend yourself, go for it, but you're not taking me with you. Jerk."*

You look up at the Big Boss, and with a tad of disgust in your voice, you say, "I see your commitment to modeling our values. I'm sure the employees would be touched by such a fine example of using taxpayer money to fulfill our mission. Come to think of it, we should all use the company vehicles for personal reasons. That will look great in the press."

You look down and start typing an email. The director looks at you with a scowl and snaps, "Who do you think you are to speak to me like that?" As he walks away, he turns to you and adds, "If you want to stick around here you might work on that attitude of yours."

Option Three: Thanks, but No, Thanks

You think to yourself, *"Wow. Really bad idea. No-brainer: this is not happening. But he is the boss. I should pick my words carefully."*

You turn to him and say, "Wonderful news about the

wedding. Congratulations! In terms of the car, I can't actually authorize that. It puts a lot at risk when we get fuzzy about the rules. I know you want to do the right thing, and it's better for everyone if I err on the side of caution. I do hope the weekend is beautiful, though. I'm sure it will be."

When the boss turns to walk back down the hall, you aren't sweating. You simply turn to the next item on your to-do list.

And the Winner Is?

Which of these choices seems most like you? Can you see yourself in any of them? What you say in that kind of moment, and how you say it, says something about your inner Warrior. As you can guess, these are images of a Warrior who is low, high, and balanced.

In the first case, a Low Warrior compromises her values, because she can't imagine saying no to the boss. She caves in immediately. In the second case, a High Warrior holds the line, but exerts her will too strongly. Instead of just stating her opinion, she responds with irony and sarcasm, nearly mocking the director. In the third case, a Balanced Warrior stays true to herself without attacking him. She doesn't submit blindly like the Warrior did in the first scenario. And yet she doesn't act aggressively, either. She takes action to do what she thinks is right, while still respecting her boss.

The Balanced Warrior avoids some pitfalls of the other approaches. The Low Warrior response—allowing the director to take the car for a private function—puts the organization in jeopardy. This would look terrible if people found out. On the other hand, the high response may put the employee in harm's way. She protects the policy but earns a reputation for insubordination. Using that approach over time could lead to the unemployment line. The Balanced Warrior doesn't shy away from power, but uses it with care.

The Warrior in Daily Life

A Balanced Warrior enables you to say what you need to say, like when you need to cancel social plans because you're simply too tired to go out. Or you want to tell your partner what you need from her. Or you want to tell the senior leader on your team that you find his treatment of the junior team members unacceptable.

Your Warrior helps you take actions that can feel like a stretch if your favorite strategy is running low, but seem perfectly appropriate to the Balanced Warrior. Like going back to the store and asking for a replacement for something you bought that isn't working. Or sending your food back at a restaurant because you don't like the way it's prepared. These are seemingly small ways your Warrior protects you, but they're not trivial at all. They let you know if you're letting your Warrior do his job. If these things are tough, then the harder Warrior tasks might seem impossible.

Higher-stakes moves for the Warrior include asking for a raise because you feel underpaid. Ending a relationship that isn't working for you anymore. Telling your spouse you want to take a big cut in salary to go back to school. Telling a job candidate who made it to the last round that someone else got the job. With the right preparation on the inside, these conversations become manageable. If you focus only on the textbook guidelines for the right words to say, these moments can go up in flames.

When balanced, your Warrior can communicate directly and clearly, without attacking anyone and without backing away from the hard truth.

Your Warrior can deliver messages like these:

- "I know you worked hard, but the job isn't done yet."
- "I'm sorry, but this doesn't work for me anymore."
- "You didn't meet your goals for three quarters in a row, so unfortunately, we're letting you go."
- "I don't think Dad can take care of himself anymore without institutional help."

None of your Big Four can make conversations like these easy or entirely comfortable. But your Warrior enables you to stop putting them off, stop hedging when people ask you what's happening, and step up to the plate when the time comes.

One very common Warrior challenge is finding a way to say no. Your Warrior helps you to set boundaries—what you will or won't do—*and* stick to them. A Balanced Warrior helps you draw the line in tricky situations, like when:

- your cousin asks if you'll serve on her Board of Trustees for a cause that doesn't interest you
- a colleague expects you to revise a document that you've already reworked several times
- your fifteen-year-old asks to spend the weekend with her college boyfriend at his fraternity's "Spring Fling" festival
- your boss wants you to fly eighteen hours to Singapore for one day to close an important deal—in the same week as your family vacation

- your kindergartner asks to hear the story "one more time" when bedtime has long passed

The Warrior also steps forward when you need a push to get moving. Your Warrior operates with a results-orientation, so you can do things like:

- Create and maintain a performance culture at the office
- Talk to your brother about your concern over his gambling
- Face the application still sitting on the kitchen table
- Get out of bed to go running
- Put away the holiday decorations from last month
- Speak up when you see discrimination
- Do your physical therapy exercises
- Implement your parts of this year's strategic plan
- Stand firm when you say that you're *done* breastfeeding the baby
- Collect the last set of hours of supervision you need to get certified for your clinical practice

Putting Principles into Practice

Warrior Sweet Spots

There's a Spanish proverb that says, "It's not the same to talk of bulls as to be in the bullring." The Warrior's power source is **willpower**, and her strongest muscle is **courage**. The Balanced Warrior provides *protection*, and specializes in the skills you need for *accomplishment*.

The Warrior's sweet spots enable you to:

1. **Speak Hard Truths**
2. **Hold Your Ground**
3. **Take Action**

The Warrior's inner resources include firmness, resolve, grounding, and accountability.

Let's see how these work in practice.

Speak Hard Truths

Let's start by looking at a dialogue. This is from a doctor named Mason.

DESCRIPTION:

My friend Austin and I went on a trip together. When we met, he said he doesn't wear a seat belt because it's too confining. He explained that he drives a Volvo, which is extremely safe. He tends to drive very quickly, which I know because he's complained to me about his speeding tickets.

WHAT I THOUGHT and FELT BUT DIDN'T SAY	WHAT WE ACTUALLY SAID
	Austin (while driving us): Can you hand me my phone?

WHAT I THOUGHT and FELT BUT DIDN'T SAY	WHAT WE ACTUALLY SAID
Oh, no. He's already speeding and not wearing a seat belt. Now he wants to make a call? He has our lives in his hands.	Me: [*Silent.*] Austin: It's in the back.
Is it safe to drive with him? I think I'll look up the accident records on Volvos. I should really put my foot down about making calls while driving. Maybe next time I should drive?	Me: [*Silent. I hand him the phone.*] Austin: I know you don't believe in talking on the cell while driving. I'm a very safe driver in a completely safe car. If you're going to ride with me, deal with it. Me: [*Silent.*]

Mason strongly prefers that Austin not talk on the phone while he's driving. But so far, Mason can't confront his friend over what he sees as dangerous behavior.

Austin's making it plain: take it or leave it.

And Mason takes it.

If your Warrior also runs low, you might recognize Mason's

situation. He's grappling inside of himself, but not saying anything out loud. Maybe you don't remain silent like he does. But you compromise or accommodate other people to avoid conflict. Whatever your specific favorite strategy is, your Low Warrior is getting in your way.

In contrast to Mason's Low Warrior, my client Cody's Warrior ran high. Warriors in overdrive don't hold back. They can be domineering, intimidating, and at times can appear mean. It's easy to spot people running a High Warrior in a crowd—the condescending boss, the parent yelling at the ball game. But it's often tough to recognize this strategy in yourself. Here's an example Cody brought to one of our coaching meetings.

DESCRIPTION:

I asked a vendor to give me a quick rundown of his proposal. I needed a simple solution, and I needed it fast.

WHAT I THOUGHT and FELT BUT DIDN'T SAY	WHAT WE ACTUALLY SAID
	Vendor: Let me explain what we can do for you and what we would charge per hour.
Don't give me a whole song and dance. I asked for one small bit of help. Don't you dare try to charge an hourly fee for what should be a small flat fee.	**Me:** I don't need all this. It'll take too long and be too expensive. Cut to the chase.

WHAT I THOUGHT and FELT BUT DIDN'T SAY	WHAT WE ACTUALLY SAID
	Vendor: Well, let me break it down for you, step by step.
I hate these sales guys.	
	Me *(annoyed)*: I just said it will take too long and be too expensive. Give me the quick-and-dirty version.
How many more meetings do I need to waste until someone will just answer my damn question?	
	Vendor: If I explain how each step builds on the next, I think you'll see how the whole package fits together.
I hate this guy.	**Me** *(yelling)*: Look, we can do half of this in our sleep! **We don't even need you! JUST FORGET IT!** [*I slam down the phone.*]

In this phone call, Cody did what he usually does: he said what he wanted, and when he didn't get it immediately, he demanded it. When that didn't work, his agitation went through the roof. He quickly wrote off the other person as a "useless sales guy" and became hostile. Cody let loose with his belligerence, scolding the vendor and terminating the potential transaction.

What was he left with after all of this?

He'd lost the opportunity to get the services he needed. In the moment Cody felt gratified by dumping his anger. But as usual in these situations, he hadn't *actually* solved his problem. That's not to say that Cody is "wrong" to get mad. The vendor wasn't listening, or giving him what he wanted. But a High Warrior like Cody turns legitimate anger into rage. He turns disagreements into combat. A Balanced Warrior would *assert* himself without crossing over into *aggression*.

Neither Mason nor Cody relates to his inner Warrior in an effective way. They avoid the problem or assault it. But neither one gets an outcome he wants. They can both close their Performance Gaps by discovering the Balanced Warrior. Then they can communicate clearly and directly, without silencing themselves or attacking other people.

Below is an example from a workshop participant who does a good job balancing her Warrior with her Lover. As you'll see, she's angry, but she communicates in a candid and respectful way. Her Warrior takes a stand. Yet her Lover empathizes with the school and its small staff. She appreciates that it's rough to serve a constituency of demanding parents. She doesn't choose *between* the Warrior and the Lover. She draws on them both.

DESCRIPTION:

I have stepchildren who attend a school near their mother's home. Three years ago, when the school directory was published, my husband Charlie and I were not listed—they listed only the mother of all divorced children. As an involved parent, this enraged my husband, and after a tense PTA meeting, the school agreed to make a change. The following year we were listed in the directory, but under "Alternate" after the mother. This year, once again, we were omitted as well as all the other divorced parents. I sent an angry email and met with the school administration the next day.

ME: Charlie and I are very angry we've been omitted from the directory *again*.

ROSALIE: I am so sorry. My staff caught the mistake, but didn't tell me until we got your email. The software program we used bumped the "alternate" parent out. We also had a big time crunch getting the directory out.

ME: I understand you have time pressure. I'm sure you want the directory to come out within the first few weeks of school.

ROSALIE: Yes, exactly.

ME: At the same time, you need to serve all families in this school. You have more than a thirty percent divorce rate for kids here.

ROSALIE: Well, what can we do if the software program has a mind of its own?

ME: For one, you can have someone proofread the directory before it goes out. But that's not the point. The issue is that you determine an "alternate" parent at all. We have joint custody of our kids, and we are *not* "alternate" parents. That designation doesn't fit our lives, and it's not yours to make for any family. I know these are delicate issues for the school. I'm sure it's difficult. But this directory situation is destructive and needs to get fixed. When can the interested parents meet with administrators? We're willing to work with you. But this *cannot happen* again next year.

In this conversation, her Warrior's message is clear: she doesn't accept the current situation and wants to know when they will address it. At the same time, her Lover expresses understanding for the school. As a Balanced Warrior, she empathizes with their difficulty, and that in no way diminishes her resolve to get this fixed now, once and for all.

Hold Your Ground

Speaking your mind is one thing, but what happens when other people push back? If something matters to you, then you need the conviction to keep standing for it even when others disagree. Let's say you think your young son spends too much time watching television and playing on the iPad. When he asks for more screen time, you easily say no. But then he starts to beg and plead, asking again and again to finish the video game he started earlier in the day. Or your friend asks if she can borrow your car, and you say you prefer not to loan it out. But she doesn't let it drop. "Oh, please, *just this once*, can you help me? I'm *really* in a bind, and *you're the only one I can ask*."

It's moments like these when you need your Warrior's perseverance to hold your ground, rather than giving "fifteen more minutes to finish that same video game, but no starting a new one" to stop the whining. Or agreeing to loan your car "if you keep this just between us."

Warrior resolve is famously needed in the writing process. Anne Lamott talks about this in her book *Bird by Bird*. When she was starting out as a young writer, her father told her, "Do it every day for a while . . . do it as you would do scales on the piano. Do it by prearrangement with yourself. Do it as a debt of honor. And make a commitment to finishing things." Prolific novelist Stephen King has a similar attitude about the resolution that writing requires: he advises writers to set a routine, and stick to it every day, no matter what. "Don't wait for the muse," King writes. "He's a hardheaded guy who's not susceptible to a lot of creative fluttering. . . . Your job is to make sure the muse knows where you're going to be every day from nine 'til noon. Or seven 'til three. If he does know, I assure you that sooner or later he'll start showing up."

In the next dialogue, my workshop participant Ming captures the endurance that's sometimes required to get results. She is *determined* not to pay fees she sees as unfair. As you'll see, Ming will stand her ground to the end.

DESCRIPTION:

I went online to pay my credit card because it was due that day. When I went to click the "pay" button, it was faded out so it couldn't be clicked. In fine print next to it, it said that payments were due by 5 P.M. Eastern Standard Time (EST) on the due date. It was 4 P.M. in California where I live, which is 7 P.M. on the East Coast. I called Customer Support to make the payment so I wouldn't have a late fee. I reached a credit card representative—I'll call her CC rep.

WHAT I THOUGHT and FELT BUT DIDN'T SAY	WHAT WE ACTUALLY SAID
	Me: Hi, I'm calling because I'm trying to make my payment on time and I can't do it online because it says I missed the five p.m. Eastern

WHAT I THOUGHT and FELT BUT DIDN'T SAY	WHAT WE ACTUALLY SAID
	time deadline. Can I pay you and not incur a late charge?
I'm mad I have to spend time sorting this out. And I'm *really* mad about this 5 p.m. EST cutoff policy—that is completely arbitrary.	**CC rep:** The deadline was five p.m. EST.
Hopefully I can get this done quickly.	**Me:** I understand that. But it is still the twelfth and I'm hoping you can help me make my payment and not incur a late penalty.
	CC rep: Well, it is considered late because it is after five pm EST.
How can she not care that this policy is completely dishonest??? It's intended to earn revenue from "late" payments that are *not* late in the local time zone.	**Me:** I understand that. But it is still the twelfth and I'm hoping you can help me make my payment and not incur a late penalty.
	CC rep: The only thing I can do is make a special exception

WHAT I THOUGHT and FELT BUT DIDN'T SAY	WHAT WE ACTUALLY SAID
	for you and waive your late fee, but you'll need to pay the phone payment charge.
This is *such BS*!!!!	
	Me: Could you please also waive the phone payment charge? I would prefer to pay online. I'm only calling because I can't pay online, even though it is still the twelfth.
	CC rep: No, I can't do that.
Is this woman human?????? I hate credit card companies.	
	Me: This is a bit frustrating for me. I don't feel this payment is late, and I would have preferred to have paid this online, saving everyone this hassle.
	CC rep: Well, you missed the deadline.
AGHHHHHHHHH!!!!! I am *not* taking this lying down.	**Me:** But I didn't. My credit card bill says payment is due on the twelfth. I live

WHAT I THOUGHT and FELT BUT DIDN'T SAY	WHAT WE ACTUALLY SAID
	in California. It is *still* the twelfth. If you are going to have a midday cutoff, you need to make that clear on the statement, or list the due date as the day before.
	CC rep: Our policy is five p.m. EST.
	Me: Then I need to speak to your manager.
	CC rep: Okay, then, please hold.

Ming holds her ground, even escalating to speak to the manager, to get the results she wants. *No matter how many times* the customer support representative turns down her request, she stands firm.

Notice that while she's increasingly angry, she doesn't lose self-control. Ming has the fortitude to stay on the line and insist on fair treatment. Notice she doesn't raise her voice, insult the representative, or get so inflamed that she slams down the phone. Any of those behaviors could have led to her paying the fees.

Ming told me that, in the end, the manager came on the line and waived *both* sets of fees—the late fee *and* the "payment by phone" fee. He also apologized for the hassle. Ming embraces the attitude described by Yogi Berra when he said, "It ain't over till it's over." If your Warrior runs low, I recommend that you find people like Ming in your life. Spend time with them, and pay close attention to the way they handle situations like this one.

Take a Stand for Your Principles

Your inner Warrior is particularly important when someone crosses one of your ethical lines. The workshop participant below is fairly balanced in dealing with his colleague Wes, who's playing games with company policy.

WHAT I THOUGHT and FELT BUT DIDN'T SAY	WHAT WE ACTUALLY SAID
	Wes: They refuse to reimburse my travel expenses since I can't provide them with all the receipts.
Ah, here we go again on the claims. I'm not surprised they turned him down for reimbursement. I saw the bills—they were clearly not attributable to work.	**Me:** Yes, they are very strict with that.
	Wes: Well, at least I have another claim against them, and I'll get that money back for sure.

WHAT I THOUGHT and FELT BUT DIDN'T SAY	WHAT WE ACTUALLY SAID
What the heck does he come up with now? I really don't like his tone. It sounds like he is *against* the organization instead of working *for* the organization.	**Me:** What are you talking about? **Wes:** I found out that I can claim my Internet bills, and I found those for the last six months—ha!
Ah, of course, how could I expect anything else from this guy? He uses the Internet for private purposes, but if he can claim his expenses, he'll do it.	
	Me *(agitated)*: Not everyone in the department claims his or her Internet bills, you know. We should get rid of that rule because everybody has Internet for private use anyway. **Wes** *(acts surprised)*: What?! Lots of people are claiming it. **Me:** Well, it's up to you. You are free to do it, of course. But like the insanely high phone bills, it's an issue of ethics and morals.

WHAT I THOUGHT and FELT BUT DIDN'T SAY	WHAT WE ACTUALLY SAID
Yeah, buddy, morals and ethics. That is something you probably never heard of, but plenty of people actually have some.	
	Wes: My bills were over the limit, but I never knew we were only allowed a limited number of minutes on our phones.
	Me: Wes, I told you that myself when you started, remember? I went through the whole routine with you, and I explained to you to be careful with your phone usage because it is bound by strict rules.
	Wes: I don't remember any of that. Otherwise I would have watched out. Nobody gave me clear instructions on the phone rules. So how can I be expected to follow them?
Don't give me that. That is an outright lie. I told you. I can even picture the exact situation when it happened.	
Damn. I should have documented the meeting when I gave him a formal run of the rules. Now I have no evidence.	

WHAT I THOUGHT and FELT BUT DIDN'T SAY	WHAT WE ACTUALLY SAID
Note to self: Next hire, make sure you make a formal document of the discussion. Regardless, it's his responsibility to learn and follow the rules.	**Me** *(sounding a little annoyed)*: Okay, Wes. Here's the thing. I am one hundred percent sure that you knew about this, because I told you myself. But even if you forgot, it is still your own responsibility to find out about the rules. If your employer gives you a phone, it is silly to assume there are no limits. I suggest you stop blaming other people and take some responsibility for your own actions here.

Hold your ground. Especially when defending your values.

Take Action

Taking action is about getting something done, whether it's fund-raising for a cause you care about, gathering all the things your kids need for summer camp, or getting rid of clutter from your home office. Actions include all the activities involved in fulfilling a contract, restocking supplies and inventory, and showing up where you're supposed to be, on time and ready to start. It's the Warrior in you that keeps track of three kids' schedules, from playdates to doctor appointments to cello lessons, and keeps all the trains on track even when you need to travel out of town. It's your Warrior that makes sure all of the materials are in place, accurate, and professionally produced before you walk in to make a client presentation.

Think of Sarah Palin, the former governor of Alaska who became Senator John McCain's running mate in the 2008 campaign for the White House. Palin coupled her Dreamer's vision for America with her strong Warrior drive to create results on the ground. She didn't want to just *talk* about politics—she was in it to win it.

Palin demonstrated the Warrior commitments to speaking one's truth and holding one's ground. She also role-modeled the Warrior as social activist. Palin shook things up by delivering the Tea Party as a grass-roots movement, forcing moderate Republicans to support more conservative ideals. In the next election cycle, Palin Warriors mobilized to support Tea Party candidates. In many cases, their campaign engagement determined who made it to Congress and who lost their seats. If your Dreamer feels inspired to create change, then negotiate with your Warrior to make it a team effort. Together you can set goals *and* do what it takes to reach them.

Seeing a grand vision, and devising plans to pursue it, won't produce the impact you want until your Warrior also takes action. When you combine these together, and add the Lover's care for people, the Big Four can accomplish amazing things. Think of British chef Jamie Oliver and his campaign to improve unhealthy eating habits. His dream, his beliefs, and his concern for people's health are all powerful forces. But ultimately what makes Oliver so influential is his Warrior's massive effort to educate the public about nutritious diets.

It's the Warrior that takes the direction, reflection, and connection of your inner team and supports them with protection. You see this in the courageous actions of Ellen Johnson Sirleaf, Africa's first female president, and her fellow Liberian peace activists, such as Leymah Gbowee. These leaders dreamed of a society without child soldiers, where violence wasn't a fact of daily life. They planned tactics such as the use of sex strikes to get their men's attention. They grieved for the overwhelming losses in their country. Then, ultimately, they activated their inner Warriors to take a firm stand. They took formidable action to protect their children's lives as well as their right to live in a free society. Years after the Liberian civil war, the women of Togo and then Kenya followed their lead.

Most of us don't need the will to forge a revolution. We just want to cross things off our to-do list. In far less daunting circumstances, we sometimes lack the grit to get off the couch and face the tasks of the day. Sirleaf and Gbowee remind us of the determination, discipline, and conviction of the inner Warrior. We can move from the worlds of our dreams, our ideas, and our feelings into powerful action, too.

If your Warrior runs low, you might struggle to tap the willpower you need to get up and get going. You might procrastinate when your team is waiting for your section of a memo. You might have a habit of finding *some* of your receipts, but then not collecting the rest that you need to submit an expense report. Despite your good intentions, you get stuck before all of the dishes are put away, or all of your emails are answered. Low Warriors aren't big fans of completing things because they're not drawing fully on the inner resources that would support them to finish fully and on time.

If your Warrior runs high, you can get stuck on overdrive. You jump out of one task and into the next without catching your breath or eating your lunch. Balanced Warriors have a results orientation. But High Warriors get fixated on constant activity. They're prone to burning out their teams, and if they maintain this profile long enough, they'll burn themselves out, too.

The High Warrior is often out of balance with the inner

Dreamer. Activity has taken on a life of its own, divorced from the purpose or mission behind it. Reaching for your Dreamer will connect you to the meaning behind all of this hustle and bustle that you're doing. That can help slow you down a little, and then inspire you to prioritize. Now you'll put more of yourself into the important topics, and delete a few that were adding weight to your to-do list but weren't mission critical.

Take Accountability for Your Actions

Taking action includes the ability to make promises and fulfill them. It also means you have the stability to accept your role when things go wrong. To take accountability for your mistakes. If your accountability muscle is weak, then you might not complete what you start, only half fulfill your promises, or not step up to take responsibility when you drop the ball.

In the exchange below, you'll see that John's Warrior runs low. When he's confronted by his boss about a problem in the office, he starts giving excuses. John points fingers everywhere but in his own direction. Now, on top of making mistakes in the task itself, John's getting in hot water because his Low Warrior can't accept accountability. John would turn the situation around more quickly if he could acknowledge that he'd made some mistakes, and commit to trying harder next time.

BOSS: Why is this recruitment process not done yet?
JOHN: I don't know. Why are you asking me?
BOSS: Because you're responsible for the process.
JOHN: Well, technically speaking, I'm not actually in charge of it.

Long silence.

JOHN:	Several of the candidates didn't send in all of their information yet. So we're waiting for that to arrive. On top of that, lots of other managers make demands on my time. So I can't be responsive to all of them *and* do all of the reference checks on these candidates.
BOSS:	If you were falling behind on reference checks, you should have asked someone in the office to help you.
JOHN:	But no one told me that I was allowed to ask someone else to check references.
BOSS:	If candidates didn't complete their application packets, it was your responsibility to remind them, and then to follow up until each one was complete. If you saw a breakdown you should have informed me that we had a problem.
JOHN:	I sent reminders and people still have information missing.
BOSS:	It sounds like everyone around here is at fault for this delay except for you. Do I have that right, then?

The nobility of the Warrior doesn't come from never failing. On the contrary, it reflects the willingness to stand tall, even in the face of mistakes.

Strive for the Balanced Warrior

In this last Warrior situation, you'll meet Frida. She wanted to establish a relationship with a potential new business partner. Her tendency toward taking action was positive. But she was so eager to close the deal that she agreed to share all of her ideas without any commitment from the other side. In this first of two dialogues, her Warrior is all over the place.

DESCRIPTION:
I wanted to establish a relationship with a potential new alliance partner.

WHAT I THOUGHT and FELT BUT DIDN'T SAY	WHAT WE ACTUALLY SAID
	Them (other firm): I need to get to my next meeting. How can I help you?
	Me: I'd like to partner with your firm to bring this idea to the market.
	Them: Tell you what, why don't you send me, say, a list of your five main ideas, and the steps for how you would develop this idea, and a good source I can reference for more information.
What? We don't even know each other yet. On the other hand, how will I let him know I've got the goods? Maybe I'm being paranoid here.	
	Me: You want me to send you a list of my five best ideas,

WHAT I THOUGHT and FELT BUT DIDN'T SAY	WHAT WE ACTUALLY SAID
	and a strategy for bringing this to market?
	Them: That's right.
This is really rushed. I'm afraid to give him anything without an NDA. I should have prepared better.	
	Me: Confidentiality is an important issue here. I think maybe we should discuss an NDA.
	Them: Well, you said you're interested in partnering with us. Do we have a problem?
Uh-oh, now he's mad at me. I really need this business. We can always work out the details later. I need to show him I'm trustworthy.	
	Me: Oh, no, no problem at all. I'm very interested in working with you. I just thought we would discuss an NDA before we shared a lot of information.
	Them: That will just delay everything. If you don't think we're the right partnership, I can look elsewhere.

WHAT I THOUGHT and FELT BUT DIDN'T SAY	WHAT WE ACTUALLY SAID
Now he sounds really pissed off. I really can't afford to lose this deal. I'll send over the info and the NDA. It'll be fine. I'll get the business first and nail down the details later.	
	Me: No need! I'll send over my proposal this afternoon. I'm sure we can work everything out later if we decide to go forward together. Thank you for considering me as a partner. I have a really good feeling about this.

Frida is balanced in her Warrior abilities to take action and to communicate clearly. To a point. She doesn't speak up when she feels rushed, or request to slow down a minute so she can consider the NDA issue. Instead, when she gets pushback about the NDA, she drops it immediately. That's not a good outcome on the substance, or for the potential future working relationship.

In the workshop, Frida had a chance to rewrite her dialogue from a new vantage point. This came after we did Warrior exercises on grounding yourself, both to stabilize your conviction and to firm up your commitment to your goals and purposes before going into a meeting. As you'll see below, she changed the internal dialogue she had with herself based on the exercises we'd done. In turn, that led to a different conversation with her potential business partner.

DESCRIPTION:

I wanted to establish a relationship with a potential new alliance partner.

WHAT I THOUGHT and FELT BUT DIDN'T SAY	WHAT WE ACTUALLY SAID
	Them (other firm): I need to get to my next meeting. How can I help you?
	Me: I'd like to partner with your firm to bring this idea to the market.
	Them: Tell you what, why don't you send me, say, a list of your five main ideas, and the steps for how you would develop this idea, and a good source I can reference for more information.
Not on your life. How dumb do I look?	
	Me: You want me to send you a list of my five best ideas and a strategy for bringing this to market?
I need to talk to you about a nondisclosure	

WHAT I THOUGHT and FELT BUT DIDN'T SAY	WHAT WE ACTUALLY SAID
agreement and you're rushing me out the door. I'm not giving you anything without an NDA.	
	Them: That's right.
I need you to decide *now* whether you'll commit to confidentiality going forward.	**Me:** You're moving a little too fast for me. Confidentiality is an important issue here. I think we need to start with an NDA.
	Them: Well, you said you're interested in partnering with us.
	Me: Yes, I'm very interested in working with you. I just need a signed NDA before I can start sharing information.
	Them: That will just delay everything.
Unbelievable. Should I thank you for stealing from me? I need to buy time and regroup, and ask you again to decide whether you'll sign the NDA.	
	Me: Well, as I mentioned, confidentiality is important to me. Why don't you think about the idea of working together? Meanwhile, I'll send an NDA over to your office, and if

WHAT I THOUGHT and FELT BUT DIDN'T SAY	WHAT WE ACTUALLY SAID
	you decide to sign it, I'll be very happy to continue our discussions.

Looking at her revised dialogue, Frida said it felt uncomfortable, but at the same time empowering, to hold her ground. She guessed that if she'd handled the meeting like this, then the partner probably would have signed the NDA in order to keep exploring the potential. She knew it would take some practice, but Frida set some goals about remaining firm on issues that matter the next time something like this comes up.

We've now explored the strengths, sweet spots, and favorite strategies of all of the Big Four negotiators—your Dreamer, Thinker, Lover, and Warrior. That brings us to the end of Part Two.

In Part Three, we'll look at the Transformers—your Lookout, Captain, and Voyager. We'll take them one at a time so you can appreciate each one's unique role, and specific ways each of them helps move you toward the lasting changes you want in your leadership and your life.

Reflection Questions

- Do the Warrior's worldview and sweet spots come easily to you? Is it challenging for you to see how the Warrior operates in you?

- How do you relate to courage, firmness, resolve, grounding, and accountability?

- How do you use your Warrior's power of willpower?

- When have you let your Warrior take bold action, or fight for you and your values? When have you held your Warrior back from taking action or fighting for you and your values? What did you learn from these experiences?

- What conversations would your Warrior like to have these days, with your permission to speak the hard truth as skillfully as possible? What unfinished business would your Warrior like to close with your consent, provided it can be done safely and ethically?

- What are you noticing about your Warrior's common strategies? Does your Warrior step out in front of the rest of your Big Four? Does your Warrior tend to get left behind? What happens when your Warrior takes over, or gets shut out?

- How can you experiment to foster better balance among your Big Four?

PART THREE

Connect to Your Core

CHAPTER 9

Perception: Awaken Your Lookout

What lies behind us and what lies ahead of us are
tiny matters compared to what lives within us.

—HENRY DAVID THOREAU

Bill shows up for a 9:00 A.M. meeting to settle a dispute for his client. He's a lawyer, and he'd exchanged letters previously with Spencer, the lawyer on the other side. Bill expects to meet with Spencer one on one. Instead, Bill gets ushered into a large conference room. A team of eight attorneys is waiting for him.

Immediately, Bill's body reacts. His muscles contract. His adrenaline starts pumping. His mind spins. He thinks to himself, "You won't bully me. Two can play this game." Before the other side can say a word, Bill charges ahead, making an extreme demand. Antagonism grows quickly. Before long, the two sides are threatening to sue each other, though both know their clients could do better by avoiding litigation. As Bill exits the meeting, he makes a condescending comment, just to seal the adversarial tone.

Given that Bill expected one, familiar attorney, and not a room of strangers, his pounding heart and defensive thoughts are understandable. He's human, after all. The glitch is that Bill *doesn't notice* that these lawyers have hit a nerve. Now he's hooked. His focus has moved from the best interests of his client, toward showing his muscle. That's a bad outcome if you're the client depending on Bill to represent your interests at this meeting.

I can relate. I got hooked.

In the spring of 2012, I had the opportunity to meet Barack Obama, and get my picture taken with him. I was excited.

Growing up, I'd spent countless hours talking with my dad about American political history. I then attended the Woodrow Wilson School of Public and International Affairs at Princeton, where I wrote my senior thesis about trends in Congress. In law school, I'd mused about running for office someday. Meeting Obama was cool.

Given my long love of politics, on the night before meeting the President of the United States, do you know what I was thinking about? What an honor it was to meet a sitting president? How to thank him for his service? What one question I might ask about world affairs if given the chance?

Nope. None of that.

On the night before meeting the president, I was focused on the fact that my "nice earrings" were in Amsterdam and not in Boston, where I was. Seriously.

Once I made the unhappy discovery, I became *obsessed* about not having the right jewelry for the magic moment. *How could this happen?*

Outside of my radar, an internal storm was bearing down. It turned from bad to worse when I started thinking, "Apparently this transatlantic life isn't going to work. If I hadn't married Bernardus, then I wouldn't have divided my things between Amsterdam and Boston. *Then* my nice earrings would be *right here* when I needed them, and *then I could* wear them to meet the president." By then, I was getting totally soaked by my inner storm.

Before I allowed myself to reevaluate my entire marriage, I listened to a voice in my head. It asked me: "Are you really going to miss out on the excitement of meeting the president by focusing on your earrings?"

Well, when you put it that way.

The clouds started to clear.

The night before meeting the president, I was generating an internal tidal wave of anxiety without realizing it. My Lookout performed job number one: it helped me see that I was in trouble *in time to do something about it*. As I was busy getting in my own way, I saw what I was doing to myself, and got out of the hole before it was too late.

That's the transformational power of your Lookout.

What Is a Lookout?

A lookout is a person who observes a setting for what's important. If they spot something, they report it to someone else who'll do something about it. Lookouts *don't take action* on the problems they see. They pass on a message, and leave it to someone else to resolve things. As we'll talk about more in the next chapter, in the Winning from Within method, when Lookouts get information, they pass it on to your Captain.

In department stores, salespeople are lookouts for shoplifters. If someone catches their eye, they tell their manager. In national forests, "fire watchers" stand post in lookout towers. They monitor the wilderness, and act as communication relays with crews on the ground. Talent scouts roam the country on the lookout for young athletes. When they spot big potential, they notify the owner of their team.

You go "on the lookout" when you pay close attention to something you don't want to miss. Maybe it's the latest sale on Zappos.com, or Springsteen tickets before they sell out. You might look out for job announcements on LinkedIn, or for a text that lets you know your sweetheart arrived home safely. Some of you look out for a twelve-step meeting when you're in a new place. Others look out for weekly sales, to anticipate hitting or missing your quarterly targets. At one point or another, most of us have monitored the bathroom scale in the morning, looking out for that magic number that says we've reached our goal.

The "lookout" mode is fairly constant. At work, you watch your email, calendar reminders, and tweets that ping you day and night. At home, you scan for who or what needs you most: family, taxes, laundry, the endless stack of paper on the table, the search committee for the new pastor, the sick dog. You look out for time to get to the gym, or to return the call from your mother.

In between *all that*, you keep an eye on the world. You watch the market and global financial stability. Small nation-states building nuclear capability. Earthquakes. Civil unrest. You pay attention to election results, unemployment levels, new treatments for depression, and advances in fuel efficiency. You know when scientists find a new planet and who's playing at Wimbledon. If you're me, you try to follow big developments in the news, from shifts in the global balance of power to the latest addition to Brad and Angelina's family.

With so much going on, choosing *where to look* and *what to look for* can get complicated.

The Role of *Your* Lookout

As you know from your everyday life, attention is one of our scarcest resources. Ironically, most of us put the least attention where it can help us most: ***inside of ourselves***.

That's the job of your Lookout.

The Lookout's role is to notice what's happening inside of you, and to get your attention by sending an "instant message."

Lookouts monitor two basic things:

1. What's happening with your Big Four?
2. Are you connected to your center of well-being?

Based on how they answer those two questions, they'll decide what instant message to send. If you're listening, you can hear your Lookout's voice before you miss something wonderful. Even in a messy situation that's already under way, your Lookout can get you a message when there's still a chance to make things right.

Let's say a guy driving a shiny red Ferrari cuts right in front of you, forcing you to slam on your brakes. You fantasize about accelerating into the back of his fancy car to teach him a lesson. Before you hit the gas pedal, your Lookout feels the rush of adrenaline and notices your desire for revenge. The moment you get the instant message, you picture the hassle of explaining this "accident" to the police. You think to yourself, "I don't want to waste my time on this stupid guy." So you leave the scene with both cars unharmed.

In this case, your Lookout notices what's up *with you*, and sends you an "instant message" *before* you act counterproductively. Sometimes this instant message is all you need to *see the Performance Gap there in front of you*, and *walk around it instead of falling into it*.

At other times, the Lookout has an instant message for you, and you're just not listening. When you watch sports or a great drama on television, your Lookout sees how many snacks you're eating, but you don't. It's as if your hand moves by itself, reaching again and again for more chips. Only when your hand hits the bottom of the empty bowl do you sit up and ask, "Hey, what happened to all the potato chips?!" The Lookout tried to warn you. But it was more fun to eat the whole bowl of chips.

At still other times, Lookouts notice when you're letting a great opportunity pass by. Let's say you're waiting eagerly for a chance to work with the dean of faculty at the college where you just started teaching. At a faculty meeting, she asks for volunteers to support a joint initiative between the Office of the Dean and the academic chairs. You don't move. Other new faculty members express interest, but not you.

Your Lookout notices what's happening on the inside: the tightness in your stomach, the fear of not getting chosen, the self-doubt about tenured academics taking you seriously with your short list of publications, insecurity about whether the dean even *wants* to work with you. At this rate, you can forget about joining this group, despite its sounding like just the shot you'd wanted to get your foot in the door.

Your Lookout can't raise your hand for you. But they *will* hold up a mirror so you can see what's going on. Your Dreamer has a vision of getting more involved on campus, with a specific interest in getting to know the faculty dean. Your Lover feels nervous, shy, scared to try and fail. In this moment, the Lover calls the shots, so you're sitting still. When you get the instant message from the Lookout, you can see what's happening in that moment. Now you can decide to let it go. Or let your Dreamer negotiate with your Lover about volunteering. Once they engage, there's a good chance your Dreamer and Lover can find a meeting of the minds. The alternative is to not try. Then you'll follow your Lover's favorite strategy, fall into your typical Performance Gap, and watch other people get to know your new dean.

Your Lookout Separates You from Your Big Four

Like your other Transformers, your Lookout stands outside of your Big Four and watches how they work. While the Big Four tug at you to identify with them completely, the Lookout knows there is more to you than their voices, opinions, and competing views of the world.

Lookouts are transformative because *they disentangle you from the chatter of the inner negotiators*—the burst of emotion from your Lover, the rumination over options of the Thinker, and so on. They remind you that these feelings, thoughts, fantasies, or impulses to act are *parts* of you. But by themselves, they don't define who you are. Your Lookout is the first of three transformers because it provides the first step toward separating you from your Big Four. Your Lookout also helps you to notice when one inner negotiator takes over, or one is left behind.

Remember Sofia, the working mother from Brazil? Her Lookout noticed that in her struggle to decide about the conference, she only listened to two of her Big Four: her Dreamer and her Lover. Her Lookout sent that message to her Captain, who then called in the other two—her Thinker and her Warrior. That new operating system led to a new result.

Each of the Big Four sees itself as more than capable of handling anything. Your Transformers have a broader view. Your Lookout provides valuable distance between you and the voices of your inner negotiators in everyday life, at work or at home.

So your Lookout is watching the Big Four and noticing your typical reactions. How does this relate to closing your Performance Gap? When the Lookout starts looking around inside, you start to have an entirely new experience: *you can observe these reactions without needing to act on them*. As we'll explore more in the next chapter, this puts your inner Captain in charge of steering your ship, rather than you getting tossed around by whatever storms are brewing inside the Big Four.

See Your Reactions Rather than Act on Them

When the Lookout knows what's happening with your inner negotiators—and you receive the instant message—you'll start to get big breakthroughs.

What will change?

You'll see your reactions without needing to act on them.

In other words, when life hands you a situation, your Lookout sees where you're headed. Before you do or say anything, the Lookout lets you know. With that information, you might or might not choose to change course. If you do, you'll get a different outcome than what you've gotten before. Developing your Lookout skills over time will create the lasting change you want, in your leadership and in your life.

A seminar participant named Guillaume questioned me on this dynamic. In his mind, there was no space between his feeling furious and his screaming at his client. Like hitting your head and feeling pain, it all happened at the same time.

I asked him to explain.

Guillaume was a senior program officer at an international financial institution. He was passionate about financial support for developing economies. He sought to connect global funders with projects he thought could conform with all the rules and regulations, while creating a substantial impact on the ground. Given the labyrinth of policies, procedures, and multinational systems, this was no small feat. But Guillaume loved his work and had a strong track record.

Guillaume said the exposure for the funders was quite high. Loans and other financial instruments required careful structuring and risk mitigation. Still, the firm's partners supported development goals, and they knew a return on their investments was vital to sustainability over the long term.

Toward the end of a long bureaucratic process, Guillaume would often encounter roadblocks from the clients, the would-be funding recipients.

"I go see them to collect the documentation we need, and they tell me 'a few more weeks,'" Guillaume said. "This could already be the third or fourth time I came for the documents, and each time they tell me the same thing—'a few more weeks.'"

Guillaume said this is the point when he becomes furious.

"When they tell me that, I start screaming at them: *'What is wrong with you?! Don't you see I'm trying to help you?!* **You know the timetable! Without these documents, we lose everything! If you don't want this loan, don't waste my time!'"**

The clients are stunned by his harsh reaction.

"Honestly, what do they expect me to say?" he asked me.

In addition to having nervous clients, Guillaume was in hot water with his Director. This was hardly the protocol for interacting with the firm's clientele. Despite success at getting loans signed, Guillaume had a big problem at his office. He was on notice about cleaning up his act, and he had no idea how to change these interactions.

For Guillaume, the road to the Performance Gap is a straight line, as you can see in Figure 9.1. He gets angry that his clients are dragging their feet, and he starts yelling at them. This is how the world works when you're not getting messages from your Lookout.

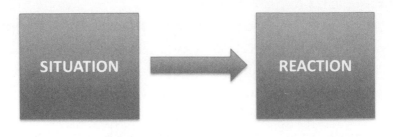

FIGURE 9.1

If we put the moment that Guillaume snaps at his client in the two-column format, it would look something like this:

WHAT I THOUGHT and FELT BUT DIDN'T SAY	WHAT WE ACTUALLY SAID
What??! The papers aren't ready? *Are you kidding me? How can you be THIS disorganized!!! Do you know I've put my neck on the line for you? Why do you make my life so difficult?!!!*	
	Guillaume: *What is wrong with you?! Don't you see I'm trying to help you?!* You know the timetable! Without these documents, we lose everything! If you don't want this loan, don't waste my time!

Guillaume doesn't see another way. But there is one.

When you introduce your Lookout into the mix, *you can interrupt the straight line* from provocation to lashing out.

In fact, Guillaume *did* start to handle his upsetting client visits differently. Over nine months, he turned his performance evaluation at work around. How?

He learned to hear his inner Lookout. That meant he started to *notice his own reactions before taking any action on them.* His experiences started looking more like this (see Figure 9.2).

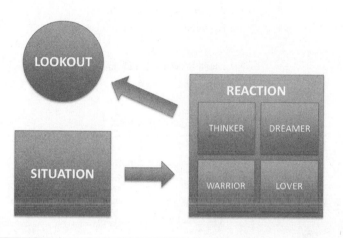

FIGURE 9.2

WHAT I THOUGHT and FELT BUT DIDN'T SAY	WHAT MY LOOKOUT NOTICED and FLAGGED FOR ME	WHAT WE ACTUALLY SAID
What??! The papers aren't ready? *Are you kidding me? How can you be THIS disorganized!!! Do you know I've put my neck on the line for you? Why do you make my life so difficult?!!!*		
	My face feels hot and my heart is racing. My blood pressure just shot through the roof. I'm furious. I feel exploited.	
	I need to take a deep breath. Maybe two.	
	I want to scream at them.	
	Come back to my center of well-being. Catch my breath.	
	Remember what I practiced.	
		I'm very disappointed. I'm working so hard on your behalf, and you're not meeting me halfway. If we don't have those documents in a week, all of this was for nothing. Can you promise me you will have them ready when I come back in a few days?

Who Has Time for All This?

But what about time? These things happen so quickly. There's no time for all that Lookout stuff before you're already throwing punches.

Yes and no.

Yes, on the one hand, you're right. When you do something new, it takes time to integrate it into your routine. Like any other skill, this takes practice. With repetition, the process gets much faster.

Remember when you first learned to drive a car. Getting behind the wheel, adjusting the seat, fixing your mirrors, checking the dashboard settings—it could take ten minutes before you put the key in the ignition. Today you do those things in ten seconds while also eating breakfast and taking a conference call.

On the other hand, this story is told in slow motion, so you can see it unfold step by step. It only takes one second to notice what you're saying, and then you can say something else.

Let me show you how the Lookout can work more simply, and more quickly.

When I was younger and practicing law, I stayed very late at the office. I felt enormous pressure to produce memos and drafts of motions, while also feeling exhausted. I had nearly the same conversation every night around midnight with my then-boyfriend, Noah. Had either one of us known how to listen to our Lookout, we could have changed this tense, repetitive discussion.

NOAH: Why don't you come home if you're so tired?

ERICA: I can't. This motion is due to the partner at
           seven A.M., and I'm nowhere near finishing it.
           This is so stressful. I can't stand it.

NOAH: Get a cup of coffee.

ERICA: I can't. I've had three coffees today already, and I drink soda constantly. If I have more caffeine I'm going to be sick. I'm just so tired, and so stressed, because I have to finish this motion tonight, and I'm not even sure I'm doing it right.

NOAH: Splash cold water on your face.

ERICA: I'm the only one here. I don't want to walk down the hall in an empty building at midnight. The thing is that I'm feeling very overwhelmed. I have so much to do, I'm totally worn out, and I'm not sure I'm even doing what the partner wanted me to do.

With your knowledge of the Big Four, you can tell this is a conversation between Noah in his Thinker/Warrior mode and Erica in her Lover mode. As clear as that seems now, we didn't see it, or have language to name it, at the time.

Noah and I are both well-intentioned people. Though we drove each other crazy in these conversations, we were both genuinely trying to communicate. No one here is "in the right" or "in the wrong." You have a Thinker/Warrior and a Lover who keep missing each other, in part because neither person hears their Lookout. How could the Lookout transform this conversation—*and quickly?*

By talking to either one of us.

Noah's Lookout could've whispered in his ear, "Your Thinker is giving options and your Warrior wants to *fix* things. She's upset. I notice your Lover isn't saying anything." With that momentary heads-up, he might have changed gears, saying something like "You sound overwhelmed. How can I help?" Then I could've told him how he could actually help me—which didn't include suggestions about coffee or splashing water on my face.

Likewise, my Lookout could have sent me an instant message, something like "Your Lover is the only one talking. Is that the best way to connect with Noah?" Just that realization and question would've prompted me to make a change.

Maybe I'd stay in the Lover mode but switch my focus from my own needs to Noah's emotional needs. I might say, "It must be hard for you to hear me complain all the time about how stressful this is, and not know how you can help me." Or I might have moved to another negotiator and said something else entirely. Either way, it would take *one moment* for my Lookout to get my attention.

In fact, that one Lookout moment holds the potential to transform not just this argument, but our whole relationship. The Thinker/Warrior vs. Lover disconnect was a challenge we never overcame. Once the Lookout helps you see what's happening, you can do things differently—and *change the outcomes you're creating.*

One more thought on the concern about time. You'll find that as you listen to your Lookout more consistently, the communication might not even require words. Your Lookout can signal you with a twist in your stomach, or a flashing sense that something's not right. That's all you might need *to take a deep breath and consider your next move* rather than proceeding as usual, on autopilot.

Lookouts Help You Capture Opportunities

Lookouts don't only keep you out of trouble. They also wave a flag so you can capture great opportunities.

Danny is the teenage son of a former workshop participant. He came along to the conference center with his dad, hoping to spend quality time with him in the evenings. Since Danny joined our group every day for meals, he listened to all the debates, discussions, and insights people had over lunch and dinner, and in turn we got to know him.

I learned that Danny adored photography and dreamt of becoming a renowned portrait photographer. I also found out that while his parents generally encouraged him, they worried he'd start wanting fancy, expensive equipment and eventually lose interest in what ended up being a pricey hobby. When a new camera came out that was ideal for portraiture, Danny desperately wanted it. But the camera was expensive and his parents said no.

Before coming to the training center, Danny had largely given up on his dream, sulking around the house and feeling deprived. However, during mealtime discussions about the Big Four, he'd identified with the idea of his inner Dreamer, realizing he was moving too quickly to allow one setback to discourage him from pursuing what he loved. His Dreamer got pumped up.

Danny recalled that a cousin, Jasmine, was getting married in the spring. He texted her with an offer to photograph her wedding in exchange for the camera. This was a good start, but only got him halfway there. Jasmine texted back:

JASMINE: That's thoughtful of you, Danny, but we have a professional photographer for our wedding. It's a very big day, you know, so we want a "real" photographer.

DANNY: Oh, I understand.

Danny paused. Another dead end.

He told me that at this point he *almost* shrugged his shoulders and walked away. But then he remembered our talks about the

Lookout. His Lookout saw that he'd tried once, and his Dreamer was ready to give up. With a momentary pause, he saw that all was not lost. He needed to hold steady, with his eyes on the prize.

He texted his cousin again.

DANNY: But you know, Jasmine, these days a lot of couples have a website for their wedding. They put photos on the site along with information for their guests. I could take portraits of you and your fiancé to put on your website, all for just the cost of the camera.

JASMINE: Actually, that's a good idea. We haven't thought about pictures for the website. I think that sounds terrific.

Despite a first rejection, Danny forged on undeterred. Danny resisted the pull of his Dreamer's favorite strategy by listening to his Lookout. He got the camera. And closed his Performance Gap.

Find Your Center of Well-Being

I said earlier that your Lookout has two areas of interest: your Big Four, and your connection to your center. Now you see how the Lookout works with the Big Four. Let's go back to your center of well-being.

At the hub of your Wanting, Thinking, Feeling, and Doing, lies the core of who you are. We can call that core your Being, your center, or your center of well-being. They all point to the same essence—something true about you that's deeper than your thoughts, your emotions, your desires, or your impulses to take action.

All of the Transformers—your Lookout, Captain, and Voyager—are connected to your center. In their own ways, they can link you back to your core, to centeredness, to the felt sense that everything will be okay. We'll look at centeredness in different ways in each chapter of Part Three. For now, let's start by thinking about two fundamental states of well-being: centered, and off-center.

What Does "Centered" Mean?

Your Lookout is constantly scanning—not only your Big Four, but also your state of well-being. Both of them relate to your capacity to make choices with your eyes open, one of the goals of the Winning from Within method.

Centeredness is the sense that you're in harmony with yourself and the world around you. For simplicity's sake, let's say you have two states of well-being: centered and off-center. The reality is more complicated. But this works well enough for our purposes.

To start, centeredness reflects what's happening in your body. Think about how you act when you're well rested and sated versus when you're sleep-deprived and you haven't eaten all day. In the first case, it's easier to be patient with people. When you neglect your physical needs, you snap at people without thinking. Or in a long-term relationship, when you go through ups and downs in physical intimacy. When you're having sex with your partner often, you feel generous, kind, forgiving. When you haven't slept together in too long, you might shut down, feel closed or distant. Centered versus off-center.

As opposed to the frenzy of daily life, centeredness is associated with a sense of calm. You might feel centered when you walk in the woods, sing with your choir, or sit by the window during the first snow of the season, watching the snowflakes fall. If you have a cat who sits by the window—especially in the one ray of sun coming through it—you've seen centeredness, big-time. Ask your cat: all is well with the world.

Think of anything you do that gives you a sense of well-being. It doesn't require sitting still. It could be downhill skiing. Playing piano. Cooking. Yoga. Teaching. Journaling. Relaxing with friends at a great restaurant. Poking your head into your child's room to check on him when he's sleeping. Your center is home to an essence in you that lives in a state of well-being. As it is for your cat when it sits by the window, well-being is available for you when you tap into it.

Going one more step, saints and sages have taught that your center is the source of your innate wisdom. They say that when you're centered, you can access essential virtues, like beauty, awe, humility, perseverance, and grace. Some traditions ground the center of being with a physical place: Olympus, Rome, Jerusalem, Mecca. Others teach that when you drop into your center, you find the opposite of physicality, what they call simply "awareness."

Philosopher and psychologist William James talked about expanding into our "wider selves." I relate to this as an image of centeredness, because it describes how I feel when I move from the tight space inside of Bernardus' boat to the more open space outside on deck.

I'm not comfortable yet inside the boat. I can't stand up to get dressed, or move anywhere without hitting my head. I don't feel happily relaxed in there. On the contrary, I feel claustrophobic. When I feel nervous in that little space, I recall a prayer I learned as a girl, asking God to free us from our "narrow places."

In that same prayer, we ask God's help to bring us out of our constriction and into our "expansiveness." I feel that expansion literally in the center of my chest when I step outside onto the boat's deck. The sea stretches out wide in front of me. The sun is shining. The Little Dude is manning the rudder and Bernardus is chilling out with a coffee. Life is good. I take a deep breath, and come back to my "wider self." Self-protection melts away into love for my family and appreciation for this beautiful day.

Two states of well-being: off-center, and centered.

What Does "Off-Center" Mean?

If the experience of feeling centered isn't clear to you, I'd bet you do know what *off-center* feels like.

Imagine a day like this.

You wake up, you're in a fine mood. You go about your day, checking things off your to-do list. It's all good. Then, all of a sudden, something happens. Something bad.

- Your colleague criticizes you in public.
- Your ex-wife leaves *another* blistering voice mail.
- Your tax estimate comes in *nearly double* what you'd expected.
- Your nanny calls at 6:30 A.M. to announce she's taking the day off, *today*.
- Your client insists on talking to you *now*—with a "quick question"—despite your *clear policy* of taking calls on the weekends *only for emergencies*.
- Your daughter with a midnight curfew walks in the door—*at 2:05 in the morning*.

- Your insurance company *finally* answers your *appeal* based on *their* mistake, and *it's denied.*
- Your best friend shows up *an hour late* for lunch—and acts like *nothing happened.*
- The printer you fixed two weeks ago *will not print.*

That feeling—the one you have at moments like these—is *the opposite* of feeling "centered." Personally, in these moments, I hate everyone: my friend, my colleague, the tax authority, my insurance company, and whoever designed this pathetic, dysfunctional printer. This is the same day I'm going to trip over the laptop cord and sprain my ankle as I fall to the floor. While I'm at it, I might as well eat a box of cookies. Then later I can hate myself, too.

Beauty? Awe? Grace?

Not so much.

When we're centered, we feel the ground beneath our feet. We see challenges in front of us but know we have the resources to figure things out. When we fall off-center, we feel like a hero from *The Avengers.* Just a minute ago, we were the sane, world-renowned scientist David Banner. Then something knocked us off-balance. The next thing you know we're turning green. We're the size of a giant. We're the Incredible Hulk, destroying everything in our path.

Respect—and Transcend—Your Animal Wiring

To some extent, we are unwitting participants in a destructive chain of events. When things like these happen, our bodies react immediately with a form of self-protection. If we register a threat, then—boom!—our involuntary responses kick into action. Hearts start pounding. Stress hormones release into the bloodstream. Bodies swing into alert. We experience different symptoms of sudden acute stress, from sweaty palms to feeling sleepy. However you show it when *you're* off-center, it shows up in our brains and bodies as well as our general sense of well-being.

Daniel Goleman, author of *Emotional Intelligence*, has researched extensively about the amygdala, a primal part of our brain designed to protect us from imminent danger. He's written about the way it "hijacks" us when it gets provoked. In this less advanced part of our brain, we have blunt tools hardwired to keep us alive. We share some instincts with our reptilian cousins. Lashing out. Running away. Even playing dead is a tactic to survive attack.

In the mammalian part of our brain, developed later, we have other survival instincts. When these neurons fire, we race to shield and guard offspring, and we reach for other people to create mutual protection. We understand instinctively about safety in numbers. All of these reflexes start with neurological impulses.

There's nothing inherently wrong with these biological, defensive reactions. On the contrary, many times they serve us well. If a moving car is approaching a child, the "rush" provided by our fear response alerts us to shout, run, do whatever's needed to save the child from harm. The trouble is that our nervous systems can't always tell the difference between an oncoming vehicle and a personal insult from a co-worker. Both can set off survival reactions in our bodies.

In many day-to-day high-stress situations, we aren't alone. We're fighting with someone we love, or in a tense discussion with people whose opinions fly in the face of our own. We're delivering bad news, giving a painful answer, or arguing our way through an emotional confrontation. Now it's not just *our* amygdala that's "hijacking" us. We've got *two* frightened animals who can't tell they've left the wild and entered the conference room. Multiply that even more when you're on a team or committee, in a family, or disputing a new policy with the entire board of your condominium association. Once alarm bells go off, more is definitely *not* merrier.

Whether we fire back or retreat to the bunker, once we react from self-protection, other people respond in kind. Almost without fail, their way of coping further inflames *our* fears. We take an *even more* provocative defensive action against them. And on it goes. Tensions ramp up. Clear choice disappears. Each person's reaction drives a counter-reaction until it becomes a dizzying cycle we can't seem to stop.

Again, your Lookout can help.

Learn to Spot When You're Off-Center

Like Guillaume, for many of us the link between our fear response and our defensive behavior happens so quickly, we can't imagine they could be separated. In addition to happening suddenly, fear and survival instincts are powerful forces. They lead to strong reactions. I saw a potent example of this after September 11, 2001, when I consulted to a reinsurance company.

Reinsurers are the people who insure the insurance agents. At that time, they were writing *a lot* of policies for large office buildings in the event of a terrorist attack. Statistically speaking, the likelihood of another terrorist attack on an office building in the United States was infinitesimally small. Yet in the aftermath of the attacks of 9/11, suddenly everyone needed a policy to protect them from this potential disaster. Unlike going back inside to check that you turned off the oven, in this case raw fear was driving a multimillion-dollar industry.

I tell you that story to convey that I don't underestimate the power of what we feel when we're off-center. Nor do I doubt the force of the urge to act—even drastically—when we feel threatened, unloved, or unsafe. I don't question that in part of our brains, we perceive that our very life could be on the line, even in a common argument at home or at work.

Here's where I do depart from some conventional wisdom on this topic. Yes, we have little discretion in the moment over our *physiological* reaction to a perceived threat, and, yes, we feel a pull to take action for self-protection. But beyond that, *we do have a choice about how we respond*. We've evolved beyond our mammal friends, and we can interrupt the cycle of fear and reactivity. We can find our way back to center, to our sense of well-being.

Developing your own centering practice is a fundamental life and leadership skill. In the next chapter we'll explore how you can do that. At this point, I'd ask you to consider that if your Lookout notices fairly quickly that you're off-center, and sends you an instant message about it, then you start to be positioned *to see the reactivity but not act on it*.

This is a crucial part of the Winning from Within method, because it empowers you to make your own choices rather than live at the whim of your neural patterning. You can stand firmly, as a centered man or woman, as a centered person, and as a centered leader. That gives you freedom, as well as accountability, for the world you create.

Can You Be "Centered" All the Time?

Unless you're an enlightened being—and I suppose there could be some, though I've never personally met one—you aren't going to feel centered all the time. Like the rest of us, you'll get annoyed, scared, or provoked—and hijacked. I wouldn't even aim for that. I'd say a good goal is to lead your life as much as you can when you're centered, and equally important, **aim to notice** when you're off-center. **That's the key to reclaiming choice.**

Once you know you're off-balance—*in the moment of feeling off-center*—you're ahead of the game. Now you'll consider your next moves carefully, because you recognize your inner state. Since most of us *rarely* notice until much later that we've lost our way, this is a whole new way of leading and living.

I've gotten much better and faster at spotting myself becoming that green superhero from the Fabulous Four. I hadn't known my inner Hulk that well before the last year. It turns out that all this time, my Hulk was living in The Netherlands. That's why I really got to know him when I moved there.

In one of my visits with my off-center inner Hulk, I came home to tell Bernardus that I'd nearly totaled the car.

"You what???!" he wanted to know.

"I turned onto this crazy road with huge holes in the street, and I couldn't drive around them, so I had to drive right through them. It was really scary," I told him.

"You know what you did?" he continued, nearly yelling. *"You drove on a bus-only lane.* Those are paved that way so that *cars can't drive on them.* Didn't you see the sign? There's a sign right there, *clear as day*—it says, Buses Only."

And then, to add insult to injury, the dreaded rhetorical question.

"You do realize you could've totaled the car, right?"

By now I was clearly not getting sympathy, but worse, I was falsely accused of being an idiot.

"There is no such sign," I insisted. "Obviously I pay extra attention to road signs when I'm driving here. *There was no Buses Only sign on that road."*

Bernardus continued to insist that the sign was right there, *clearly* indicating *Buses Only*. I insisted, too. So we had no choice. Late at night, tired and annoyed with each other, we *had* to drive back to the scene to see who was right.

Here is the sign at the entry to the road in question (Figure 9.3).

FIGURE 9.3

Does this sign "clearly" communicate *to you* that cars cannot enter this road?

Give me a break.

It's not a picture *of a car with a big X through it*. It looks nothing like a stop sign. No, this sign is an empty circle. I was supposed to know *from this sign* that I couldn't drive a car there without totaling it.

Really?

I can't say that either one of us was "centered" for the rest of that evening. That's why I say don't bother trying to be "centered" all the time. Who can do that? We're human. We trip over wires on the floor. We get upset when we burn dinner. We drive down the wrong road. It's okay.

The power of the Lookout isn't to make us Super-Humans who transcend all troubled states that emerge in daily life. Developing your Lookout enough to let you know when you're centered or not *is a huge step forward by itself.*

The night of the "buses only" incident, we weren't centered enough to talk about it. But *we knew from our Lookouts* that we were too upset to have a decent conversation. That recognition led us to hold off until the next morning to discuss it, including making a plan for me to learn the Dutch street signs. The night before, it was *not* funny. By morning, we could laugh about it.

CHAPTER 10

Presence: Let Your Captain Steer the Ship

No need to hurry. No need to sparkle.
No need to be anybody but oneself.
—VIRGINIA WOOLF

It was January 15, 2009, when Chesley Burnett "Sully" Sullenberger III was the pilot in command of an Airbus A320 heading from New York to North Carolina. Less than one minute after takeoff, the plane hit a large flock of birds and lost both engines. Within five minutes from takeoff, Captain Sully had safely landed the plane in the icy Hudson River. He saved the life of every person on board.

In the precious few minutes available, Captain Sully had to choose what to do under incredible pressure. Should he return to LaGuardia Airport, or try to land at Teterboro Airport in New Jersey? The captain spoke to air traffic controllers about both options in the brief time he had.

He could tell that neither one would work.

Both airports were located in densely populated areas, and he sensed the risk of catastrophe. If he missed the target, it wasn't just the passengers on board who'd lose their lives. Sully wasn't sure he could even clear the George Washington Bridge. So, in the blink of an eye, he opted to use the Hudson River as his runway. It worked.

Sullenberger exemplifies a great captain. He delivers the power combination: *skill*, *presence*, and *centeredness*.

First, years of experience gave him the technical skills to land the plane. He didn't just land it in the water. Sullenberger had the grace under fire to ditch the plane in one of the busiest stretches of the river, where the most rescue vessels were nearby. Landing somewhere else would've cost the emergency crew precious time, and possibly people's lives. Sully later told investigators he'd hoped that location would "improve chances of recovery."

Second, he demonstrated tremendous situational awareness, to use a term of art that explains presence in a helpful way. We'll come back to that in a little bit.

Third, he remained centered and steady throughout the ordeal. New York City mayor Michael Bloomberg dubbed Sully "Captain Cool" for his poise and calm during the crisis.

It was this combination—skill, presence, and centeredness—that led to the "Miracle on the Hudson."

Let's look at each of them, one at a time.

What Is Your Captain?

Where your Lookout watches *what's happening inside of you*, your Captain watches *what's going on all around you*. Taking that together with news from the Lookout, the Captain makes the calls about what to do.

Lookouts are a key member of your inner crew, observing your internal experience and passing information to your Captain. Then it's the Captain who takes the lead. Your Captain senses your situation, considers your values, and chooses an optimal route. To paraphrase Harry Truman, the buck stops with them.

To be sure, noticing what's happening inside you, *as it's happening*, is a big step forward. *It's huge.*

But it's not enough to generate lasting change in the favorite strategies you've used and honed over decades. It's the first step. But not the last.

Why?

Because seeing that you're about to walk into quicksand, while helpful, doesn't yet tell you *what to do instead.*

An email from a client of mine expresses this stage in the learning process well. He'd completed one week of a two-week leadership program, and was in the monthlong interim between the two sessions. He sent this email to the group:

> You know what's really annoying? When you are in an amygdala hijack and you know that that's what's happening and you can't stop it. You want not to yell back at your wife knowing that it's not really you, but you just can't help it. It really SUCKS! Now I have to sleep on the couch tonight knowing that it didn't have to be this way!

The good news is that he'd put his Lookout tools into practice. In the very moment of his hijack *he saw what was happening.* But as you can hear from his frustration, seeing what's going on isn't enough to change your behavior. *That's* why you need your Captain. Because Captains take that information from the Lookout— but then have the resources and skills *to do something about it.*

Captains Guide with an Inner Rudder

There's another reason why you need your Captain.

Values.

Lookouts are values-neutral. They send you a message that tells you what's happening. That's it. They observe without judgment. They pass updates along.

Your Captain, on the other hand, has a values-orientation. Captains carry a moral compass. They want to act with integrity. They pull you to express what Abraham Lincoln called "the better angels of our nature." This is a crucial dimension to your inner team when it comes to leading wisely and living well.

Operating from your center of well-being, the Captain grounds you in a bigger-picture perspective on life. It's your Captain who whispers in your ear, "Just a minute, buddy. What are you about to do?" before you take a convenient but questionable shortcut.

Every once in a while, something enters the culture that reminds us about the deeper wisdom we hold. For a while it was *The Last Lecture*, given by Carnegie Mellon professor Randy Pausch when he had terminal cancer. Before that it was a moving exchange between newspaper columnist Mitch Albom and his former professor, Morrie Schwartz. In *Tuesdays with Morrie*, Albom captured the conversations they had about love and life while his professor lay dying. In both cases, there was a widely felt sense that these men had expressed simple yet fundamental truths.

I sometimes wonder, do we need to reach our deathbeds before we wake up to what really matters to us? Can't we start now, with whatever health we have, to love, live, and lead from the profound insights we already know? Do we need a terminal diagnosis to focus our lives around basic wisdom and simple truths?

All of us lose touch with our values from time to time. We fall short. We miss the mark. That's normal. The question is whether we're engaging actively with these questions, or we're too busy day to day to think about "big topics" like our character and ethics. Connecting with your Captain can help.

In the Jewish tradition I grew up in, the entire community, everywhere around the world, gathers for twenty-four hours on the same day every year to acknowledge all the ways we didn't meet our own standards in the past year. On this day, we fast together, and we commit together to do better next year. The fact that this tradition is *annual* means our ancestors understood that we're all trying, yet not always succeeding. The Captain is the part of us who's trying to align how we live with who we hope to be when we stand there next year, evaluating how we're doing.

Losing contact with our Captain clearly causes problems in our personal lives. The stakes get even higher when we lead other people. Business strategist Gary Hamel talks about this in his book *What Matters Now*:

> If you are a leader in any organization, you are a steward— of careers, capabilities, resources, the environment, and organizational values. . . . If you're a manager or an executive, your stewardship obligations extend far beyond yourself and your family. Yet in recent years many business leaders have blithely dodged those responsibilities. . . . So ask yourself . . . am I really a *steward*?

In the terms of Winning from Within, you might ask yourself, *Who is steering my ship?*

Or in more general terms: *Who is leading my life?*

Is it my Thinker? My Warrior? My Lover? My Dreamer? A combination of two of these? Or *is my Captain steering the ship*? When *that* happens, you carry the Big Four along as helpful passengers. And everything works a lot better.

Only your Captain has the worldview of a steward. And that's reason enough to let your Captain steer your ship.

The Role of *Your* Captain

To close your Performance Gap and generate lasting change, you need to empower your Captain to steer your ship.

How does that work? What does the Captain do?

With the right mandate from you, your Captain will choose the best course of action in your current situation. In addition to your level of skill and what they believe you can do well, they'll make that call based on three things:

1. Receiving and filtering messages from your Lookout
2. Using their presence to sense your environment
3. Drawing on the values and wisdom in your center

In the last chapter, we'll complete the inner team by exploring the Voyager. For now, let's understand the Captain's role and how to deploy your Captain to get optimal results.

Let Your Captain Make the Calls

Each one of the Big Four will always speak for itself. It will always see the world through its specific lens, and its actions are constrained by the skills it has. If it acts alone, for instance, a Warrior isn't going to express compassion, just as a Dreamer isn't working hard to set firm boundaries. Each of the Big Four has a unique function, strength, and skill set. As we looked at in Part Two, you gain access to the strength and skill set of each inner negotiator as you gain capability with it.

Your *Captain* is unique in the potential to call on *any* of the Big Four. Because of that, Captains can draw on *all of their strengths* and *use all of their skills*. This is how you move from your current reactions to your optimal ones, to closing your Performance Gap. It's also a way you become the leader of your own life. As Pythagoras said, "No one is free who has not obtained the empire of himself. No man is free who cannot command himself."

Letting your Captain direct your actions is a big shift for most people in how they operate. First you need to develop all four inner negotiators, so they're active when the Captain needs them. Then you can learn to let your Captain "steer the ship." Like choosing whether to lower the sails or travel onward, your Captain makes the calls so you can unlock the full range of skills and get the best possible results.

As you sail along the river of life *now*, you likely experience one or two of your Big Four acting in the role of Captain. They call the shots. They consider your options and they decide what you'll say and do. If you want consistent high performance and lasting change, one of the best things you can do for yourself is **put the Big Four in the passenger seats** and **let your Captain steer the ship**. This is how the Captain becomes a Transformer in your leadership and your life.

Captains Take In the Full View

I've only recently started to experience life on a boat, since I got married last year. My husband is a lifelong sailor, so I'm taking a crash course in pulling ropes and raising the sails while on a moving vehicle that splashes water in your face. As a first-timer, my concerns tend to focus on me. Am I too cold? Am I wet? Am I going to be sick? From time to time my thoughts turn to the same ones I had at six years old in the backseat of my father's station wagon: *Are we there yet?*

My husband has other concerns. He's the captain of our little crew, which includes me as First Mate, and the Little Dude as support Helmsman. The Little Dude and I can do small things here and there, but it's our Captain who says what happens. Will we stay the course? Change direction? Lower the sails and call it a day? There are good reasons for the Captain to make those calls, too. Because like the Big Four, each of us as a passenger has our own agenda to advance.

If you ask me what we should do, I'll suggest we find the nearest harbor where we can dock the boat. Then we can take a nice walk, get some lunch, maybe sunbathe on dry land. I might forget to ask if anyone else is hungry. And I might overlook that I'm sunburned already.

Ask the Little Dude and he'll say find the closest beach to search for crawling creatures beneath the sand and shallow water. He won't consider the timing of low tide. He won't realize that if we stop now to look for crabs we'll get stuck overnight and never get to the harbor.

Only our Captain takes the full overview of our situation.

He'll consider the preferences and needs of his passengers, yes. But he'll also check the timing of the tides. He'll assess the strength and direction of the wind. He'll also bear in mind a bigger picture, beyond the immediate interests of the Little Dude and me. He knows we want off the boat for our own reasons. But he holds a higher vision for the long-term good of our family. To be able to take boating adventures over the years, the Little Dude needs to learn how the sails work. I need time to find my sea legs. The Captain chooses what to do from a centered perspective, one that knits all the fragments together.

Like the Little Dude and me, your inner Dreamer, Thinker, Lover, and Warrior each has its own wants and needs. They see the world differently. They value different things. That's normal and healthy. For you to succeed in leadership and life, you want to put your inner Captain in charge of directing these "passengers" because the Captain considers all of their interests simultaneously. The Captain also sees a wider picture beyond the preferences that any one of the Big Four can appreciate within their own world.

The Captain in Action

Getting where you want to go is the most basic reward of closing your Performance Gap. That starts with developing your capacity in each of the Big Four. As we explored throughout Part Two, you need access to the strengths of each inner negotiator in order to call them out at the right time and for the right purpose. That's why we started by looking at each of the Big Four, one at a time. All things being equal, you want to activate all of them. Then you can learn how to balance your profile across all four.

Once you *can* use any of the Big Four, how can you choose *which to use* at any given time?

That's the job of your inner Captain.

Part of "getting out of your own way" means that you stop letting one or two of your Big Four lead every conversation, meeting, or negotiation that you have. Once you have access to all four, you empower your inner Captain to choose which voices to bring out and when.

Leading wisely and living well involves the full range of your inner resources. It also requires your ability to deploy the inner negotiator best designed to hit your target in any given situation. That's your Captain's job. Your Captain determines your optimal reaction in any given moment, and directs you to implement it as best you can.

Justice Elena Kagan is the best example of someone I've met who lets her Captain lead. I heard her speak at a celebration of alumnae of Harvard Law School when she was the dean. A large audience of impressive women fired questions and criticisms at then-Dean Kagan. She demonstrated an amazing agility to hear each person's concern and respond in a tailored way to each of them.

She spoke the analytical brilliance of the Thinker to a very heady question on a recent legal decision. That was immediately followed by the warmth and relatedness of the Lover in response to an alienated alumna who felt her specific minority group was being ignored by the school. She inspired the audience with her ambitions for the next generation of Harvard Law students, and from that Dreamer's vision she moved into action, describing a multimillion-dollar capital campaign and using the "can-do" orientation of the Warrior to get the crowd to open their check-books.

As law school dean, Kagan showed an uncanny ability to move from one negotiator within to another in a flash, and to express each one with elegance. This is precisely what the Captain can do when we pass her the baton. Just as the chair of the board can be tasked with making sure the CEO, CFO, VP of HR, and COO work together to produce results, the Captain aligns the inner Dreamer, Thinker, Lover, and Warrior. The Captain operates at the center of them all.

Your Captain can bring in each inner negotiator at the right time and for the right purpose. Captains call on the Dreamer to paint the vision of what you want; the Thinker to provide insight into a different perspective; the Lover to share how you feel; or the Warrior to protect your values.

Only the Captain Can Use All Four

Here's an example from a participant of mine who also let his Captain lead.

Marcos worked in a government office near The Hague. He was reassigned to a new post in his agency. Marcos told our seminar group that he would now report to Lars, and that Lars had been his peer before the reorganization.

Before the dialogue below happened, Marcos had run into a few colleagues in the hall. They'd agreed to meet for coffee to brainstorm about his new role. Lars heard about the meeting and told the colleagues to cancel it. He then sent Marcos an email to direct him to cancel the meeting. Lars insisted that Marcos meet with him first, before speaking to anyone else.

This is how Marcos described what happened next.

DESCRIPTION:

I received an email from Lars telling me he'd canceled the meeting. This caused an immediate peak of adrenaline in my veins. I started to type a reply to Lars, but halfway concluded this might not be such a good idea (knowing how easily emotionally charged email escalates). I decided to step into Lars' office, three doors down the hall.

Before we get to the dialogue, we can already see that Marcos' Lookout is on the job. He notices the adrenaline rushing through his body, and feels himself getting rattled. With this information, his Captain makes a centered choice not to send a reply by email, but instead to talk with Lars face-to-face. This is how the Transformers can influence a conversation before it even starts. Not because this will go perfectly in person. It won't. Yet talking in person will improve the conversation relative to the email exchange they would have had otherwise.

Here is the dialogue that Marcos submitted, with my comments in italics in the brackets.

MARCOS: Lars, can I talk to you for a moment?

LARS: Well, I am very busy, have very little time, but, okay, let's take a few minutes.

MARCOS: I read your email. I'm very upset about it [*allowing his Lover to say how he feels*]. This is not the way I want to work with you [*his Dreamer, commenting on his vision for the kind of working relationship he wants to have with Lars*]. Next to that I don't see any reason to cancel the meeting this afternoon [*his Thinker, saying that the decision doesn't make sense to him*].

LARS: I didn't mean to upset you, but there is a lot of commotion about your reassignment to my team. We should talk about it before you start discussions with other people. Once I've talked to you, you'll realize that yourself. And, further,

I think it's normal that you should discuss these things with your boss first.

MARCOS: Well, Lars, this isn't the kind of relationship I want to build with you [*the Dreamer, again raising his vision for their relationship*]. We've known each other a long time, and we respect each other. If you're worried about something I'm doing, you can ask me to bear a few things in mind, and then trust me to handle it appropriately [*the Lover, appealing to the history of their relationship, trust, and respect*]. The meeting this afternoon is no more than an inquiry. I don't intend to take any positions at all [*his Thinker, providing information*].

LARS: Really, this is a minefield. I'm doing this also to protect you. I think it's far better to write down on paper first what you're going to do. Then you and I can discuss your memo, and after that, we'll discuss it with other members of the team. Then it will be clear to everyone what exactly you're going to do.

MARCOS: I can't write it down, because I don't even know myself. That's what the inquiry discussion is for. That's the way I've worked for years [*his Warrior, speaking his truth and holding his ground*].

LARS: [lots of talking] . . . and as your boss, I urge you not to hold this meeting this afternoon and discuss this with me first on Friday.

MARCOS: I'm not able to promise you that. I need to think it over [*his Warrior, while not becoming aggressive, still holding his ground*]. On Friday let's talk further.

LARS:	I'm your boss. Trust me, after we've talked you'll understand.
MARCOS:	See you on Friday.
LARS:	See you on Friday.

As you see in these examples, your Captain needs access to all of the Big Four in order to steer your ship effectively and close your Performance Gap. A mature Captain like now–Supreme Court Justice Kagan has the flexibility to call on any of the Big Four at the right time. She isn't attached to making a certain impression: as the consummate legal scholar, or the kinder-and-gentler face of the law school. She's embraced her Big Four. So she can use any of them to steer toward her current destination.

Marcos also appreciates the different roles the Big Four can play when his Captain leads the way. He moves smoothly and easily among the Big Four in a single conversation, from one sentence to the next. Because he's embraced all of them, Marcos' Captain can draw on any of the Big Four, even in a heated and high-stakes situation.

Both Justice Kagan and Marcos offer examples of what Captains are capable of, when they're able to call on *each of the Big Four* in a given situation. To be clear, that *doesn't* mean that in *every* conversation, you *need* to bring out *each* of the inner negotiators. It depends on the situation. Captains tune in, and from all four options, call on the inner negotiator—or negotiators—that seem most useful in taking you where you want to go.

Captains Receive *and* Filter Instant Messages

Think for a minute of the famous ship *Titanic*. The captain relied on his lookout to flag potential dangers, including icebergs. But the lookout didn't report the huge blocks of ice in the water. By the time the captain found out, it was too late for him to save the ship and most of the passengers. Clearly, on the *Titanic*, the teamwork between the lookout and the captain didn't work.

When that relationship *does* work, though, the lookout and the captain are effective partners. The lookout tells the captain what's going on, and the captain uses that information plus their own assessment to determine how to steer the boat.

This is how it works with your Transformers. Your Lookout has a specific target of observation: what's happening with the Big Four inside of you. The Lookout pays attention to what you're thinking about, how you're feeling, what you want, and what you're drawn to do. As you know, Lookouts send an "instant message" to the Captain when they have something meaningful to report.

The Captain takes those messages from the Lookout. However, the Captain will then **assess the context** of what's happening around you. Where the ship captain considers the tides and the wind, *your* Captain listens to the tone of conversation in a meeting, and takes *that* into account to determine if this is an appropriate time for you to speak up.

Let's say your Lookout sends an IM to your Captain. The Lookout notices you're upset, and your Warrior wants to speak up. The Captain gets that information, and then asks some quick questions about your context. Things like:

- Is it wise to confront your friend about his drinking in front of other people?
- Are your colleagues *also* telling personal stories, or will this be "too much information"?

- Are you about to accept blame for something that wasn't your fault?
- Who's the right person on the team to discuss late payments with your client?
- What's the best way to talk to your husband about canceling date night again?
- How can you raise this discussion within the cultural norms of the country you're visiting?
- Before you say anything else, shouldn't you offer an apology?

This is the Captain's domain. To figure out what's best for you, given what's happening inside of you, **and** what's happening all around you. It's a critical role that the Captain plays, to keep you from getting in your own way. Otherwise, the Lookout would report an urge you feel and the Captain would just implement it, *without discernment.* That's not a good idea.

Let's say your Lover feels enthralled over dinner. Your Lookout notices and reports it to your Captain, so you say, "I'm falling in love with you." That *could* be okay in some situations. But given that you're on a first date, not so much.

Or your colleague shows you a draft of the presentation you're giving together. Your Thinker finds the draft pathetic. So your Lookout tells your Captain that you're highly unimpressed. Unless your Captain takes that Lookout's report and *applies his own judgment*, you're going to tell your colleague that "your work stinks." This is not the way to go.

Instead, your Captain takes the observations of your Lookout, and then asks a few questions before taking action. Table 10.1 lists three categories of good Captain subjects, and some sample questions to keep in your back pocket.

Goals and Strategies	Context	Your Inner State
What's my purpose? What's the best outcome? Is this a step in that direction?	Is this a good time for this conversation?	Is the inner negotiator who wants to speak in a centered mode, or should I wait until later?
Am I talking to the right person? Is there a different stakeholder or decision-maker in the hierarchy whom I should speak with first?	Is this the right place?	Does the inner negotiator who wants to speak have the skill to do this well? Do I need a bit of coaching to succeed in this conversation?
Am I moving too quickly?	Should I raise this at all?	Am I using my Big Four's favorite strategies? Is that the best choice right now?
What coalitions can I build to help me achieve my goals? Who might have influence on the person I need to say yes?	Does making this comment here and now account for the politics in the organization?	Am I outside my comfort zone, given my profile? Can I use this as a chance to balance my profile?
Who in my network would be helpful in this task? Is there anyone outside my network that I could bring into my network?	Do I have a mandate to raise this in this group?	What impact am I having already?

TABLE 10.1

Filtering Is How Captains Watch for Safety

Filtering messages from your Lookout is one way your Captain monitors safety. On a boat, the captain makes sure you're wearing your life jacket. Safety requires moving carefully around the ship. Moving slowly. Moving thoughtfully.

The Captain in you keeps watch on safety, too. That means watching over your context, and working to prevent you from hurting yourself. Or from hurting your relationships, your job, your health, or your reputation. The Captain has your back.

Remember what we said at the end of every chapter in Part Two: *none of the Big Four should "go it alone."* Your Captain pays attention to this balance, recognizing that your Big Four will always pull you toward their respective favorite strategies.

When you decide to let your Warrior speak after a long time of keeping quiet, your Captain will aim to bring your Lover along. That way you can speak your truth while not dropping bombs in your relationships. Likewise, Captains don't want you to leave your Dreamer or Thinker at home while the other one speaks their mind. They want you to say what you want *and* consider the consequences as well.

In the spirit of former U.S. surgeon general C. Everett Koop, here is a safety label:

> SAFETY WARNING: *Let your Captain temper your message, your actual words, your tone, and your timing.*

Here are some examples of what you *could* be tempted to say, absent your Captain's eye on safety and purposeful decision-making.

- "I quit!"
- "It's over!"
- "I know I said that, but I never actually believed it."
- "I do *everything* around here, and you do *nothing*!"
- "Why can't you see that no one thinks you're going to make partner in this firm?"
- "Do you really *need* those French fries? Haven't you eaten enough?"
- "I told you so."
- "You're fired."
- "Take it or leave it."
- "I know a *fabulous* painter who could make this room look *so much better.*"
- "She's not good enough for you."
- "Why do *you* get to be the 'nice parent' and *I'm* always the 'mean' one?"
- "What made you think you *would* succeed at cooking school?"

Here's the bottom line: *Wear your life jacket.* Yes, it's good to express yourself. No, it's not good to do that mindlessly. Move thoughtfully. And let your Captain lead the way.

Safety is particularly crucial in three situations:

1. **Affiliation.** The relationship involved is *very* important to you. You don't want to say things you can't take back later.
2. **Office Politics.** You're not talking to peers, but to people with higher rank professionally. Saying the wrong thing to a superior (or saying the right thing poorly) can hurt your reputation or cost you a job.

3. **Literal Safety Risk.** Your actual security or well-being is at stake. Saying the wrong thing in some cases (or saying the right thing without proper preparation) can put you at risk—emotionally, financially, physically, or spiritually. If you're in circumstances like this, *please don't improvise.* Prepare, and consider consulting professionals. They can help you design a safe and wise course of action for you and everyone involved.

Captains Lead with Presence

Let's come back to the nautical metaphor. On a ship, the captain takes a panoramic view of a situation, considering the tides, the wind, and other boats in the sea. Likewise, the Captain *in you* steps back from the action to sense what's going on *around you* before deciding what to do. As your Lookout watches what *you're* thinking and feeling, your Captain *picks up cues from your environment.*

What does it mean to "pick up cues"?

Have you ever been to a sports event at a big stadium, and felt there's "excitement in the air"? Have you ever given a talk, a presentation, or a seminar, and sensed you need to shift gears, because you were losing your audience?

Some people explain this ability to sense what's happening by saying, "Well, yes, you changed gears in your speech, because you saw people checking their email, or looking at their watches. So you could tell they were bored." I think that's too easy. This doesn't result only from super-fast data processing by your Thinker.

In moments like those above, you're exercising one of your Captain's unique traits: *presence.* That means you're tuning in to the environment around you, and making some sense of it. You probably use presence to tune in to what's happening around you more often than you realize.

Consider times in a relationship when *you* were the one pressing an important conversation. Times you wanted to talk about things like these:

- I think you need to get that spot on your back tested.
- You need to work harder to find a job.
- We need to start planning for our retirement.
- You want us to be vegan, but you're still eating steak?
- We can't afford to keep supporting your brother like this.
- I'm worried our sex life has fallen apart.
- Our son might need a special needs school.
- We need to tell our families we are *not* just "room-mates."
- *Please* tell our daughter that she *cannot* treat me this way.
- I'd like us to explore our spiritual lives—*together.*
- I don't want any more kids.
- I think you're having an affair.

In delicate situations like these, you're careful about the way you move things forward. You watch for little signs that it's still okay, that you haven't pushed things too far. You work hard to sense when you're getting close to that line, when your partner's going to snap. If you cross it, they won't see the doctor anytime soon. You might never come out to your families. Or go together to a yoga class. Worse still, they'll make you promise not to bring it up again. Then you feel *more* stuck than you did before.

What's the Captain's role here?

You know your Big Four will do the talking. One of your inner negotiators will step up to say what you want to say. Your Lover might take the lead when you talk about not wanting more kids. You know this is a letdown to your partner. Your Warrior might come forward to insist that after all these months, you *need* your other half to start earning some money. Even if their "dream job" isn't available, you can't support your household by yourself.

While all that's going on among your Big Four, *it's your Captain's sense of how things are going* that lets you know how to behave from one minute to the next. Is your partner opening his mind, or getting defensive? Is she listening, or pushing you away? You use your Captain's presence to pick up on what's happening around you, in your environment, and with the people who matter to you.

All of those cues steer you away from your Performance Gap and toward a more optimal set of reactions. When you're *present* in a conversation, you're paying close attention to the other people, not just to yourself. Your responses reflect what you're learning from them right now, not just what *you expected them to say* when you prepared the night before. Drawing on your Captain's way of tuning in and connecting—your presence—turns what could be a two-sided debate into one conversation where everyone's on the same side.

Understanding Presence

Presence is a commonly used word but few people understand what it means. We use it in different ways, like when we confront someone we love and ask, "Are you listening? I'm talking to you, but I feel like you're not *present*." Or we treat presence like charisma, describing a person as having "a strong presence." But what are we really saying?

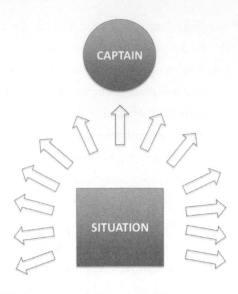

FIGURE 10.1

I advise people who get feedback about working on their presence. It's often paired with coaching to develop their "authenticity" as a leader. More often than not, the first question these people have for me is "What are they talking about?" Presence is now considered important to leading and living well, but mostly we don't know how to explain it.

Here's a way to understand presence, and to illustrate the power of the inner Captain. Presence is a way of paying attention, one that involves absorbing all kinds of information from all around you. It's what people in law enforcement, counterterrorism, and air traffic control call "situational awareness." This is an excellent way for the rest of us to understand "presence" (see Figure 10.1).

As synthesized by researcher Mica Endsley, situational awareness drills down to three things: you notice what's going on around you; you immediately appreciate the significance of it; and you can predict what's needed in the short-term future. This capability is very helpful, for example, if you're in a high-speed chase in pursuit of a getaway car after a robbery. You have unclear information. Moving parts. Variables changing every minute. No time to think. And high-stakes decisions to make.

You also need to get ahead of the criminal in order to catch him. You can't just follow him. Yes, you need to know exactly what's happening right now. But you also need to anticipate his next move, to cut him off at the pass. *You need to sense this moment fully, in order to sense the future.* What will happen next?

Answering that question isn't accomplished through a cognitive exercise of prediction or diagnosis. You have no time for that. Situational awareness is a way to understand a dynamic set of events as they emerge. Think of Captain Sully. Thankfully for the passengers of US Airways flight 1549, Sully had this capacity in spades. People in the aviation industry said after the incident that they didn't think it was a "miracle." They saw a great example of presence, or situational awareness, in action.

This capability makes all the difference in dynamic situations, like the one Captain Sully found himself in—suddenly flying a plane with no working engines. It's a huge asset in police work. Whether you're investigating a crime, pulling over a driver for a traffic violation, or acting as an emergency first-responder, you need all of your radar collecting information so you can connect the dots.

But situational awareness involves much more than collecting or managing complex information. Those activities can be performed by your Thinker. This is a form of *presence* that I can best explain by sharing two examples, one personal, the other professional.

My husband Bernardus has a remarkable connection to his center of well-being. And not just because he goes from the sauna to the freezing-cold pool. It's because he can call on his inner Captain as needed. He is steady, calm in the midst of chaos, and a grounding force to people around him any day of the week. He makes great use of presence, one of the Captain's special traits.

The woman he married—me—can sometimes seem like a "take-no-prisoners" international leadership expert who teaches at Harvard Law School. The woman who moved in with him as his wife, on the other hand, can sometimes come across a bit differently, as revealed when I yelled *at him* because my earrings were in Amsterdam the night before I was to meet President Obama.

And then, as you know, I struggled with the washing machine, the coffeemaker, the oven, and the claustrophobic boat. I nearly totaled his car. I haven't been the easiest new roommate.

In a particularly low moment after my relocation to Amsterdam, I discovered a phenomenon known as "trailing spouse syndrome." That's a name for the discontent you feel when you move to a new country to join your partner. It's common when one partner serves in the military or as a diplomat, is an academic, or works in the private sector in a global company. When they get assigned abroad, their spouse uproots their entire life to "trail" their beloved.

You only need three minutes on the Internet to get the lowdown on this: commentary about the misery of trailing spouses abounds. I told Bernardus about my discovery, and my concern that I might share an unhappy destiny with these despondent trailing spouses. That night he went out for a while and came back with a goldfish for me. "I thought you needed a friend," he said.

I loved that little fish. I named him Larry, because the name sounded so American to me, and that meant I wasn't the only American I knew there.

When the Little Dude met Larry, we had a momentary setback. Upon laying eyes on Larry, he squealed with joy, shouting his own name for the fish: "Nemo!" I wanted to be a grown-up, but I'd already become attached. "Actually his name is Larry," I said. There was a pregnant pause. I could see Bernardus' face, torn between the love of his child and the need of his wife. And then, from the mouth of babes, came an excellent suggestion.

"What if his *first* name is Nemo and his *last* name is Larry?" the Little Dude proposed. "Then we can call him Nemo Larry." And so we did.

Nemo Larry was my first friend in The Netherlands.

Presence Is About Now, *and* About What's Needed *Next*

Bernardus' gesture was sweet—but it was more than sweet. It was intuitive and wise. He'd listened, felt into the situation, and sensed what might help. If we'd sat down to brainstorm, in a million years I wouldn't have put "get me a goldfish" on the list of things that might cheer me up. When in fact, it hit the spot perfectly.

Presence is important not only because it tells you what's going on around you. It's vital because it clues you in to **what you can do next**. It tells you what steps you can take that will make the situation better, whether at home or at work.

Failure to develop presence has measurable business consequences. I saw this firsthand when I did a short project for a client called Gavin. He'd asked me to run a diagnostic process with one of his teams, because their business unit was not meeting targets. After I did the assessment, I gave Gavin my strong conclusion that the leadership team was in trouble.

"Oh, no—that's not the problem," Gavin told me. "The team is in great shape. I think their line managers have a bad attitude and low accountability."

I repeated my clear sense that the primary issue was broken trust. A near-complete breakdown of communication within the leadership team had become toxic for the whole business unit. I recommended that Gavin convene a meeting right away to facilitate a dialogue with these leaders and clear the air. But he refused. Gavin didn't perceive any issue with the leaders at all.

Gavin's inability to tune in had significant fallout. In due course, one member of that team transferred into another business unit, one exited the company, and the third was left holding the bag without a clue how to lead by himself. Many other people had felt the tension among the leadership team. Indeed, few were surprised when the group fell apart. Except for Gavin. Since he wasn't present to the real issues in the first place, the dissolution of the team took him by complete surprise. The unit's performance continued its downward trend.

This situation could've turned around with the right intervention done in a timely way. But that would have required Gavin to have the quality of presence to sense the real issue, or at least to pick up that he didn't know what was really causing the trouble. Despite going to the effort to hire an outside consultant, Gavin couldn't take in what was happening. Not even enough to take a leap of faith and bring the team together to talk.

Captains Lead with Values, Wisdom, and Character

Your Captain supports you from a core of personal strength. With resolve. Grit. Trust. Recall the Chilean miners trapped underground in a collapsed mine for sixty-nine days. The shift supervisor, Luis Urzúa, organized the miners into a functioning, democratic community. He led from his center of well-being, keeping the men alive physically, mentally, emotionally, and spiritually, under life-threatening circumstances. Against all odds, every one of them survived.

Your Captain's fortitude can see you through adversity. Remember Christopher Reeve and his wife, Dana Reeve. He became famous playing the hero Superman in the movies. But then he fell off a horse, tragically incurring a spinal cord injury that paralyzed him from the neck down.

After the accident it wasn't clear if he would ever move again. In such a situation, it's easy to imagine someone giving up. But the Reeves found a reservoir of resilience, hope, and love, in themselves and in each other. Despite life-altering events, they stayed in touch with their centers of well-being.

Christopher Reeve went on to become the most vocal and impactful American advocate for research on spinal-cord injuries, before or since. He and his wife created the Christopher and Dana Reeve Foundation, devoting their lives to speeding up research and improving the quality of life for people living with paralysis. The Reeves pulled on their inner resources to take a devastating injury and create new lives imbued with meaning.

When you're anchored in your center, you follow the call to do what's right, even at serious risk to yourself. The civil rights movement in the American South gives countless examples of such individual actions taken in the service of creating an equitable and open society.

One of the well-known stories from that time is about Rosa Parks. She famously got arrested for violating the Alabama segregation law when she refused to give up her seat in the "white section" of the bus. Parks kicked off the long-planned Montgomery bus boycott. Howell Raines writes about the events of that time in his book *My Soul Is Rested*. He recounts a memory of Martin Luther King, Jr., who was talking with an elderly woman. She was participating in the boycott of segregated buses, and Dr. King thought she needed a break. This is the story that Raines shares:

Martin asked this old lady, he said, "Now, listen . . . you have been with us all along, so now you go on and start back to ridin' the bus, 'cause you are too old to keep walking."

She said, "Oh, no." She said, "Oh, no." Said, "I'm gonna walk just as long as everybody else walks. I'm gonna walk till its over."

So he said, "But aren't your feet tired?"

She said, "Yes, my feets is tired, but my soul is rested."

To me this woman embodies living from your center. She got up each morning with a clear sense of purpose. She wanted to play her part. Despite what must have been physical challenges, she rose to the occasion. Like Christopher and Dana Reeve, she illustrated what Joseph Campbell taught when he said, "People are not necessarily looking for the meaning of life. Rather they're looking for a meaningful life."

Through your Captain, you tap into something bigger than yourself. That enables you to take honorable action for the common good. Think of Presidents George H. W. Bush and Bill Clinton. Formerly political adversaries, these men have looked beyond their differences for higher causes. Together they've marshaled amazing resources in times of crisis, like helping in Haiti after the devastating earthquake in January 2010. They also role-model how to separate political agendas from personal relationships by publicly remarking on what good friends they've become.

Where your Big Four focus on you, your Captain's circle of concern extends beyond your own life, pulling you to look where the need is great and you have something to offer. You see the Captain's power in Muhammad Yunus, an economist who witnessed rampant poverty among the rural poor in Bangladesh. Conventional banking wisdom said clearly that his target clientele was not creditworthy. Yet Yunus and his Grameen Bank found ways to provide "microcredit" and other banking services to the poorest of the poor. His immensely successful models have spread to dozens of other countries.

Yunus' influence was profound not only because he delivered resources to people who needed them, but also because his actions demonstrate a set of values. Yunus regards all human beings as worthy of dignity and respect, as well as capable of discipline, hard work, and accountability. He sees all people, including those who are poor, illiterate, and unemployed, as full of potential just waiting to get unleashed. For him these aren't lofty beliefs, but strong motivators to get engaged and to provide leadership.

Living from your center isn't reserved for elected officials or Nobel Prize winners. It's the pull any of us can feel to make something right, though admittedly our heroic nature often shows itself in the face of extraordinary need.

Remember the young Japanese workers who braved radioactivity to protect their fellow citizens. In 2011, following a lethal earthquake and a tsunami, Japan faced a nuclear meltdown at the Fukushima Daiichi Nuclear Power Plant. It was the worst nuclear disaster since Chernobyl. An article in the *Scientific American* reported on a maintenance worker in his twenties who volunteered to enter the plant to help control the situation. He did this knowing that his action would jeopardize his health, his future, and his life.

> He knew the air was poisoned and expected the choice would keep him from ever marrying or having children for fear of burdening them with health consequences. Yet he still walked back through Fukushima's gates into the plant's radiation-infused air and got to work—for no more compensation than his usual modest wages. . . . "There are only some of us who can do this job," said the worker, who wished to remain anonymous. "I'm single and young, and I feel it's my duty to help settle this problem."

Mary Fisher shows us another example of a regular person following the lead of her inner compass to do the right thing. She wasn't famous. She was a private citizen who lived in Florida with her husband and two young sons. She became a public figure only when she felt called to step forward to serve the public good.

Three years into their marriage, in 1990, Fisher's husband asked for a divorce. A year later, he revealed that he was HIV positive. Tragically, it turned out that Mary was HIV positive, too. Her disease ran counter to the widely held perceptions at the time about who was—or wasn't—at risk for exposure to the deadly virus. Mary contracted HIV as a white, married, heterosexual, politically conservative, financially secure, monogamous woman. Given the stereotypes, she felt a duty to teach people about the reality of the disease.

In August 1992, Mary Fisher stood before the Republican National Convention in Houston to deliver what has been called "one of the best American speeches of the twentieth century." Anchored in her center, she felt connected to a purpose that reached far beyond herself. Fisher told her private, intimate story on national television, in a convention center filled with thousands of people.

> Tonight, I represent an AIDS community whose members have been reluctantly drafted from every segment of American society. Though I am white and a mother, I am one with a black infant struggling with tubes in a Philadelphia hospital. Though I am female and contracted this disease in marriage, and enjoy the warm support of my family, I am one with the lonely gay man sheltering a flickering candle from the cold wind of his family's rejection. My call to the nation is a plea for awareness. If you believe you are safe, you are in danger. Because I was not hemophiliac, I was not at risk. Because I was not gay, I was not at risk. Because I did not inject drugs, I was not at risk. To the millions of you who are grieving, who are frightened, who have suffered the ravages of AIDS firsthand: Have courage and you will find comfort. To the millions who are strong, I issue this plea: Set aside prejudice and politics to make room for compassion and sound policy.

> To all within the sound of my voice, I appeal: Learn with me the lessons of history and of grace, so my children will not be afraid to say the word AIDS when I am gone. Then their children, and yours, may not need to whisper it at all.

Mary Fisher was an ordinary if wealthy citizen whose Captain led her to play an unexpected role in public health education.

Your inner Captain guides you to rise to the occasion and act from a sense of common cause. Like Navy SEAL Chris Kyle, who dedicated himself to ailing veterans after a decade of service in the military. In a wrenching twist of fate, Kyle lost his life on one of the outings he led to help troubled vets. Despite his pre-mature passing, friends noted in a *Time* magazine article that he'd found his calling as a healer. "Chris died doing what filled his heart with passion—serving soldiers struggling with the fight to overcome PTSD [post-traumatic stress disorder]." Inner Captains aren't reserved for a small group of noble people. They exist in every one of us.

Each of you has your own moral compass. Some of you are bound to codes of honor under professional mandate. Doctors take the Hippocratic Oath, vowing first and foremost to "do no harm." Teachers and health professionals are required to report suspicions of abuse, even when it violates confidentiality, to protect children from getting seriously hurt. Board members and business partners are bound by "fiduciary duty." Food handlers are bound by rules of health and safety. Businesses are bound to comply with "truth in advertising." Yet all of us share a fundamental code of decency toward each other. Our Captains remind us of this if we're at risk of temporarily forgetting.

You could say, "But my inner Captain isn't a certified professional." Yes, that's true. But every day citizens have basic responsibilities to one another. We owe each other a duty of mutual care, not only when the law requires it, but also because our inner Captains know it's the right thing to do.

When you and I get caught up in our Big Four, we care so much about ourselves that we can lose perspective on everything else. Yesterday I took a flight from Albuquerque, New Mexico, to Los Angeles, California. Before I got to my gate, I stood in line to send my shoes and laptop through the metal detector. A couple stood behind me, and in front of me was a man with physical disabilities who was putting his things into the plastic bins. Because of his physical challenges, he was moving slowly, which was apparent to those of us waiting in line. All of a sudden, the couple lurched from behind me, cut in front of the man, and slammed their belongings into plastic bins in front of his. With audible irritation, they stomped through the body scanner before he and I walked through it.

As luck would have it, we were all on the same flight, and we all waited for the same twenty minutes at the gate before we boarded the same plane. Guess what? We all arrived in Los Angeles at the same time, too. Was it worth the scene that likely embarrassed him to get to the gate three minutes earlier?

In our busy lives, we're all prone to focusing narrowly on what we want. At the same time, we also have an inner Captain who *doesn't* lose sight of the world around us. In ways big and small, we can draw on our Captain's principles and sense of fellowship to keep an eye on broader needs and the common good.

When I teach leadership development workshops, I often ask groups to call out names of "great leaders." It takes fewer than thirty seconds before someone shouts, "Nelson Mandela." Why? It's that power combination again: skills, presence, and centeredness. Mandela was imprisoned for twenty-seven years by the South African government. Yet on the day he was released from his small cell on Robben Island, he gave a speech asking for unity and forgiveness. "We call on our white compatriots to join us in the shaping of a new South Africa," he said. Four years later, on May 10, 1994, Mandela gave another speech in which he called for reconciliation. This was his inaugural address as the first president of a fully democratic South Africa.

In both of these historic public appearances, Mandela let his Captain lead, orchestrating and directing the Big Four inside him. He demonstrated the *Dreamer's* vision for a united South Africa, a *Thinker's* view of the long-term difficulties of brokering a new peace, a *Lover's* feel for the pulse of a troubled nation, and a *Warrior's* laserlike focus on purposeful action. His Captain attuned him to the extraordinary delicacy of leading a fledgling nation toward a new kind of freedom. Mandela demonstrated the Captain's presence to tap into what's going on around him and discern what's needed. When I ask people why they pick Mandela, they also quickly comment on his character. They use different words, but nearly every group points to "who he was," his "humanity," his "dignity," or what they sometimes call his "philosophy." Time and again what I hear is that *it wasn't what he did* that sets him apart. It's something hard to name about *his character.* Mandela's story reminds us that letting your Captain lead involves more than mastering skills. It's a willingness to connect with something bigger than yourself—and then do what's best for the highest good of all concerned.

Mandela was a steward. Your Captain is, too.

CHAPTER 11

Path: Grow with Your Voyager

Not all those who wander are lost.

—J. R. R. Tolkien, *The Lord of the Rings*

In November 1975, William Henry "Bill" Gates took a leave of absence from Harvard College to start his own computer company. This made him both a college dropout and something of a maverick. Over the next few decades, Bill Gates seemed to evolve, as a person and as a leader, in front of our eyes.

He started out as a tech wizard. His Thinker could crack technical problems others didn't understand. His Dreamer was an innovative genius as a software developer, and as a visionary in the market for personal computers. He built Microsoft and launched a social revolution with his Thinker and Dreamer in the lead.

As Microsoft grew, so did Gates. He developed a tough leadership style and competitive business practices. The computer nerd and entrepreneur were making room for the hard-hitting businessman. Soon he faced antitrust litigation and a judge ruled that Microsoft had violated the Sherman Antitrust Act. The dazzling Thinker-Dreamer had empowered another member of his inner team—the Warrior.

Of course the Thinker-Dreamer never went away. With audacity and unique problem-solving in new products, Bill Gates' material success ballooned. His wealth at one point surpassed $101 billion, causing the media to call him a "centibillionaire." For most people, this would be a complete life story, undeniably one of enormous triumph and contribution.

For Gates, these achievements in the corporate world offered another opportunity to reflect: on his focus, his life purpose, and how to realize his full potential. Attuned to the Voyager's call to keep learning and growing, Gates changed course yet again.

In 2010, Bill Gates surrendered the top spot on the Forbes list of the world's richest men—a position he'd held for fourteen of the previous fifteen years. He did this by giving away more than $29 billion of his personal fortune through The Bill and Melinda Gates Foundation. Rounding out his profile, he expanded on his previous favorite strategies to take on yet another role, as a Lover of humanity. Gates embraced a new chapter in his life as a philanthropist, dedicating The Gates Foundation to improving global health, development, and education.

With Gates' support, U2 front man Bono applied his rock star swagger to the bland issue of debt relief for impoverished countries. Together, they convinced wealthier nations to retire $40 million of debt that could be redirected for AIDS research and prevention, eradication of malaria and tuberculosis, prenatal care for pregnant women, and more.

We see the Voyager's imprint over the course of Gates' life. Time and again, he expanded his profile and his favorite strategies to take his leadership and his life to new levels. In his current endeavors, we see: the *Dreamer* who started Microsoft innovating a movement he calls "creative capitalism"; the *Thinker* who created Windows convincing the wealthiest people to hand over half of their fortunes to better the world; the can-do *Warrior* who fought the government on antitrust matters, now delivering tangible results that improve the lives of the disenfranchised; and the *Lover*, redirecting Gates' formidable life force toward humanitarian ends.

So, who is the "real" William Henry Gates? The college dropout? The captain of industry? The computer pioneer? The philanthropist? The social entrepreneur? The humanitarian?

He is *all of these*.

Bill Gates' biography continues to move and transform, pulling him forward to the next part of his life story. You might think we'd *obviously* define Gates as the genius of Microsoft. But his voyage keeps going. As Bono has said of Bill Gates, "He's changing the world twice. And the second act for Bill Gates may be the one that history regards more."

What Is a Voyager?

A Voyager sees life as an adventure. As a series of explorations, with one learning opportunity followed by another. Voyagers seek new experiences because they know they can gain wisdom as they travel through life. It's no accident that the first shuttle into space was called Voyager. Nor a coincidence that the same name was given to the *Star Trek* ship traveling the farthest into uncharted space.

The "voyage" is a timeless motif for self-discovery and fulfilling your potential, both as a person and as a leader. As Voyagers we live in a state of paradox. We need audacity *and* humility. The hunger to grow *and* acceptance of where we are now. The urgency to act *and* the patience to let things ripen.

As you know, I hit a personal low when I discovered I was a "trailing spouse." Notwithstanding my good friend Nemo Larry, I did wonder about the voyage I'd undertaken. Whether things would get better. And when. Then I got a card in the mail from my sister Heather, the social worker, who understands the passages of life as well as anyone I know. I taped the card to the window over my desk, because it summed up the spirit of this chapter in my life so well.

It said:

It will all be okay in the end.
If it's not okay, it's not the end.

And so it goes.

We feel lost, we get found. The Voyager in us keeps us moving, rolling with the punches, falling down and picking ourselves back up. We adapt to new circumstances. Rise to meet new occasions. It's our Voyager who learns from our successes and our mistakes.

Why do we need our inner Voyager?

For one thing, because life throws us curveballs.

I know a woman whose husband had a vasectomy. About two months later, she learned she was pregnant—*with twins*. Turns out the impact of that procedure *is not* immediate. That couple faced a journey of adapting expectations. I know lawyers who've turned nearly suicidal when they lost a huge case for a client, and they believed it was their fault. Their journey is one of self-forgiveness.

We also need our Voyager to help us rise to new opportunities.

I work with lots of professionals as they enter leadership roles. They're crossing a bridge to jobs that create new demands on them. Success will *require* them to expand their profiles and their favorite strategies. They'll need to welcome new inner negotiators to their table. It's the Voyager who builds their capacity over time, as they lean in to their new roles.

Brett is a perfect example. He worked as a tax accountant and had excellent technical skills. In time, his company promoted him. Until then, Brett's rising-star status came from his capacity as a Thinker-Warrior. His Thinker prowess was central, as it is for most knowledge workers. And his Warrior enabled him to get things done well and efficiently.

Now Brett enters management.

He needs to expand his profile to succeed in his new position. Brett needs his inner Lover to manage people successfully. That's not something he can do simply by snapping his fingers. If he's left his Lover behind years ago, he'll need his Voyager to stretch into the role of people manager, and help integrate his Lover back into the scene.

Very often, people in Brett's shoes continue applying their Warrior and Thinker instincts. While those skills are still valuable, they're not fit-for-purpose now as a manager. The Voyager plays a crucial role in these transitions if new leaders are going to succeed.

In fact, in many workplaces, people follow a track that goes something like this: *project leader*, which requires Thinker and Warrior strength; to *team leader* or *client leader*, which requires Lover strength, and ultimately, to *firm leader* or *organization leader*, which stands on Dreamer strength. It's the Voyager in you that helps you to *evolve your profile and your favorite strategies over time*, so you can meet each set of opportunities and challenges with the inner team that serves you best.

The third reason we need our inner Voyagers is to overcome our fears. Like learning to manage people, facing fear and learning to live with it differently takes time, intention, and sometimes professional help. It can't always be done. But there is growing evidence that, even in the aftermath of severe trauma, healing, growing, and integrating are possible.

Daniella is a home care nurse who attended a workshop of mine. She told the group her story about this kind of voyage.

"I never thought I had a fear of dogs. So when I went to see my new patient, I wasn't worried. I arrived to a massive circular driveway in front of a beautiful New England mansion. A pretty blonde woman came to the door, tailored from head to toe, along with two very large dogs. They were barking at me, jumping up on the window panes inside the door. The woman said, 'Don't worry. They won't hurt you,' as she opened the door, and both dogs came plowing past her, jumped up and bit me."

Daniella was shocked and ran from the house.

She was bruised black-and-blue the next day, but the real damage was on the inside. "For a while I turned new patients away. I'd call a house to schedule an appointment, and I could hear a dog barking in the background. I guess people could hear my anxiety, because they'd say things like, 'Oh, she's a little dog,' or 'Don't worry, he's harmless.' But I didn't believe them. So I'd tell my nurse manager to send another nurse."

Daniella said her job wasn't in jeopardy. Her nurse manager "was great" and told her if she felt unsafe going to anyone's house, she didn't need to go there. But after a while, she felt angry that this fear was choosing her patients for her. She wanted to deal with it so she could move past it.

At first she asked people with dogs to put them in another room, or in the garage, before she arrived. At times she heard a dog barking but knew it was a safe distance away. Once she felt comfortable, Daniella let families bring a dog into the same room, *if* they were on a leash, supervised by an adult, and didn't come *too* close to her.

She told us that she still feels anxious going to a new patient if they have a large dog. "But I'm dealing with it," she said. "It still feels like I'm on a journey. But I don't feel like it controls me anymore."

The Voyager Helps Us Grow Over Time

We'd like to think we can pull off anything we want with the knowledge and know-how we have now. Let's face it: we've been around the block more than a few times already.

But we also know it doesn't really work like that.

A colleague and friend of mine, Aryeh Ben-David, leads an organization called Ayeka in Israel. Aryeh is a lifelong scholar and teacher of Jewish wisdom. Like me, he's more interested in the power of education to transform than to inform. He talks about the tension between wanting to fulfill our potential, while also wanting to stay right where we are. He wrote on his blog:

"There is nothing as daunting as personal change and growth. I am who I am. Isn't that enough? No, it is not enough. I am infinitely more than I am. My soul is vastly beyond what I am presently. I am not nearly what I will and can become."

The path to fulfillment, high performance, and lasting change requires the journey to an expanded self. That's where your Voyager comes in to point the way.

The Voyage Motif Is Timeless

Since ancient times, people have taken voyages to move forward in their lives and societies. The classic path involves the hero or heroine going on a physical voyage, while undertaking a transformational journey within. Like the Greek hero Odysseus, who leaves home and wanders for ten years. He develops as a man by facing fearful enemies. Only then can he return home, at last ready to lead Ithaca.

Or the biblical character Joseph, well known for his "Amazing Technicolor Dreamcoat," portrayed in the Andrew Lloyd Webber musical. Joseph's story illustrates a path that appears throughout history, in the lives of prophets, literary figures, mythology, and popular culture. An archetypal journey often involves a birth or rise; followed by a fall or death; followed by rising again, or rebirth. Depending on the context, this can happen literally or symbolically. And the cycle can repeat.

In the book of Genesis, Joseph starts off as the beloved son, publicly honored as his father's favorite. Then comes his fall: thrown into a pit by his brothers, Joseph is sold into slavery. He rises to become a trusted advisor to the wealthy Potiphar. Then he falls again: falsely accused by Potiphar's wife, Joseph gets thrown in jail, abandoned by the world. In the end, he'll rise again, all the way to leading man of Egypt, second only to the Pharaoh.

From his all-time low in prison, Joseph will even regain his original stature as first among equals. Caught in the famine that Joseph had predicted, his brothers are forced to turn to him for help, begging for food and mercy. By the time they reunite, Joseph has taken a physical voyage to Egypt, but "traveled" so much more through his experiences. He stands before his brothers not only in power, but also empowered.

At the story's close, Joseph takes back his amazing dreamcoat and returns to his father's side as a changed man. This is the kind of experience T. S. Eliot described when he wrote, "We shall not cease from exploration / And the end of all our exploring / Will be to arrive where we started / And know the place for the first time."

In the Christian Scriptures, the life of Jesus follows a path like this. Born in poverty in a manger, Jesus rose to preach a ministry of love and humility alongside his growing number of disciples. When he caught the attention of the Roman rulers, however, Jesus seemed to fall: he was tried and convicted of sedition and was crucified. The Scriptures go on to teach that Jesus rose from the dead on Easter Sunday. To this day Christians celebrate the voyage of Jesus from birth to death to resurrection as an inspiration for their own individual voyages.

In other traditions, the voyage to develop, heal, and evolve as fully as possible isn't limited to one lifetime. The journey extends from one body to another, and the path toward awakening plays out from one form to the next. The journey is completed when the soul awakens to its original divine essence and is liberated from the cycle of birth and rebirth.

In the West, we might call the voyage of life a path to self-actualization. In the East, perhaps a path to enlightenment. By whatever name, societies around the world converge on the notion that we develop as we travel. They likewise agree that the journey to growth has an outer expression and an inner dimension. There is a part of each of us designed for this very process. That's the part of human nature that I'm calling the Voyager.

The Voyager Expands Your Horizons

When we hear the word *Voyager*, many of us think of explorers and adventurers. Like Edmund Hillary, the mountaineer renowned for making the first solo ascent of Mount Everest. Or Ernest Shackleton, legendary figure among pioneers of the Antarctic. After

Shackleton's ship, *Endurance*, got crushed and sank in a pack of dense ice, he famously persevered through unimaginable circumstances to bring every member of his crew home alive.

Other explorers travel to discover foreign lands, like cultural anthropologist Margaret Mead. Or Isak Dinesen, whose experiences in Kenya formed the backdrop of her book *Out of Africa*, on which the movie is based. And Elizabeth Gilbert, who memorialized her passages across the world in *Eat, Pray, Love*.

For other voyagers, exploring involves taking flight. Like famed astronaut Neil Armstrong, the first person to walk on the moon. And extreme sportsman Felix Baumgartner, renowned for freefalling from amazing heights. His motto says it all: "Everyone has limits—not everyone accepts them!"

But for most of us, our voyages are less about climbing literal mountains. They're more about meeting and navigating the moments that we face, and the stages we go through, over the course of our lives. In these developmental voyages we also traverse challenging ground and travel large distances. Think of American senator John McCain. His life journey took him from a prisoner-of-war camp to the nomination for President of the United States. Or Wael Ghonim, a person who stretched himself to meet a moment in history. His unexpected turn as the leader of a movement demanded big changes, and expansion of his profile.

Ghonim was a technology executive, the head of Google marketing in the Middle East. He was shocked at the police brutality he witnessed against another Egyptian citizen, Khaled Said. Activating his inner Dreamer and Warrior, the Internet businessman turned social activist. Ghonim uploaded a page on Facebook proclaiming, "We are all Khaled Said." The page amassed 350,000 fans, whom Ghonim invited to a peaceful protest in Cairo's Tahrir Square. Just weeks later, the Egyptian people removed Hosni

Mubarak and his regime from office, ushering in the "Arab Spring" of movements for democratic reform.

Some journeys take you from humble beginnings to greatness. Maya Angelou dropped out of high school to become San Francisco's first African-American female cable car conductor. She worked as a cook and a waitress to make ends meet as a young single mother. Angelou became the author of thirty bestselling books of poetry, fiction, and nonfiction, and she delivered the opening poem at the inauguration of President Clinton. We can only imagine how much she grew over time on the inside to travel *that* distance on the outside. Embracing all of her experiences, Angelou said, "I can be changed by what happens to me. I am not reduced by it."

Of course, our lives don't follow a straight line north. Somewhere along the way, we fall down. We can't expect otherwise. If we can find a route to get back on our feet, the "failures" and setbacks become one more chapter in our life story. Think of Al Gore. He spent most of his life preparing to serve as President of the United States. He came as close to fulfilling that dream as a person could—without seeing it come true. That devastating loss could have been his last hurrah. But it wasn't. After that tumultuous period—for Gore and for America—he went on to win the Nobel Peace Prize for his efforts to educate the public about climate change.

Up and down and back again. We just need to keep walking.

Voyaging Can Start Where You Are

It's true that in many journey stories, protagonists "leave" where they are to take a voyage. At the same time, throughout folklore of civilizations, people search for things in faraway places, only to find what they seek right where they already are. Like Dorothy in *The Wizard of Oz*, who needs only to click her heels three times to get home, the lesson you need is available the moment you recognize it.

Consider this tale about a stonecutter.

All day he labors in the heat, cutting stone with the hot sun beating down on him. Each day he yearns to be more powerful than a humble stonecutter. And what is more powerful than the sun? So one day he calls out and prays to become the sun, the most powerful being on earth. His wish is granted.

With his warm rays he beams down on flowers and makes them grow, shines on children playing, and drains away puddles from the ground. All of a sudden, a large cloud moves in front of him, and he is completely blocked. Shocked by his realization that the cloud is more powerful than the sun, he begs to be made a cloud. His wish is granted.

And he moves around the sky, raining on the grass, making fog over the cities. He is delighted with his newfound power, until one day the wind comes along and blows him out of the way. Distressed by losing his powerful role, he prays to become the wind. His wish is granted, and he blows around the sky, casting a breeze past lovers on the beach, turning umbrellas inside out.

He is content. Until one day he hits up against a mountain. He can move around the mountain, or over it, but he cannot move through the mountain. "Aha," he thinks to himself, "the mountain is the most powerful of all." So he prays and begs to become a mountain. His wish is granted.

And he rules over all the land.

Until one day, when he feels the chipping away of the stonecutter.

Endlessly searching to acquire more "tips, tricks and techniques" is like wishing to be the sun, the clouds, and the wind. There is always the next thing to learn, the next tool to add to your toolbox, the *next* effective habit. You can find yourself at the top of the mountain only wishing to be the stonecutter—*again*.

This parable holds a key that unlocks the door to high performance and lasting change. Yes, you need to develop skills to perform out in the world. But the real moral of the story lines up with my mother's good advice about cooking. *You become masterful by cultivating what's inside of you.* You can start doing that right here, right now.

Whether you're working with the best tools or the worst ones, at the end of the day it's *you* who's putting them to work. If you skip the inner journey, then a pile of dirt and water is just mud. Once you start learning about yourself—what makes *you* tick, what hits a nerve in *you*—those same materials *in your hands* become the start of a blossoming garden.

You don't need to leave home for the Holy Land or wander in the desert for forty years. You don't need to give up your house and move to an ashram in India. You already have all the raw materials you need, inside of you, living as unrealized potential. *Your voyage takes off the moment you realize you're already on it.*

Your Voyager Can Shape Your Life

In his play *Hamlet*, William Shakespeare handed down a timeless challenge: "This above all: to thine own self be true." Pulling that off can take a lifetime: you have to figure out what living truly to yourself even means, and then find out how to make it happen in your life.

Hard as it may sound, that's the invitation that your Voyager gives you. *This is your life.* Can you live well and lead wisely, while being true to yourself? Only you can decide. As Charles Dickens' David Copperfield writes, "Whether I shall turn out to be the hero of my own life, or whether that station will be held by anybody else, these pages must show."

In the last chapter I told you that Nelson Mandela is always mentioned when I collect names of centered leaders from a group. Throughout his years in prison, Mandela had a poem engraved on the wall, written by William Ernest Henley. These are the last two lines of the poem, clung to by a man imprisoned by authorities for nearly three decades, a person who seemingly lacked all autonomy or power to create his own destiny:

I am the master of my fate
I am the captain of my soul.

Your Voyager stands for the idea that you have choices, and that ultimately, *you create your life*. Yes, your biology makes a difference. Yes, of course, the life circumstances into which you're born make a *large* impact on where your journey begins. Your health. Your financial reality. Your status in society. Your opportunities for education. The degree of freedom granted to you by your government. *Absolutely true.*

At the same time, think of John McCain, Maya Angelou, Wael Ghonim. Remember what they were up against, and how far they came. The challenge is to hold it all at the same time. Acknowledge the constraints that life has given you. They are real and significant. *And*—you can still ask yourself the question posed by Mary Oliver in her poem "The Summer Day." To paraphrase her well-known inquiry, what will you do with the unique and precious gift called your life? No matter where you've come from, *that* is the question beating in your Voyager's heart.

Change Isn't Easy, but Neither Is Standing Still

Change is hard. Sometimes it's gradual. Sometimes it happens in a flash. Either way, it often involves growing pains. Spending Christmas in The Netherlands has involved both kinds of change.

I practice the traditions of Hanukkah, but I grew up in America. That makes Christmas part of my cultural heritage. I wasn't raised with the religious significance of the day. So Christmas to me meant a few reliable, if secular, things.

Rudolph has a red nose. Mr. Scrooge will discover a change of heart, and help Tiny Tim. Santa and his reindeer live in the North Pole, where elves make presents. On Christmas Eve, December 24, reindeer pull Santa's sleigh to deliver the gifts, and children wake up to them on Christmas morning, December 25.

These facts were as much "a given" to me as four quarters make a dollar.

Then I moved abroad.

The Dutch celebrate Sinterklaas on Saint Nicholas' birthday, December 5, so they exchange gifts then. Santa doesn't have a sleigh or reindeer—he rides a white horse with black spots. He also doesn't have elves. He has servants called *"Zwarte Piet"*—"Black Peter"—who look terrifyingly like African slaves (admittedly from an American point of view). Perhaps most shocking of all, and the adjustment I *cannot* seem to make, is that in The Netherlands, Sinterklaas is *from Spain*.

Spain.

He arrives every year—by steamboat—from Spain.

This is a level of change that goes to the heart of my cultural DNA. How can Santa Claus *not* live in the North Pole? It feels like saying our capital is not in Washington, D.C., or that Arizona isn't home to the magnificent Grand Canyon. "We hold these truths to be self-evident." Isn't one of those that Santa lives in the North Pole?

I share this example to acknowledge that change is rough. It's painful. It's hard to wrap our heads around. Let's face it. Santa's residence is not an important fact. Indeed, *it's not a "fact" at all.* Add to that, Santa comes from a tradition that's not my own. All of that said, I find it difficult to accept that Sinterklaas comes from Spain.

In contrast to my ongoing Santa transition, my young Dutch nieces made a much bigger one with a lot less fanfare. Until last winter, these little girls were more than happy to write letters to Santa, listing all of the gifts their hearts desired. But this winter, something changed. They started to ask questions, ones that poked holes in their formerly satisfying blind faith.

"If there are millions of houses, then how can Santa get around to all of them in only one night?" they wanted to know.

"If Santa comes down through the chimney, and some houses don't have a chimney, then how can Santa get into *those* houses?"

After about a week of these searing inquiries, one of them made a nine-year-old declaration.

"I know," she said. "Santa doesn't exist."

And that was that. In a snap. For the rest of her life, she will never again live in a world where Sinterklaas is real.

Voyagers Know You're a Lifelong Learner

Crossing this threshold for my nieces marked more than learning *a new skill.* That's a line the Little Dude will cross when he masters tying a knot in a rope. *This* shift in perspective indicated *development in their capacity*—to think, to make meaning, to explain their world. They'd taken a step away from simplicity toward a higher level of complexity, a move that marks the kind of change people call transformation.

You're older than my little nieces. You might or might not be older than I am, as I try to embrace Santa's Spanish domicile. Either way, you're growing and learning, too. We all are. No matter what stage of life you're in right now. Like everyone you know, you're subject to a basic law of the human condition: *you are a work-in-progress*.

You might think you stopped "developing" a long time ago. Perhaps when you entered adulthood, or completed your formal education. Perhaps you were fully cooked when you got a license to drive. Or when you left home for the first time. Maybe you were all grown up when *your last child* left home. Or on your fiftieth, sixtieth, seventieth, or eightieth birthday.

But it isn't so.

Although the changes were more *visible* in the first twenty years of your life, this law applies forever. Regardless of your age.

You are always a work-in-progress.

Full stop.

One Voyage with Two Sides

The movement of our times is to remember *both sides of our journey*, to reunite our outer and inner lives. The deeper truth of the Voyager is that the human experience isn't one or the other: it's both at the same time. Anchoring in your center is about embracing opposites—even seemingly contradictory ones—and finding ways to hold them together, side by side.

By and large, we don't see our lives from this view. We mostly value what happens in the outside world. For a sizable majority, at least in Western countries, the inner life doesn't get too much attention. We're far too busy doing important things in the world. For those of us who *do* take our inner lives seriously, there's a tendency to believe that the inner journey is *all* that matters. We operate from the premise that our inner life is our *only* true self, and everything else is egocentric hogwash. Whichever way you go, you're embracing half of your life.

The approach of Winning from Within stands for the idea that both outer and inner experience constitute who we really are. The Big Four aren't more or less important than the Transformers. The Transformers aren't the only aspect of human nature that really counts. It is one system with seven elements, each of which has a role to play in our inner development as well as in our interface with the world around us.

We'll come back to this idea shortly. Let's pause, to look more closely at the common separation of the outside world and interior experience.

We Value the Outer Voyage

You've likely heard the saying that "the journey *is* the destination." What does that actually mean? It means that you are changing over time. As long as you live. And those changes operate on two levels: in your outer world, and in your inner world. If you're like most people, you pay more attention to events in your outer world. This maxim points you to also notice your inner journey along the way.

Our common tendency is to signpost our lives by the successes and failures we see in our outer world. The formula is simple: we set a goal—and we arrive at the "destination" when we meet the goal. You long to buy a home someday, and you finally do it. You've arrived. You hope to start your own nonprofit. When you open the doors for the first time, you've made it. If you work for nearly a decade to become a partner in your office, then you feel you've "arrived" when the title is finally yours. You're *almost* finished with the paperwork on your divorce. When the court documents arrive in the mail, you've crossed the finish line. You stop smoking. You lose the last ten pounds you've carried around since pregnancy. You're done. You made it.

On the outside, your journey will include recognizable milestones. Depending on your circumstances, they will vary. Here's a sample of common experiences that people give in workshops when I ask about passages in their lives *that other people can see* when they happen.

You might ask yourself as you read the list: Have I experienced something like this? Can I remember a moment in time, or a period in my life, when this was happening? Can I recall when they "started," and a time or even a moment when I felt like they were "done"?

- Finding a job; losing a job; getting promoted; retiring
- Choosing a career; getting educated; changing careers
- Living with family; moving out; moving back in, and out again
- Periods of sobriety; of addiction; of recovery
- Periods of good health; of illness; of completing treatment
- Years on your own; in a couple; in a family; in a community; on your own again; years in a new relationship or starting a new family
- Starting a new project; working on it; completing it; starting something else

- Periods of fidelity; of infidelity
- Not having enough money; gaining wealth; losing wealth; gaining or losing it again
- Giving birth to a child; adopting a child; infertility; gaining stepchildren; sharing custody of your children; losing a pregnancy; choosing not to have children; ending a pregnancy; becoming grandparents; losing a child.

These kinds of experiences—and many other milestones not listed here—are *how we mark time* and *how we measure our lives.* They show us how things are going. They let us know if we're on track.

That means that in truth, **we don't believe the journey** is the destination. **We believe that meeting our goals** is the destination.

We use things like these as indicators of whether we're succeeding or failing, moving forward or backward. Looking at the world around us, we think we can tell if these are good times, or bad times. To some extent, that's true. These kinds of experiences tell us *something* about whether our lives are coming together, or falling apart. But surely that's not the whole story.

The Outer Journey Tells Half of Your Life Story

A parallel track—as significant as the first—is the development path you travel *inside* of yourself. In fact, the advice to seek wisdom and truth by paying attention to your inner landscape is one of the oldest teachings in the world. It's also one of the most universal.

There is a famous precept inscribed at the temple of Apollo at Delphi—*gnothi seauton*—that means "know thyself." With a similar message, Jesus said in the gospel of Luke: *Physician, heal thyself.* One of the first injunctions in the Bible is in Genesis 12:1, when God says to Abram, *"Lech lecha."* This command is often translated as "go forth" or "go out." But the Hebrew words literally mean "go to you" or "go to yourself." Twenty-five hundred years ago the Buddha instructed followers to observe the inner workings of their minds. The Chinese Zen master Tung-Shan taught, "If you look for the truth outside yourself, it gets farther and farther away." Myriad traditions direct us inward.

Winning from Within starts with a focus on *what's happening inside of you.* That's because what's happening *in here* will directly produce what happens *out there.* Teaching you tips and tricks for new behavior that you'll implement *from your original internal landscape* won't get you much better outcomes than you got before.

I saw this up close when I helped a global business prepare for a "culture transformation." In a business, the inner world is often called your mindset, and what you do on the outside is your behavior. Put in those terms, to get lasting change in your behavior, you need to make some corresponding shifts in your mindset.

For this client, the corporate culture of "every man for himself" wasn't capturing synergies across businesses: they wanted to end the "silo" mentality. Related to that, they aimed to create a less closed environment, and one less driven by fear. In the "new world," colleagues would share information, give each other constructive feedback, and bring opportunities to each other's attention. They'd see each other as teams rather than as internal competition. Over time, the company hoped to build a culture of trust.

A task force got to work on writing guidelines for the "new world." They circulated a draft of the new rules for comments. It was a classic example of trying to do the right thing, *but not making any shift in the internal mindset* before jumping into action. In other words, they wanted to pull off a transformation in people's behavior but bypass the inner learning they needed to enable it. Like so many change efforts, this one would fail because of this oversight, if not addressed.

When I got their new rules, I read things like this: "Everyone Must Be Open" and "Everyone Will Collaborate." I don't know about you, but to me, starting a statement with "everyone must" already lets me know this is *not* an open environment. Even if the same statement tells me that what I "must do" is *be open*. Likewise, *compelling* people to collaborate through proclamation—because *everyone will*—hardly instills the feelings of trust and free exchange they were seeking to foster.

I knew what they were trying to say, despite the way they said it. My biggest concern wasn't the rules themselves. It was that they didn't see the irony in giving "mandates" for openness and teamwork. Going for outer change without the parallel inner development doesn't fly. Have you ever experienced a change process like this, and watched it break down? If you have, then you know what I'm talking about firsthand.

This dynamic is not limited, by the way, to the private sector. This is a truth about the way lasting change happens, whether your context is a nonprofit, a government agency, or a church. It applies in a hospital, a school, a music studio, a candy store, or your condo association. **Do the mindset work. Behavior change will follow.**

After these new guidelines went around, we took a few steps back to look at the underlying drivers of the current culture. This was the ground from which these "new" rules came: competition, fear, control, survival of the fittest. Whether you're working as an individual, an institution, or a society, you're going to grow new flowers when you plant seeds *in new soil*. Otherwise, you might wish for a different garden, but when spring comes, that flower bed is going to feel darn familiar.

The Complete Voyage Includes Both Sides

At the end of the day, it's not about *choosing* between the inner journey and the outer one. You don't need to figure out which is the important one, or which one will impact the "real" you. The Big Four and the Transformers are all part of who you really are. Your inner world, *and* what happens at home and at work in your daily life, are all part of who you really are. The approach of Winning from Within fosters transformation and lasting change precisely because *it weaves the two of them together.*

The most well-known symbol for this idea is probably the Taoist image of yin and yang. That's the circle with two halves, one black and one white, with a curve moving down the middle where the two sides meet. You've likely seen the image at some point. Both sides include a smaller circle in the opposite color. Its curved lines suggest motion, while the interchange of opposites, black and white—all held in a circle—conveys completeness.

We need a symbol for these times, to represent our collective journey toward wholeness. The Winning from Within method uses the Mobius strip. Its design comes from mathematics, making it both universal and secular. In a Mobius strip, the interior seamlessly becomes the exterior, and then it reverses. What is outer becomes inner; what was inside moves outside. Like the yin and yang symbol, there is no beginning and no end. It's a steady motion, like breathing. You inhale, and exhale. Inhale, and exhale (see Figure 11.1).

FIGURE 11.1

This image stands for the union of opposites that happens when we come back to our center of well-being. It also harkens back to one of Jung's central ideas, one that we talked about near the start of the book. Jung taught that we all know things about the universal voyage called the human experience. That's how we recognize archetypes, even though we never learned about them in school. We also all follow our own unique path, the voyage that is ours alone. A life is like the Mobius strip: it exists on the inside and on the outside, but it's one piece of paper. We are at once parts of the collective journey, and at the same time, singular travelers. One voyage with two sides.

The Inner Journey Involves Getting Centered

In business conversation today, I often hear the word *pivot*. People seem to be looking for the magical "pivot point" that will turn everything around. When I'm designing leadership programs for companies, the two things that come up most often are whether the program will provide "lasting change" and whether the participants will "pivot" after the experience to the next level of performance.

I tell clients the same thing: let's help your people to develop centering practices, and then support them to practice them. This is a fundamental aspect of the inner voyage, which in turn supports lasting impact in the organization.

Why?

Because the reliable road to that treasured pivot point is to activate your Transformers. Knowing how to tap those inner resources, and how to harness them for effective action, *is the game-changing move.* All of your Transformers—the Lookout, the Captain, and the Voyager—reside in your center. As you develop ways to connect to your center of well-being, you learn to draw out your Lookout's capacity for reflection-in-action, your Captain's ability to assess your context and make the best decision for your current situation, and your Voyager's skill at helping you expand your profile and strategies over time.

Explore Ways to Center Yourself

Centering is a practice of turning inward to connect with your core of well-being. From time immemorial, countless practices have evolved for helping us get back to our center. Like Bernardus and his friends when they jump from the sauna to the freezing water, people have used centering practices to quiet the mind, still the heart, and reconnect to what's important.

Everyone should have a centering practice.

Whether you run a household or a private practice, manage a charity or a hedge fund, develop children's minds or research drugs for new medicine, this applies to you. We all need a trustworthy path to our sense of well-being. The wisdom of centuries says you learn how to center yourself through the discipline of a practice.

Centering practices are making a comeback in the twenty-first century. Because we need them. When things are changing so quickly, and the layers of complexity and uncertainty make your head spin, you realize that you can't count on the world "out there" for orientation or stability. What's here today may be gone tomorrow. Arthur Andersen. Bear Stearns. Lehman Brothers. All things of the past. It's unthinkable. But it all happened. That's why this age-old wisdom is coming back: because the times demand it. When you feel lost and things are crumbling around you, don't look *out there*. Look *in here*.

Your center of well-being is an essential part of you that can't get lost, damaged, compromised, or tarnished. It can't go bankrupt. It can't go out of business. It can't leave you for a younger woman. It can't gain weight, go bald, or forget where you left your keys. Your center is *right here*, and you owe it to yourself to have a practice that helps you remember that, even when things look bleak. When you can feel your center, *that's* when you can say to yourself, "It will all be okay in the end. If it's not okay, it's not the end."

A growing number of CEOs are practicing mindfulness meditation to get back to their center. One example is Ray Dalio, CEO and founder of Bridgewater Associates. Dalio is widely considered one of the most successful investment managers of all time. He told *Business Insider* magazine that "it's 20 minutes in the morning and 20 minutes in the evening," and that meditation gives him "clarity" and "creativity." The same article reported that Legal Sea Foods CEO Roger Berkowitz also meditates twice a day for twenty minutes. This trend is so significant that sessions on mindfulness were oversold at the 2013 World Economic Forum in Davos, Switzerland.

Apple cofounder the late Steve Jobs practiced Zen meditation.

Many organizations, from Google and Genentech to parts of the United States military, have instituted mindfulness programs. Other companies, like Bill George's former stomping ground, Medtronic, have dedicated a conference room in their office as a quiet place where people can go for a bit of tranquility. Imagine the world when every office has one room designated for quiet. Everyone at work knows there's an assigned space, available at any time, for a few minutes of silence during the day. That will be a big step in the right direction.

The key isn't *what* your centering practice is—it's that *you choose a practice*, and then you actually *practice* it. Like going to the gym, building new strength requires discipline. If you commit, you'll see dividends from your investment. A leading brain researcher, Richard Davidson of the University of Wisconsin, puts it like this: "In our country, people are very involved in the physical fitness craze, working out several times a week. But we don't pay that kind of attention to our minds. Modern neuroscience is showing that our minds are as plastic as our bodies. . . . [You] can train the mind in the same way exercise can train our body." Brain researcher Rick Hanson has written about "self-directed neuroplasticity." That means not only that your brain is changing throughout your life, but also *that you can play a role in the changes that it makes*.

More than a decade of scientific research shows that sustained repetition of contemplative practice fosters measurable changes in the brain. For example, brain scans of long-term meditators show reduced activity in the limbic system, where the amygdala sits. By meditating as a dedicated practice over time, people have stimulated their brains in ways that lower their emotional reactivity. Admittedly, subjects in these studies included Tibetan monks who've been meditating their whole lives. That said, self-directed neuroplasticity is a brand-new subject. Who knows what we'll learn about how to direct our own neural pathways in the years to come?

Find Something That Works for You

No one can tell you what kind of practice fits you best. But you have an enormous set of options to explore for learning how to find your center when you fall off-balance. Just think about the vast range of practices used for centering over time.

Saying the rosary. Repeating a mantra. Prayer. Walking in nature. Atonement. Whirling like a dervish. The Japanese tea ceremony. The Catholic centering prayer. Contemplation of a koan. Walking the labyrinth. Chanting. Lighting candles. Martial arts.

The list goes on.

Reading psalms. Taking vows. Playing music. Silence. Dancing. Dialogue. Drawing a mandala. Singing. Bowing. Cooking. Drumming. Confession. Repeating the serenity prayer:

> *God grant me the serenity*
> *to accept the things I cannot change;*
> *courage to change the things I can;*
> *and wisdom to know the difference.*

Observing the Sabbath as a day of rest. Fasting. Sacred calligraphy. The sweat lodge. And *so much more.*

In our times, we have informal and formal practices for centering ourselves. You might find centeredness when playing sports, going for a run, or engaging in intimate conversation with a dear friend. You might take yoga classes, where feeling centered means not falling out of a posture and instead achieving a deeper stretch.

You might write in a journal or simply take walks. You might find peace and quiet when you're gardening.

You can attain a sense of centeredness and well-being by doing what feels right. Like participating in a walk-a-thon to raise money for breast cancer. Or choosing not to tell a lie. By helping a friend who needs you, or turning down a business opportunity because you have insider information. By saying no when you mean no. Or taking a stand for justice.

To see yourself grow as a person and as a leader over time, though, finding your center can't be a casual thing you do once in a while. That's why it's called a *practice*.

Think back for a minute to Elena Kagan when she was the law school dean, and the way she responded with so much agility to the alumnae crowd. It would have been easy for her to get offended or defensive. You and I probably feel insulted for less troubling reasons—*she* was accused publicly of racial discrimination. Ouch. She held her ground while respecting her audience **because she knew how to stay centered under pressure**. Yes, she'd developed the skill set of each of her Big Four. But it was her centeredness in that moment of heat that enabled such high performance.

We Don't Travel Alone, and We Travel Alone

Let me close with one of those paradoxes I mentioned, a pair of opposites that sound like they'd cancel each other out, though they're both true.

The presence of support for our journey through life is a timeless principle. As one example, traditional Chinese fishermen prayed to Kuan Yin for a safe return from their fishing voyages. Along with her masculine counterpart, Avolokiteshvara, Kuan Yin embodied compassion, and she sustained the voyagers. Throughout human existence, people have prayed for help to a higher power—a source many people call God, and many people know by another name.

From generation to generation, people have expressed the idea that reality operates on more than one level. In one way, we're separate from one another; each of us is alone. But on another level, we're all connected. Ralph Waldo Emerson called this collective meeting place the Oversoul. Vietnamese monk Thich Nhat Hanh refers to it as "inter-being." Scientist Albert Einstein was searching for what he called a "unified field theory" to explain how the whole world works. He wrote this:

> A human being is part of a whole, called by us the "Universe," a part limited in time and space. He experiences himself, his thoughts and feelings, as something separated from the rest—a kind of optical delusion of his consciousness. This delusion is a kind of prison for us, restricting us to our personal desires and to affection for a few persons nearest us. Our task must be to free ourselves from this prison by widening our circles of compassion to embrace all living creatures and the whole of nature in its beauty.

The overwhelming message from history is that we don't walk alone.

With all of that said, we also walk alone.

And we can.

As I've navigated this roller-coaster year, I've experienced both of these realities. At different times, and sometimes both at the same time. I've known that I'm not alone, and also that I am ultimately alone. I found for myself that my journey to wholeness requires me to live in both of these truths. To find a solid place to stand in both of them.

Catholic monk and teacher Thomas Merton wrote that "humans have a responsibility to find themselves where they are, in their own proper time and place, in the history to which they belong. . . ." This resonates with me as something we each have to do for ourselves. This is our time and place. These unprecedented times are the history to which we belong. Now each of us is on our own journey, our unique voyage to find ourselves where we are, and to discover where we are going.

Laurence Gonzales is the author of several books, among them *Deep Survival* and another called *Surviving Survival*. He wrote a passage that I've read many times, because it brings me back to my center of well-being. It says: "Not being lost is not a matter of getting back to where you started from; it is a decision not to be lost wherever you happen to find yourself. It's simply saying, 'I'm not lost, I'm right here.'" This feels like an important piece of wisdom for us as we live and lead in uncertain times.

In whatever work we do, and wherever we live, we want to do more than just survive: we want to thrive. Whether we're making decisions that impact our own lives, the people around us, tens of thousands of people working in the same global company, or millions of people through multinational organizations and international affairs, it would be nice to know that we're not lost. As we figure out where we are and where we're going, we can take comfort in remembering: We're not lost. We're right here.

EPILOGUE

Life isn't about
finding yourself.
Life is about
creating yourself.
—GEORGE BERNARD SHAW

There comes a time in every caterpillar's life when he lets go of what he knows *before he sees what will come next.* To advance to another stage of his life, he turns inward, entering a unique place for transformation: the chrysalis. Inside the chrysalis, his fundamental structures will break down. Others will form. Bits of the original will carry on, while others get left behind. At the right time, he'll knock at the inner door, prepared to meet the world again. As we all know, he'll expand into life anew, as a butterfly.

Individually and collectively, we find ourselves in a chrysalis of our own. We feel old structures breaking down. We experience the rumblings of what we know giving way. We can *almost* sense new forms coming into shape—*but not quite.* We'd really like to know what happens next, both for ourselves, and for the societies in which we live. But that's not where we are. We haven't emerged yet. **We're still in the chrysalis.**

Smack in the middle of our own transformation, how do we make the most of it?

Carl Jung famously said "in the shadow is the gold." To paraphrase him, we don't like to enter the dark places. But when we do, we discover the good stuff. These days, we often feel like we're leading and living in the dark. What are the rules for this world where things change at the speed of light? How do we find our footing in environments that feel volatile, uncertain, complex, and ambiguous? It turns out the word *chrysalis* comes from the term *chrysós,* the Greek word for gold. Following Jung's premise, where we are right now—as dark and shadowy as things may seem—is the right place to find the gold.

As we've explored throughout *Winning from Within,* one way to "find the gold" is by engaging the voyage of your life *with your eyes open.* Of course, you *can* operate on autopilot. You can use the same favorite strategies, and fall into the same Performance Gaps, time and again. Philosophical, psychological, and spiritual traditions liken this to living in a trance. You have your routines. You go through the motions. It's not *so* bad: you get through the day. But you're not connected to your center of well-being all that much. It's a bit like sleepwalking through your life.

Over the course of this book—in different ways, with various metaphors and a range of vocabulary—we've looked at ways to wake up from the trance. You wake up by starting to recognize what really motivates you, what hooks you, and what opportunities show up that you never noticed before. You wake up by embracing qualities of *each member* of the Big Four: your Dreamer's hope; your Thinker's insight; your Lover's warmth; and your Warrior's conviction. You wake up by discovering your Transformers, learning that *you can see yourself in action*, and *you have power to shape your leadership and your life*. You realize that when you spot your familiar Performance Gaps looming in front of you, *you can choose to go another way*.

Zalman Schachter-Shalomi, a visionary Jewish teacher and interfaith leader, shared a story about waking up. Reb Zalman, as he's fondly known, was born in Poland, and you'll hear in his words that he retains his European roots. Here's what he told a journalist.

When my daughter was young, and I put her to bed one night, she asked me, "Daddy, when you're asleep, you can wake up, right?"

"Ya," I said.

Then she asked, "When you're awake, can you wake up even more?"

Joining a chorus of the ages, the message of this book to respond to that question is also "ya."

A Season for Awakening

Written in the book of Ecclesiastes—and memorialized by the folk rock band the Byrds in their song "Turn! Turn! Turn!"—is the teaching that every purpose has its time and season. For the first time in history, we have today the convergence of Eastern philosophy, Western psychology, and worldwide spirituality—all coming together in a conversation with science, or neuroscience to be exact. This allows for a trailblazing exploration of terrain each knows well, by different names. Call it the nature of mind, the psyche, the soul, the Tao, the brain. Call it Christ consciousness, Buddha nature, *neshama*, Atman, inner light, *homo imago dei*. Talk about human development or new neural pathways. Debate the roles of passion and reason, or relate the limbic system to the neocortex. The beauty of this moment is the conversation itself.

In this time and season, we're privileged to experience a far-reaching exchange. With such a vast, unprecedented investigation happening right now, we might wonder: What is the purpose? What deeper meaning does it hold for us? As we reach the end of this book's journey, I suggest it's an invitation to explore how to wake up. In other words, perhaps the purpose of this time is to encourage our awakening.

What does awakening really mean?

A full answer to that question can't be found in these pages. It can't be found in any book. What *Winning from Within* aims to do is open a door for you. Then you can explore and make your own discoveries, forge your own path. As you do, consider that awakening can include asking yourself things like this:

- Which of the Big Four do you listen to the most, and which do you ignore?
- How would you describe your current profile?
- What Performance Gaps are getting in your way, and what impact does it have when you fall into them?
- What intentions might you set today, and what steps might you take to fulfill them?

One hope of this book is to ignite your curiosity, to interest you in the voyage of awakening and what it could mean for your leadership and your life.

Some Core Principles

With all of that said, we've covered a lot of territory together. We've laid a foundation for you to move forward, taking some fundamental principles along with you.

Focusing only on your behavior won't create the lasting change you want. That approach is well tested, and proven to get you similar outcomes, if packaged differently. Thinking you can change the world by focusing *only* on what's happening *around you or outside of you* is a failing mindset. It just doesn't work.

Yes, you can get incremental change that way. Or short-term change that slides right back when the going gets rough. But as you know from experience, trying to "fix" the people around you to solve your problems is a dead-end strategy. Those challenging colleagues or impolite cousins don't change their ways because you tell them what's wrong with them. Strangely enough, it *still* doesn't work after you've told them *several times.*

Even trying to "fix" yourself by committing to "do it differently this time" doesn't do that much if it's all about new action. This is the New Year's Resolution phenomenon. You say you'll go to the gym. You'll spend less time on Facebook. You won't take work home with you. You'll lose more weight, spend less money, and find new customers. You will basically become a much better and more worthy human being. You promise. *Has that worked for you so far?*

To generate lasting change, you need to work on both *the outside* and *the inside*. Transformation happens when you *pair your vow* to take new actions *with a practice* to anchor in your center of well-being. When you recognize your life as a voyage, with predictable roads and utterly unforeseen twists. When you accept that you won't get it right the first time, or every time, but you keep moving in the right direction. Indeed, *even noticing* that your life is going in the wrong direction *is one step toward moving in the right one.* Ultimately, the journey of your life has both an outer and an inner dimension. You'll get better results, stronger relationships, and more of life's deeper rewards as you pay attention to both of them.

Part of awakening is the realization of your own complexity.

It's easy to go through life getting feedback and thinking, "Well, I'd love to do that, but *this is me*." Or answering a request from your spouse with "I'm sorry. But this is just the way I am." As we explored at length, there's more to you than meets the eye. Try to relax the notion that there's one fixed "you," singular and unchanging. Neuroscience shows the multiplicity of human nature. Neuroplasticity means the adult brain grows over time. Simply put: You're multi-faceted, and you're on the move.

You're most effective when you treat the Big Four as a team, allowing each one to balance the others. Each one of your Big Four speaks for a part of you, reflecting *one of the ways* you see the world and your role in it. *Their different needs, priorities, strengths, and styles are all part of who you are.* You'll get consistent success and satisfaction as you let them balance each other's tendencies and behaviors.

You're so much more than your Big Four. Particularly in the West, we put a lot of emphasis on human personality. Various assessments tell us our "type." We mostly identify who we are with our persona—what I'm calling your profile—which is essentially the psychological clothing we wear to present ourselves to the world. As we saw by investigating the Transformers, that profile layer of who we are is real and important, but not the full truth. The Lookout, the Captain, and the Voyager point to dimensions of our lives that are deeper than our wants, our thoughts, our emotions, and our impulses to act. If nothing else, awakening includes the exploration of who we are *in addition to all of that*, and in the language we've used here, finding ways to experience the essential well-being at our center.

Everyone needs a centering practice. At the end of the day, your effectiveness as a leader and your fulfillment as a person will deepen by developing a practice to access your center of well-being. That doesn't mean you'll feel calm all the time. Or you'll always use good judgment, or say just the right thing. It means that when you find yourself on rocky seas, you know how to find a safe harbor, if only for a few minutes. It means you know that your safe harbor isn't out there somewhere—it's inside of you. And it means you understand that the actions you take after centering yourself are more likely to be strategic, ethical, and wise.

Last Thoughts, for Today

On October 27, 2012, I attended a service of remembrance for Roger Fisher. It was held at Memorial Church in Harvard Yard, a fitting place to bid him farewell. During the service, the former president of Ecuador, Jamil Mahuad, stood to speak. President Mahuad was a close friend of Roger, and is a dear friend of mine. As ever, he spoke from his heart, about a man he deeply respected and loved. Standing before the congregation, Jamil quoted a poem written in 1915 by Amado Nervo, titled "En Paz," At Peace. Speaking from Roger's perspective, he recited these lines:

Life, you owe me nothing,
Life, we are at peace.

We nodded our heads, calling to mind Roger's extraordinary voyage over his ninety years.

This sentiment that captured Roger's final days so well, is the parting wish I have for you, and for all of us. My hope is that we make choices today, and every day, with our eyes open. That we lead, love, and live consciously. With purpose and with wisdom. That we harness our intuition, our rationality, our compassion, and our fortitude. That we find our place in something bigger than ourselves, ever mindful of the wider world to which we belong. I wish for us to find paths to integration, to wholeness, to center. To leave legacies of making a difference. To answer Dickens' charge with a resounding yes: we *do* turn out to be the heroes of our own lives. Then we can all say this for ourselves: Life, you owe me nothing. Life, we are at peace.

And may it be so.

ACKNOWLEDGMENTS

Every blade of grass has its angel that bends
over it and whispers, "Grow, grow."
—THE TALMUD

A long the winding road to creating this book, many angels
stood beside me, whispering into my ear, "Grow, grow." From
that vast group, I can acknowledge some of you here by name.
I hope the other angels in my life know how grateful I am to you.

First I thank my dear sisters, who are always with me, even
when I'm on the other side of the world. Heather, my deepest gratitude and love for always hearing where I am, and knowing what
I need. For making me laugh, and letting me cry. Art, thank you
for making Heather so happy. Michal, James, and kids, thanks for
everything we share as a family. Love and thanks to Uncle Myron
and Cousins Shirley, Alvin, Susan, and Bruce.

To my sister and business partner, Amy Elizabeth Fox, words
could never express my gratitude to you. Thank you for who you
are, and for who you aspire to become. Thank you for making
space for all of the inner negotiators who live and breathe in me.
Thank you for the magic of our synergies. Thank you for always
remembering.

To my new family, I find it hard to put in words the love and
appreciation I feel for you. To my beloved, my partner, my husband
and friend, you know this book would not exist without you. Thank
you for your loving heart, your radiant soul, your clear mind, your

beautiful eyes, and your joyful spirit. Thank you for always having my back. Thank you for Nemo Larry. To the Little Dude, thank you for waiting so patiently while Heit explained that "Erica is upstairs working on her book." Thank you for correcting my Dutch, teaching me the joys of soccer, and for lighting the Shabbat candles with such enthusiasm. I hope that one day, when you're old enough to read this book, you'll feel my love for you in the stories I share about our joint adventures. To the rest of my Dutch family, thank you for cheering me on, and for understanding when I left family gatherings to go home and write—*again*. Anke, thanks for making sure my wardrobe looks remotely European. To Eelco and Sietske Zijlstra-Pels, a special *dank je wel*.

My profound appreciation to my first professional family—my colleagues at the Program on Negotiation at Harvard Law School. To the thinkers and practitioners who shaped me, including the late Roger Fisher, William Ury, Bruce Patton, and Robert Mnookin. A special thank you to Frank E. A. Sander and Michael Wheeler, who put their necks on the line to sponsor my research project in the early days. At that time, putting "mindfulness" and "Harvard Law School" together made little sense to most of our colleagues. Without the two of you, we never could have launched the Harvard Negotiation Insight Initiative (HNII), which convened the extraordinary interdisciplinary exchanges that led to this book.

My gratitude to Robert Mnookin, Susan Hackley, James Kerwin, William Ury, and Jim Sebenius for standing by PON's commitment to experimentation that advances our field. My gratitude to Rikk Larsen and your family foundation, for the first grant that supported the action research at HNII. For your wisdom and friendship when the going got rough, deepest thanks to Jim Gimian and Ronnie Heifetz. For decades of fellowship that began at PON, thank you to Bob Bordone, Stevenson Carlebach, Enid Cherenson, Chuck Doran, Debbie Goldstein, Pete Hiddema, Kathy Holub, Michael Moffitt, Linda Netsch, Beth Scheel Pearson, Scott Peppet, John Richardson, Rob Ricigliano, Gabriella Salvatore Strecker, David Seibel and Amy Casher, and Angelique Skoulas.

To Doug Stone and Sheila Heen: How did we get so lucky to write books at the exact same time? My dearest friends, I can hardly imagine the last year without you. Thank you for sharing this crazy adventure of authorship with me. Excelsior!

Thank you to the senior colleagues who've been role models, supporters, teachers, or guides over the years, including: Daniel Bowling, Mirabai Bush, Tom Dine, Joanna Duda, Robert Gass, Jim Grant, Charlie Halpern, Robert Hanig, David Hoffman, Mark Alan Hughes, Jon Kabat-Zinn, David Kantor, Bob Kegan, Wilfried Kerntke, Lisa Lahey, Jamil Mahuad, David Matz, Phil McArthur, Bob Putnam, Terry Real, Len Riskin, Sharon Salzberg, Tony Schwartz, and Cornel West. My appreciation to the faculty of the Family Institute of Cambridge, who introduced me to psychodrama, and designed ways to adapt it for wider contexts. Thank you also to my friends at the International Academy of Mediators, particularly to Cliff Hendler and Teresa Wakeen. For your spiritual counsel and friendship, my appreciation to Efraim Eisen, Aryeh Ben-David, and Tirzah Firestone.

A special acknowledgment to Diana McLain Smith, my mentor in the best sense of that word. Thank you for everything. Likewise a salute to Carole Kammen, whom I thank for the many experiences we've shared. I've learned so much from watching you teach about the human condition. I'll reserve a few special acknowledgments to share privately.

My gratitude and respect to the faculty who taught at HNII, including: Arjuna Ardagh, Samuel Bartussek, Lee Jay Berman, Melissa Blacker, Tara Brach, Kenneth Cloke, Susan Daicoff, Tirzah Firestone, Norman Fischer, the late Rev. Peter Gomes, Anne Gottlieb, Emily Gould, David Hall, Robert Hanig, Sheila Heen, Jack Himmelstein, David Hoffman, William Isaacs, Jon Kabat-Zinn, Jeff Kichaven, Alexander Kuilman, John Paul Lederach, Doug Noll, Helen Palmer, Robert Richardson, Len Riskin, Scott Rogers, Gabriella Salvatore Strecker, Beth Scheel, Louise Phipps Senft, Peter Senge, Angelique Skoulas, Charlotte Thornton, and Bill Torbert. A special acknowledgment to my teaching partner of many years, Mark Thornton. Your wisdom, your heart, your spontaneous humor, and your grace bless every group we meet. Thank you for the pure joy of teaching with you, and for the solidarity in our friendship. And a bow to our angel Charlotte.

A singular thank-you to my colleagues and dear friends Emily Gould and Dave Savage. You've held the vision of the essence of this work for so many years, and supported its many expressions. From public workshops to a book; from keynotes to blogs; from T-shirts and pins to logos and taglines; from Harvard to a global movement with local chapters around the world. Thank you for your leadership, your skills, and your stewardship of the global network. Thank you for knowing when I need space and solitude. Thank you for always dancing with me.

Thank you to David Gould, who started that leg of the journey with Emily, Dave, and me. I am eternally grateful. My appreciation also to Robert Creo, for seeing the power of the method so quickly and so early, and for pouring your energy into sharing the ideas.

For all the years of support, shared vision, and friendship, thank you to Cristin Martineau. You held our learning community together, and took the ride with me—ups and downs and in-betweens—as we brought new ideas and methods into very traditional institutions. I hope you feel proud of your contributions to everything we built together. I certainly do.

To my partners at Mobius Executive Leadership, I can't wait to take the next step with you. Amy, Alex Kuilman, and Andrea Winter, *we've come a long way, baby.* You are core to the center where I drop my anchor. I can never honor you enough. To our partner in crime, Johanne Lavoie: every acknowledgment in the world to you. You've mastered the craft of calling on your Dreamer, Thinker, Lover, and Warrior at the right time and for the right purpose like few people I know. You're a tireless champion for transformational leaders in corporate environments, a challenge few people have the will or the guts to pull off. You show me how to bear the heat and not sweat the small stuff. Thank you.

To the Mobius core who brings the depth of this teaching to life along with my partners, including: John Abbruzzese, Iris Bagwell, Matthias Birk, Jen Cohen, Kate Davies, Devra Fradin, Jason Gore, Anne Gottlieb, Michele Gravelle, Jamil Mahuad, Linda Netsch, Priya Parker, Sam Reid, Claude Stein, Mark Thornton, Alex Trisoglio, Cat Tweedie Ball, Bill Underwood, Marcia Wieder, and Paul Zonneveld. Thank you for your incredible talent, for the way you see and hold people, for the way you love life, for the way we love each other. I know of no team anywhere that can foster transformation like you can.

To our closest allies and fellow travelers, a deep bow of thanks. You give me great hope about the future, including *as representatives of our collective global team*: Zafer Achi, Pierre Avanzo, Rajiv Ball, Joanna Barsh, Michael Bennett, Nate Boaz, Eric Braverman, Kara Carter, Natascha Catalino, Hervé de Barbeyrac, Aaron de Smet,

Amadeo di Lodovice, Véronique Dorval, Biniam Gebre, Ken Gibson, Smaranda Gosa-Mensing, Magnus Grimeland, Viktor Hediger, Elizabeth Schwartz Hioe, Jeff Holland, Alison Jenkins, Beth Jones, Matthew Joseph, Jill Krambeck, Dana Maor, Kirstan Marnane, Adriana Mascolli, Guido Meardi, Raoul Oberman, Renée Paradise, Ioana Parsons, John Parsons, Wolfhart Pentz, Michael Rennie, Tom Saar, Clare Sellicks, Ramesh Srinivasan, Oliver Triebel, Kotaro Ueda, Kristina Wollschlaeger, Inge Walters, Carol Weese, Sarah Wilson, Jeffrey Wong, Jin Yu, Mischa Zielke. My appreciation also to Stefan Heck and Kevin Lane.

To the people who keep Mobius running every day, and enable Amy, me, and the entire Mobius network to fulfill our shared mission, I salute you: Kelly Asato, David Boyd, J. J. Byun, Vanessa Cirella, Tracey Eisman, Cindy Grossi, and Karyn Saganic. You are a remarkable team, and living proof of Margaret Mead's reminder to never doubt the power of a small group of people to change the world. You surely do. Thank you to the devoted and skilled people who support the work we do around the world, including: Mary Allen, Phil Davis, Roy Edelstein, and Jeanne Waller. A special thanks to Susan Brady, for the year you spent building a business for Winning from Within. I appreciate you as a colleague, as an advisor, and as my confidante.

My admiration and appreciation for the Power Team who brought Winning from Within from a method I used to teach people in an interactive setting, to an expression of ideas people can read in a book. That is no small feat. To my literary agent, Linda Loewenthal, who was also my devoted proposal editor, there simply is no book without you. Full stop. Thank you for teaching me the craft of translating my teaching voice into a writing voice. Thank you for seeing the possibility of an orchard when we only had the seed. Thanks for always telling the truth. My gratitude also to David Black, the head of Linda's agency, for believing in this project from day one.

My praise and appreciation to my developmental editor, Betsy Rapoport, who faced the large challenge of turning hundreds of pages of my free associations into a coherent story line. Thank you for your skill, your vision for the book, your dedication, your love of language, and your belief in me.

To my book editor, Laureen Rowland, we did it! First, thank you for sharpening the main messages of this book to enable the final proposal to read so clearly and powerfully. We could not have done it without you. Second, turning complex ideas into accessible language is an art, and one I've learned much about from you. I'm eternally grateful for your ability to cut away good but unnecessary material, in order to reveal the best gems for the book. Finally, as I enter the next phase of this journey, I will miss our regular talks—about ideas, about chapter revisions, about life and love. Thank you for seeing me so clearly, and for helping me to find my voice on the page.

To Hollis Heimbouch, my editor at Harper Collins, my deepest thanks. My life changed the day you read my book proposal. Thank you for believing that *Winning from Within* can change the lives of so many people. Thank you for your warmth, your compassion, your directness, your patience, your wisdom, and your enthusiasm about bringing this book out into the world. I hope this book is our first but not our last.

To other members of the Harper team, thank you for making all of this possible. To Colleen Lawrie, Brian Perrin, and Marisa Benedetto, my special gratitude for your hard work, your passion, and your warm encouragement.

For your editing, encouraging, and collaboration to reorganize ideas, thank you to the stellar team who helped in the final weeks to pull it all together: John Abbruzzese, Matthias Birk, Amy Elizabeth Fox, Emily Gould, Chas Hamilton, Scott Peppet, and Terry Real. John and Matthias: you were heroic help at the end to get this over the finish line. And Bernardus, who played editor-at-large along the way. Thank you all.

For your expertise and your brotherly love, thank you for everything to Kevin Small. I feel blessed to know you, and lucky to work with you.

My gratitude to the professional communities filled with my colleagues and friends. Thank you to the Association for Conflict Resolution, specifically the Spirituality Section, and the people who contributed their ideas, their willingness, their energy, and their skills to refine this methodology, including: Michael Aloi, Nan Waller Burnett, Jeremy Lack, John Phillips, Keith Seat, Tina Spiegel, Ron Supancic, and Rachel Wohl. Blessings and gratitude to all of the faithful members of HNII and later the global counterpart, GNII, with special thanks to Chuck Barker, Bill Doenges, Michael Herman, David Selvanathan, Phil Shecter, and Zack Van Rossum.

Thank you to my friends at Mediators Beyond Borders, particularly to Ken Cloke, who has blazed so many trails for the rest of us to follow. And to my colleagues at the American Institute of Mediation, first and foremost Lee Jay Berman. My gratitude to the Shadow Work community, starting with Cliff Barry, a pioneer in using archetypes to foster personal development, and our colleague, Shari Marbois. Appreciation and love to my colleagues and friends at ALIA Institute, including Lenneke Albers, Christopher Baan, Michael Chender, Jane Corbett, Chris Grant, Marty

Janowitz, Susan Skjei, Susan Szpakowski, Maria Sturm, and Chris Tamjidi.

My sincere thanks to people who supported me in the very beginning. You encouraged me to develop my own methods for teaching, and you held a big vision for how it could help people. To Anna Huckabee Tull, Chaim Koritzinsky, Allan and Kathy Koritzinsky, Deirdre Fay, Jonathan Levene and Franny Elson, Michal Frankel and George Mordecai, Roy Edelstein and Sarah Birkeland, Jen Goldman and Jeff Wetzler, and Angelique Skoulas, I am forever grateful. My acknowledgment also to my early research assistants and dialogue partners for the book: Seth Castleman, Lauren Galinsky, Michael Kalikow, Madeline Keros, and Lisa Stefanac.

I want to acknowledge people whose work I'm building on—some of whom I know personally, and many I don't. I can't mention every author I've read or every thinker who's influenced my approach. But I'd like to offer appreciation to at least the following people, whose books have impacted me greatly. First and foremost, I appreciate the path-breaking work of Carl Jung and of Joseph Campbell. I'm also very grateful to others, including Chris Argyris, Jean Shinoda Bolen, Tara Brach, Anthony de Mello, Ronald Heifetz, Jon Kabat-Zinn, Robert Kegan and Lisa Lahey, Peter Levine, Dan McAdams, Robert Moore and Douglas Gillette, Joseph Moreno, Helen Palmer, Carol Pearson, Richard Schwartz, Daniel Siegel, Hal and Sidra Stone, Richard Strozzi-Heckler, Bessel van der Kolk, and Margaret Wheatley. On a purely personal note, thank you to Andrea Martins and Victoria Hepworth for *Expat Women: Confessions*.

Finally, and ultimately, my infinite appreciation and respect to all of the people who've taken part of your journey with me. To the workshop participants, leadership teams, conference delegates, clients, the global network, and all the other voyagers who've explored going "beyond yes" and "winning from within": thank you for everything we've experienced and learned together. Working with you creates many of the highlights of my life.

This global community now includes you, the reader with this book in your hands. May we all continue along the paths we've chosen, and may life bring us back together, again and again.

Meet
Erica Ariel Fox

Erica Ariel Fox, J.D., teaches negotiation at Harvard Law School, and is the president of Mobius Executive Leadership. A graduate of Princeton University and Harvard Law School, she's been teaching and consulting for almost twenty years. A highly sought-after expert and speaker by companies around the world, Erica is also a senior advisor to McKinsey Leadership Development. Mixing nearly two decades of teaching and researching at Harvard Law School, extensive experience in the hands-on world of business, and her own personal touch, Erica brings a unique voice to the conversation about leading wisely and living well.

Erica also works with public sector leaders, civil servants, members of government, and non-profit organizations to advance the common good. She is an Influencer on LinkedIn and blogs for Harvard Business Review (hbr.org).

Erica is actively exploring the meaning of life as a "global citizen," living with her husband and stepson in Amsterdam, The Netherlands, and outside of Cambridge, Massachusetts, in the United States.

To book Erica Ariel Fox please visit
www.EricaArielFox.com or
email booking@ericaarielfox.com.

Join *the* Global Community!

Go to WinningFromWithin.com to join the conversation

LinkedIn   ···:> **LinkedIn.com/in/ericaarielfox**
Follow Erica Ariel Fox through the world's largest professional networking community. She has an Influencer status.

Facebook   ···:> **Facebook.com/erica.a.fox.5**
Be a fan of Erica Ariel Fox on FaceBook. LIKE this page to enjoy all the latest news, photographs, and updates.

Twitter   ···:> **@EricaArielFox**
Follow Erica Ariel Fox on Twitter for instant updates on what's happening in the world of *Winning From Within.*

Get *the* Tools *to* Win *from* Within

Are you looking for the tools to help reconnect all the parts of yourself and skillfully engage them as you navigate your world? To help you succeed along the path, we've assembled terrific resources to help you master your inner negotiators. Use the free survey, videos, and easy-to-follow guides to get your journey going today!

Get these FREE resources now
at www.WinningFromWithin.com

Your Big Four Survey

With this survey, you can discover more about your inner negotiators. Find out about your profile, and discover the strategies of a Dreamer, Thinker, Lover, and Warrior. Then, by linking your inner negotiators to your world of work or home, you'll create brand-new results, stronger relationships, and a full, rewarding life. Go online and get started today!

Wallet Card

Whenever you need an easy recap of the path to winning from within, this downloadable wallet card will provide the perfect visual reminder. Hang it up by your desk or on your kitchen bulletin board or keep it in your wallet, and your inner negotiators will always be nearby.

Book of the Month

Looking to broaden your understanding of the topics in Winning from Within®? Let your Voyager chart your path forward to new understanding—with some help from the author herself. Each month Erica will share a book that has shaped her ideas on leading wisely and living well. Check in every month to keep your own personal learning voyage on course!

Video Library

Whether you need to persuade a colleague for an extra resource or ask a persnickety neighbor for a favor, your life is a constant series of negotiations. But that doesn't mean you have to face them alone! In these insightful, short video tutorials, Erica walks you through everyday examples of the lessons taught in the book, providing a quick and easy playbook for making the most of your daily interactions.

Discussion Questions

Build your life skills and leadership strengths by discussing these thought-provoking questions at your next team meeting or book club.

Get these
FREE
resources now at
WinningFromWithin.com

Put Winning from Within® into Action

Hands-On Workshop

Based on nearly twenty years of research, Winning from Within® training helps people transform ideas into action and action into results.

Learn how to develop leaders and drive results by bringing the Winning from Within® workshop into your organization. This two-day workshop is offered at both a basic and an advanced level:

- Winning from Within® Fundamentals
- Winning from Within® for Leaders

Senior Executive Development

Change champions in global firms look to Winning from Within® for the exclusive field and forum program, Beyond High Performance. Limited to twenty-four participants from around the world, the Beyond High Performance program gives executives an extended, experiential leadership development journey. Details and applications for consideration are available at www.WinningFromWithin.com.

Train-the-Trainer

Building a new organizational culture can begin by certifying your network of internal facilitators in the Winning from Within® training.

Your trainers can participate in a development program to learn how to facilitate the Winning from Within® workshops tailored for your organization. We will work with you to customize the workshop and then license you to deliver it with your own people.

Certified
Winning
from Within®
Facilitator